LIVING ON THE
BOUNDARIES

*Evangelical Women, Feminism and
the Theological Academy*

NICOLA HOGGARD CREEGAN
CHRISTINE D. POHL

InterVarsity Press
Downers Grove, Illinois

InterVarsity Press
P.O. Box 1400, Downers Grove, IL 60515-1426
World Wide Web: www.ivpress.com
E-mail: mail@ivpress.com

InterVarsity Press® *is the book-publishing division of InterVarsity Christian Fellowship/USA*®*, a student movement active on campus at hundreds of universities, colleges and schools of nursing in the United States of America, and a member movement of the International Fellowship of Evangelical Students. For information about local and regional activities, write Public Relations Dept., InterVarsity Christian Fellowship/USA, 6400 Schroeder Rd., P.O. Box 7895, Madison, WI 53707-7895, or visit the IVCF website at <www.intervarsity.org>.*

Scripture quotations, unless otherwise noted, are from the New Revised Standard Version of the Bible, *copyright 1989 by the Division of Christian Education of the National Council of the Churches of Christ in the USA. Used by permission. All rights reserved.*

Design: Cindy Kiple

Images: Besie Van der Meer/Getty Images

ISBN-10: 0-8308-2665-3
ISBN-13: 978-0-8308-2665-0

Printed in the United States of America ∞

Library of Congress Cataloging-in-Publication Data

Creegan, Nicola Hoggard.
  Living on the boundaries: evangelical women, feminism, and the
  theological academy / Nicola Hoggard Creegan, Christine D. Pohl.
    p. cm.
  Includes bibliographical references (p.   ) and index.
  ISBN 0-8308-2665-3 (pbk.: alk. paper)
  1. Women—Religious aspects—Christianity. 2. Feminism—Religious
aspects—Christianity. 3. Evangelicalism. 4. Women clergy—Training
of. 5. Women in Christianity. I. Pohl, Christine D. II. Title
BT704.C74 2005
230'.04624'082—dc22

                                                                    2005012101

| **P** | 16 | 15 | 14 | 13 | 12 | 11 | 10 | 9 | 8 | 7 | 6 | 5 | 4 | 3 | 2 | 1 |
| **Y** | 16 | 15 | 14 | 13 | 12 | 11 | 10 | 09 | 08 | 07 | 06 | 05 | | | | |

CONTENTS

PREFACE

—⊸⬡⬡⊶—

Initial descriptions of the subject of this book have elicited very different responses. As we've answered the question, "So what are you writing these days?"
with "We're finishing a book on evangelical women, feminism and the theological
academy," the reactions have become predictable if also disparate. Some friends and
acquaintances have responded with a flat "Oh," and the conversation has quickly
shifted to another topic. Others have responded with a second question, asking,
"*Who* is going to read *that* book?" communicating their uncertainty about whether
the intersection of issues and communities was sufficiently significant to generate
a readership. And then others, certainly more reassuring for us, have exclaimed with
surprising intensity, "I *really* want to read that book."

What makes this book more than a rarefied exploration of a very small intersection is that the three worlds it draws together are large and important to the
church. We are convinced that a closer look at the experiences and issues found in
the intersection, or on the boundaries, of evangelical identity, feminism and the
academy as it deals with theology is also important for all three communities.
While each of these worlds has received popular and scholarly attention, little work
has been done at their intersection, and rarely have women, situated in this intersection, publicly shared their experiences, insights, struggles and concerns. We
write for the sake of the church and with a deep commitment to theological education, hoping that our particular combination of description, narrative and analysis will be helpful to men and women who are also seeking to discern what is good
and true in these three worlds.

The scope of this book expanded slowly. The first ideas were hatched years ago

during a casual conversation between two close friends. Gradually we realized that
we longed for a larger conversation, with many more participants and many more
stories. And so we came up with a strategy that would allow us to interact with
many other women in theological education. We are enormously grateful to the
women who so thoughtfully and honestly engaged our extensive questions and graciously shared their stories.

Thanks also to the editors at InterVarsity Press for their confidence that there
are people who will want to read this book. We are grateful to them for hosting the
InterVarsity Press evangelical women's consultation in 2002 as well as the evangelical women's breakfast at the American Academy of Religion meeting in Toronto.
Our initial conversations at IVP were with Rodney Clapp, and his early encouragement was very helpful. In subsequent years, Bob Fryling, Jim Hoover, Andy
Le Peau and Dan Reid were consistently encouraging. Special thanks to Gary
Deddo for his editorial wisdom and direction, and to Jennifer Conrad Seidel for
her work in copyediting.

We are also grateful to the American Academy of Religion for a summer grant
in 1997 that enabled us to begin the work of processing the questionnaires.

We especially want to thank Pam Buck, Wyndy Corbin, Joel Green, David
Gushee, Maria Russell Kenney, Ron Pohl, Cathy Ross and Jim Thobaben for reading the manuscript and for offering very helpful suggestions. For their friendship
and their wisdom, we are deeply grateful. Their insights strengthened the book significantly, but they bear no responsibility for its weaknesses. While we have taken
their suggestions and criticisms seriously, the arguments are finally our own.
Thanks also to Stephanie Wells for help with the bibliography, to Linda McKnight
for assistance with the index and to Charlie Creegan for helping with the last-
minute database changes.

Thanks also to our institutions—Asbury Theological Seminary in Wilmore,
Kentucky, and the Bible College of New Zealand in Auckland—for their interest
in the project and for being the sorts of communities within which we want to continue to live.

Last, but not least, we thank our families for their love and support. Heartfelt
thanks to Christine's mother, Dorothy, for her prayers and encouragement, for her
consistent interest in our work, and for her editorial reading of the entire manuscript. Special thanks to Nicola's husband, Charlie, and to their sons, Timothy and
Andrew, for managing while she was away writing. Writing a book can take half the
lifetime of a child. Thanks for getting used to growing up with a mother at the
computer saying, "I'll be there in just a minute."

| 1 |

WHERE ARE THE GOOD WOMEN?

Revised Maps for a Changing Terrain

⟨⟨⟩⟩

"Where are the good women?"

Although this question invites all sorts of additional questions and interesting, if not jaded, responses, at times it is asked with genuine perplexity and concern. It is frequently raised within evangelical schools that are committed to including academic women on their faculties.

As search committees meet to consider applicants for positions in theology, ethics, biblical studies and church history, members wonder aloud, "Why aren't there more good evangelical women in the applicant pool?" or "Why is it so hard to find good female applicants?" Similarly, as planning committees gather to develop a speaker's roster for academic conferences, they often ask, "Where are the female experts in these fields?"

The simple question Where are the good women? condenses a host of complex issues and conflicting assumptions. It has institutional, theological, personal and practical dimensions. Are the women missing, lost or invisible? Are there, in fact, very few female academics who dwell within evangelicalism? What does it mean to be "good" in this context? Is the question asking where are the women who can agree to a particular institution's doctrinal standards and ethos as well as be experts in their field? Does it include questions about finding women who can also teach well, do excellent research and writing, sustain a good marriage, nurture children, or be faithful and single? Are the search committees also looking for women who can fit comfortably, even gracefully, in a theological world still largely defined by men's experience and priorities, and who can build on the strengths of female identity without seriously challenging a male domain? Are they asking where the women are who can recognize the significance of gender and keep their primary focus on Christ and God's kingdom?

Just as there are many significant assumptions embedded in the question Where are the good women? there are important but often hidden assumptions about gender in evangelicalism and in the evangelical academy. Any adequate answer to the question will require a close examination of evangelical culture as it engages and interprets gender.

The question suggests additional questions about the context of women's formation. How do evangelical institutions shape women for the academy? What are the practices, commitments and expectations of the families, churches, schools and communities that form them? Where are the tensions? Insights from women presently teaching in evangelical schools as well as from women who have left evangelicalism provide a window into the complex experience of personal, intellectual and theological formation.

However informally the question of "good" is raised, it also invites theological reflection. How do evangelical interpretations of the biblical story, goodness, faithfulness and gender support or undermine women as they pursue higher education or minister within the academy? What does the tradition expect of its women and of its male and female academics? Where and how do contemporary theological issues and discussions intersect with and inform the theological work being done by evangelicals—especially work by evangelical women?

Theological conversation is very different today than it was a generation ago. Feminist insights and perspectives are an important part of the larger theological conversation and are very often an element in the formation of female academics. Feminist theology has provided helpful categories through which to interpret texts and experience, while it has also caused certain difficulties. Exploring the points of contact within theological reflection that allow evangelical women to bridge both feminist insights and evangelical orthodoxy is a key step in formulating a responsible answer to the question Where are the good women?

We write out of our experience as theological educators within evangelical institutions. We have heard the question raised on those search committees, and we have been the "good" women hired and invited to speak. But we have found the experience difficult at times and the question burdensome and personal, even as it is institutionally important and intellectually interesting.

A story illuminates how complex these issues are. Because of her expertise in the field, Christine was recently asked to be the keynote speaker at a conference on Christian hospitality. As the expectations for plenary sessions were being discussed, her potential participation in the school's worship service was raised. Confused by whether she was being asked to prepare an additional plenary presentation, to read a Bible text or to pray, she asked whether they wanted her to preach on hospitality. The conference organizer on the other end of the phone responded, "Oh, no, we wouldn't ask you to do that. We don't want trouble with *that* for ourselves or for you." When Christine responded that it would not be a problem for her to preach if asked, the conference chairman explained that they would want to use a different format for that particular chapel. He noted that several trustees and faculty members had been very concerned when another woman who had been invited to speak in chapel had done so "with authority."

The invitation was simultaneously bewildering and illuminating. To be invited to speak in one's area of expertise is normal for an academic. To be warned that to speak with authority would be problematic for that sector of evangelicalism reveals the complex terrain that a "good" woman traverses.

Most invitations to speak are not this conflicted, but the tensions around evangelical women's authority and voice are often significant. It is not always possible or appropriate to name the tensions as they occur, but such incidents demonstrate how difficult it can be to have integrity when expectations clash so intensely. In this case, what does it mean to be good, or faithful or responsible to the church and kingdom?

We share in the responsibility and privilege of forming and training the next generation of evangelical pastors, academics and youth workers. Our experiences as teachers and mentors and also as students and colleagues provide the soil out of which we reflect and write. Between the two of us, we have already invested forty years in the world of theological education. Our individual disciplines of theology and social ethics shape how we ask and answer some of the questions. But the story is far bigger than our individual experiences and far richer than our particular interpretations. We have therefore invited many other women to join the conversation in the hopes of providing a fuller, more nuanced account of life on the boundary.

Because our daily conversation partners include a much broader community than evangelicalism and because we continually travel across multiple communities, which are often at odds with one another, our preference would have been to gather all of them around a single table for lively conversation. But the table would have had to be enormous and the time allowed very long. The potential for too many different conversations pressed us to frame our focus more explicitly. In this book, we have brought together voices of women in the academy, mostly those who have identified themselves as evangelicals, with theological and sociological perspectives related to contemporary evangelicalism. We have also interacted with contemporary feminist conversations about theology and women's experience. While we have drawn from very mixed literature, we are writing specifically for those who are concerned about identifying and supporting evangelical women in the theological academy. Thus, although we ourselves dwell on several maps, we will in this book primarily speak in one direction, toward those who share with us a set of assumptions and commitments.

We are writing for colleagues and administrators who believe that a school is stronger when it has both women and men involved in training the next generation of leaders and who are concerned about the well-being of female evangelical academics. We are writing for female students considering a call to doctoral studies and to work in the theological academy. We are writing for female academics who are serving faithfully in evangelical institutions and for those academic women who identify themselves as evangelicals but are working in nonevangelical environments. We are writing for male and female pastors who are concerned about nurturing the call of intellectually gifted women and men to theological engagement.

Our purpose is both descriptive and educative. We are describing a mostly unmapped territory: the boundary land where evangelical women, feminism and the theological academy intersect. Because the terrain is also the substance of our lives, it is quite personal, and we have chosen to use a modified narrative approach. The description, stories and insights from a variety of women serve a powerfully educative function because they bring to light some of the distinctive characteristics, challenges and graces of life on the boundary.

MAPPING THE LANDSCAPE

Both evangelicalism and feminism are controversial movements that provoke complex loyalties as well as ambivalence within the church and in the world at large. In spite of a considerable degree of shared history, they are quite often defined against each other. Most of the rhetoric from and about the movements assumes that there are few connections and little overlap and that individuals might locate themselves within one or the other movement, but not within both. Yet some evangelical women in the academy find themselves living on the boundary between feminism and evangelicalism or on the boundaries between the multiple forms of both feminism and evangelicalism.

Thus, while for many people it is nearly impossible to imagine an intersection between evangelicalism and feminism that has integrity, we are convinced that this intersection is precisely what needs to be explored. Nevertheless, it is a topic that makes many people on all sides nervous, and naming and addressing some of the issues, assumptions and experiences can invite some very intense responses. It can occasionally feel like an interpersonal and institutional minefield.

Evangelical women who dwell in the overlap of maps, or on the boundary of texts, are familiar with the languages and grammars of these territories and move back and forth between them.[1] We are convinced that some of the issues we have encountered are also important to other Christians and that in this overlap new insights can be found or, at the very least, a few signposts can be erected. Still, it is often a difficult journey, and while we engage issues and critiques raised by feminism, those same critiques challenge the basis for authority and meaning that is central to evangelical identity. Certainly, some feminist critiques of patriarchal society ring true in our experience, and we live with those tensions both personally and in institutional settings. In addition, the maps themselves are currently being redrawn: mainline or liberal Protestant interest in renewal and orthodoxy and evangelical interest in liturgy and tradition make discussion more complex, interesting and urgent.

In 1 Peter, Christians are addressed as literal aliens and exiles and are then encouraged to own that identity and to live as aliens in the world. Throughout Scripture, the people of God are challenged to see themselves as strangers and sojourners. We recognize that there is something normatively appropriate to our identity as followers of Jesus that contemporary mappings of the world leave us not quite sure where home is. Life on the boundary provides the kind of critical distance and alternative perspective that challenges assumptions and practices, institutional arrangements and authority structures.[2]

---

[1]In the last few decades, the theological world has been transformed by its encounter with and its immersion in postmodernism. Liberal theology has been affected by postliberalism and narrative and, more recently, by conversations with Radical Orthodoxy. Evangelical theology has also been influenced significantly by dialogue with and appropriation of some of these postliberal concerns. Indeed, evangelicals sometimes seem to be obsessed with postmodernism and with language. Evangelical theologians, at least some of them, have listened to George Lindbeck and have moved away from the propositional rationalism that so characterized twentieth-century fundamentalism and evangelicalism. Thus it is now appropriate to talk of theology and discourse as "grammar": the second-order language that describes how the first order language of faith operates and what it means. Every map and every discourse has its own grammar, the often hidden rules by which God-language and spirituality are used and collectively expressed. See John Milbank, *The Word Made Strange: Theology, Language, Culture* (Cambridge, Mass.: Blackwell, 1997), p. 2.

[2]See Miroslav Volf's excellent discussion of distance and belonging in *Exclusion and Embrace: A Theological Exploration of Identity, Otherness and Reconciliation* (Nashville: Abingdon, 1996).

Nevertheless, we have wondered why anyone would choose to live in this conflicted and frequently misunderstood position for long. And yet, there does not seem to be much choice. The regular maps do not work: the either-or of the culture-wars paradigm is not accurate to our experience. Neither pure feminist theory nor standard evangelical assumptions and practices quite resonate with our beliefs and experiences. Often we find ourselves in the middle, negotiating both worlds, caught in the hostilities between them, yet persuaded that both have rich resources we cannot abandon.

Although situated in an awkward place, we are in a position to draw on the strengths of both movements and to be sensitive to the questions and agendas of both worlds. From our location on the boundary, we hope to speak about what is best in the evangelical and feminist worlds and to be the locus of the mixing of their grammars.

There are other reasons for taking seriously the wisdom that comes from life on the boundary. All of us are embodied and institutionally connected beings. Our particular locations and loyalties bind us or loose us; they free us for answering God's call on our lives or block our moves toward maturity and faithfulness. These concerns matter as we shape and train persons for Christian ministry and, because of the conflicts, they particularly matter for women.

WHO WE ARE: OUR SHARED HISTORY

Assigned to the same women's dormitory at Gordon-Conwell Theological Seminary in the fall of 1984, we met during our first few days of seminary. We quickly discovered a particularly important experience and friendship network we had in common—the deeply formative period each of us had spent at L'Abri Fellowship in England. We had been there at different times, yet the encounter with L'Abri had shaped our understandings of Christian faith and evangelicalism profoundly.

Neither of us grew up within the evangelical world; instead, we each came to it as a young adult (Nicola from a Roman Catholic background and Christine from a mainline Protestant family). At L'Abri, both of us experienced a very unusual evangelical community; and through its ministry, we found renewed commitment to faith and church. During the 1970s, L'Abri was a remarkable movement of the Holy Spirit, a place where shared meals, worship, appreciation for art and the asking of questions went hand in hand. Although some people have experienced evangelicalism as closed doors and minds, we experienced it as a lively and intense interaction with culture and a deep compassion for those who did not believe. L'Abri workers interacted with the "cultured despisers" of religion and thought that hard questions were exciting.

Like numerous male academics from evangelical backgrounds, we found that L'Abri's willingness to address rather than to bracket questions was important in our intellectual development. The depth of this communal and spiritual experience had never been reflected in descriptions of evangelical orthodoxy that we encountered in feminist or liberal literature or in classrooms.

A second experience at the intersection of deep evangelical worship, thoughtful intellectual engagement and warm fellowship was also formative for both of us. On most Sunday evenings during our seminary years, a group of about thirty students met at the home of a New Testament professor for prayer, praise and biblical discussion. In the home of Gordon and Maudine Fee, we experienced welcome and an extraordinary blending of scholarship, love for God and passion for teaching. In that environment, the prospect of combining Christian faith and academic work became not only interesting, but also absolutely compelling. While we never formed a tight community, we found a place where gender and background were relatively insignificant. A most potent form of mentoring for us turned out to be a kind of hospitality that drew us in because of the host's love for his subject area.[3] In retrospect, we realized that a number of the women at Gordon-Conwell Theological Seminary who went on for Ph.D.s shared in this same experience; in fact, many of the men who went on to further studies also participated in the fellowship at the Fee's home.

In both L'Abri and the home fellowship at Gordon-Conwell, what drew us to go further in our studies was not individual mentoring or even personal encouragement toward additional education. At L'Abri, women were neither encouraged toward nor discouraged from advanced theological study, and in many cases the male-female roles were somewhat gender stereotypical. But in both settings, the academic component was richly theological and deeply personal. Two communities that identify themselves primarily as evangelical provided us with a place where Scripture and life, culture and theology, prayer and critical reflection came together in a vibrant way. As a result, we have found it impossible to abandon these connections and commitments.

For many evangelicals, and in many stereotypes of evangelical experience, churches are places where conversion is emphasized but questions are not encour-

---

[3]In *The Courage to Teach*, Parker J. Palmer writes about the frequency with which students describe their "great teachers" as those with "a passion for the subject." He continues, "passion for the subject propels that subject, not the teacher, into the center of the learning circle—and when a great thing is in their midst, students have direct access to the energy of learning and of life." See Parker J. Palmer, *The Courage to Teach: Exploring the Inner Landscape of a Teacher's Life* (San Francisco: Jossey-Bass, 1998), p. 120.

aged. When a crisis of faith emerges, subjectivity and objective faith appear to be in conflict. These crises for us were less burdensome because the questioning was encouraged and the Holy Spirit was so real as to be undeniable. Questioning and doubt were not defined out of the Christian's experience, but rather included as an integral part of real faith. This also gave us a more nuanced hermeneutic; there was little chance that we would assume it was possible to go directly from text to the present day without attention to context and story, a tendency in certain strands of evangelicalism. Where questions are welcomed, there is an implicit understanding that interpretation is difficult, communal and contextual.

Our friendship, formed in our first years of formal theological study, has now spanned two decades. In that time we have encouraged one another through the traumas and joys of graduate school, comprehensive exams and dissertation writing, as well as through the challenges of marriage, childrearing and singleness, job searches and job changes, interactions with colleagues, administrators, the guild and church leadership. We have upheld each other through disappointments and significant achievements, wondered together about classroom experiences and family responsibilities. And we have enjoyed decades-long conversations about theology, ethics, feminism, the church, evangelical faith and our experiences as women.

In modern typologies (as described especially by Gary Dorrien), we mostly fit into the postconservative, progressive or incarnational evangelical type.[4] We are part of a generation of evangelicals shaped by the writings of C. S. Lewis, J. R. R. Tolkien, George MacDonald and Madeleine L'Engle, and by the L'Abri experience. Also, for us, evangelical faith has provided motivation and structures within which to work for social justice and reconciliation in the church and the world.

WHO WE ARE: OUR INDIVIDUAL STORIES

While we share a long and deep friendship, many of our experiences and much of our shaping have been different. In developing the book, our differences allowed us to focus in particular areas and helped to keep our reflections somewhat nuanced. Our disciplines, though overlapping, are also different, as are our life situations and our experiences in jobs and engagement with feminism. Therefore, we thought it might be best to tell our own stories at this point.

---

[4]"[Robert] Brow observes that the influence of [C. S.] Lewis's processive incarnationalism among evangelicals deepens every time that evangelicals read the Narnia stories or Madeleine L'Engle's time-travel fantasies to their children. . . . The split between a Lewis-influenced new model and the old-model juridical theology is 'dividing evangelicals on a deep level' " (Gary Dorrien, *The Remaking of Evangelical Theology* [Louisville, Ky.: Westminster John Knox, 1998], p. 175). See also Robert Brow, "Evangelical Megashift," *Christianity Today*, February 19, 1990, pp. 12-14.

Nicola's story. I grew up Roman Catholic and from a very early age was interested in all the God questions that theology attempts to answer. Pierre Teilhard de Chardin was my first theologian and my first inspiration. Roman Catholicism, however, was a mixed heritage. There were too many sermons and too many nuns warning of the dangers of eternal damnation, and yet there was strength and mystery to be found in the great high masses of the liturgical year. Although Vatican II was changing the church during this time, it was not possible as a girl to think of studying theology.

So I studied mathematics and wondered whether God existed. In the end, this and other questions took me to L'Abri in England. I was asking, Why is the Bible so violent? Why does music mean so much? What is beauty? Are we free? In this small community in the English countryside it was all right to ask and to think. Faith, trust, the Holy Spirit and love in community were what made the world go round.

I went to Gordon-Conwell Seminary with more questions and was intrigued by Professor Richard Lovelace's postmillennialism and by the whole new world that New England Puritanism and revivalism opened up. Like many New Zealanders, I went as far away from home as possible—to the eastern shores of Massachusetts.

Embracing feminist concerns or a full feminist identity was a slow process, in part because my evangelical experience had been unusual; I had rarely encountered congregations that defined gender roles narrowly. During doctoral studies, an adviser insisted that one must study women's issues in order to be authentic. And, after some study, I found feminism to be fascinating but also lacking in transcendence. Nevertheless, I read widely in feminist theology, keeping it on hold, so to speak, for later. I focused my research on theology and freedom. However, after a number of years living in a quite traditional community in North Carolina and trying to combine child-rearing and academic life, I was converted to feminism. I had simply experienced too much patriarchy in birthing children, in churches, in small-city life, in a liberal arts college and in a so-called liberal denomination. And the more I dwelt within that world and within church institutions, the deeper the sense of patriarchy became.[5]

---

[5]We are working with a definition of *patriarchy* as that evil—manifested in language, institutions, family traditions, cultural practices and work expectations—which subjugates, dominates and excludes women from the public sphere, which caricatures women, and which precludes women's entry into and participation in many roles and occupations. Patriarchy is deemed to affect the structures of every society in history; its influence is effected by the benevolent as well as the malevolent or misogynist. Patriarchy is understood as leading to androcentrism: the structuring of life and narrative around the experiences of men, and the according of dignity and worth to men and not to women. Contemporary feminism attempts to expose and root out patriarchy in all its lingering disguises by deconstructing and reconstructing the androcentric texts, institutions and meta-theories of Western civilization. Adapted from Nicola Hoggard Creegan, "Feminist Theology," in *The Evangelical Dictionary of Theology*, 2nd ed., ed. Walter A. Elwell (Grand Rapids: Baker, 2001), pp. 447-49.

One summer I was in Europe and struggling deeply with identity questions. I was in limbo spiritually and professionally. That summer, while vacationing in France, I read Elisabeth Schüssler Fiorenza's *But She Said: Feminist Practices of Biblical Interpretation* with new appreciation. Also during that trip, I worshiped at St. Aldates in Oxford on Pentecost Sunday and resonated at that time with the unusual combination of intelligence, liturgy and charismatic spontaneity. While the theologies, communities and experiences were often defined in opposition to each other, I needed to reconcile them or at least find a place to dwell between them. I found myself now living on two maps—not sitting on one looking out at the other, but truly on the boundary.

As I reflected further on evangelical identity, I pressed hard to grasp why I continued to identify myself as an evangelical. I was returning to the same questions again. I realized that the questions I continue to find most urgent are the ones posed by authors of InterVarsity Press books, in the journal *Books and Culture*, at Wheaton theology conferences or on evangelical campuses. More specifically, in evangelicalism, there is an enduring sense that God is bigger than reason; that we do not know what we need ultimately; that however clever we are, we still must come to God as children; and that prayer is work. Evangelical grammar is the grammar of the scandal of faith, of the last being first and of the worker who turns up late being paid equally—things against reason. Identifying with evangelicalism also made sense of my ongoing interest in the interface between science and theology, an engagement that has kept me rooted in a critical realism somewhat at odds with some forms of liberalism and irrelevant to many in mainline churches. But with all of this I also had the increasing sense that the tradition was marred by a deep patriarchy.

In spite of this identification with evangelicalism, I have felt a special call to bridge the polarities of Christian existence. I am interested in what draws us together, in what different traditions have in common and in how experience, tradition and Word might interact. For this reason, I did my dissertation work on Friedrich Schleiermacher and Jonathan Edwards, the fathers of two seemingly disparate traditions. I continue to be inspired by the work of Schleiermacher, one of the first great modern apologists and pietist theologians.

In the year 2000 I moved with my family to take a position lecturing in theology at the Bible College of New Zealand, an evangelical, nondenominational theological school offering undergraduate and graduate degrees. On the surface, New Zealand evangelicalism is more irenic and less divided than its American counterpart. Nevertheless, it was a major decision for the school to hire a woman to teach theology. The student body at BCNZ is drawn partly from people in conservative nondenominational and Pentecostal churches for whom theology is at first quite threatening. While some students are very interested in gender equality and feminist insights, there are a number of women and men for whom conservative understandings of women and of male hierarchy are definitive. Thus while I am now somewhat removed from the furor of North American theological battles, there is much in the New Zealand evangelical ethos that reflects the American experience about which we write.

I belong to a mainline Anglican church of a fairly liturgical variety, and I live the chaotic lifestyle of theologian, wife and mother. Thus the questions of identity and integration we discuss in this book are those for which I, too, am always seeking answers.

Christine's story. Like many women who grew up in the mainline Protestant church in the 1960s, I received mixed messages about the significance of gender. I remember thinking, as I walked home from the youth group I loved leading, "If I were a boy, I could become a pastor." There was some freedom, but little encouragement, for women to pursue theological interests. In my world, there were no models of female pastors. When I moved toward more evangelical settings, the messages were equally mixed, though the ingredients were different. I found myself in leadership positions, especially in teaching roles, but I was usually viewed and treated as "the exception."

From my first year of college, I was involved in leading Bible study groups, a skill and commitment I learned from my involvement with InterVarsity Christian Fellowship. Through IVCF's training in inductive Bible study, I found my teaching voice and in many ways also found a research methodology that I continue to use today. I discovered that I loved studying Scripture; loved teaching at the intersection of Scripture, tradition and contemporary issues; and loved drawing out insights from others.

My first exposure to feminist discussions, especially those within evangelicalism, came in the mid 1970s when I read the book *All We're Meant to Be* and the magazines *Daughters of Sarah* and *Radix*.[6] I found the arguments simultaneously persuasive and disturbing, especially as my primary church and theological contexts were then hostile to strong egalitarian stands. Mostly, I lived quietly with the ambiguities while I served in various forms of ministry. I read the very conservative responses to the emerging feminism and took seriously some of their concerns about Scripture and authority.

---

[6]Letha Scanzoni and Nancy Hardesty, *All We're Meant to Be: A Biblical Approach to Women's Liberation* (Waco, Tex.: Word, 1974). *Daughters of Sarah* and *Radix* were important Christian magazines during that time that frequently gave voice to egalitarian concerns.

My decision to go to seminary and graduate school came as I confirmed a deep love for teaching Christian ethics and a sustained engagement with justice issues. I was blessed with very fine mentors within seminary, graduate school and family. Most were men who often could see the value of my work better than I could. From the time I was very young, my mother was sure I would be a teacher and has consistently encouraged me in the various dimensions of my call, persuaded that what I was doing was both interesting and useful to the kingdom.

In spite of years of work in social ministry and extensive studies in social ethics, for a long time I did not directly engage feminist arguments. I shared feminist concerns for empowerment and inclusion but found it easier to work within other frameworks. I was strongly encouraged by my mentor at seminary to do further study in social ethics, but in neither seminary nor my doctoral program did I receive encouragement to study feminism or explore gender questions within ethics.

Furthermore, my prolife stance and commitments made any sojourn in feminism quite awkward. I cared deeply about justice issues in general—and about race, gender and poverty concerns in particular—but found few other Christians except those in the left wing of evangelicalism who embraced a similar combination of positions. I was deeply ambivalent, attracted to feminism because it spoke truthfully about some things I knew from experience but also wary because the feminism I encountered seemed so white, middle-class and self-centered.

While not fully comfortable in evangelical contexts, I was also uncomfortable in feminist ones and often found myself silent in both. I gradually incorporated numerous feminist sociocultural and political critiques into the ways I work in ethics, but I consistently avoided theological ones for several reasons: some of the approaches to Scripture and tradition shredded what I cherished, some did not ring true, and sometimes they caused more trouble for me at the time than they were worth.

The topic of my dissertation and related academic work over the past fifteen years was recovering the tradition of Christian hospitality. This topic has allowed me to make sense of my varied commitments and has opened up many conversations among evangelical, mainline and Roman Catholic communities. My work has brought me into a new phase of bridging multiple worlds in which I take gender seriously without necessarily fully engaging feminist theology.

Adopting and being adopted into the Wesleyan tradition has made it easier to draw my life together. The long-standing affirmation of women's leadership roles and the connections between nineteenth-century Wesleyan revivalism, abolitionism and the first wave of feminism provide a narrative that makes sense of my own life and concerns. Though I would most readily describe myself as an evangelical in the

Wesleyan tradition, I have recently become involved in an Episcopal/Anglican church with strong evangelical commitments. The pastor and the congregation are deeply committed to hospitality and community, and questions of gender are clearly settled in favor of women's leadership and authority.

But gender concerns are never really settled. Working in a seminary context, I engage the boundaries all the time and see female students and faculty also struggle with them. Over the sixteen years of my teaching at Asbury Theological Seminary, I have seen many changes, but each year we also address the same issues again. With a new crop of students annually, with the move of several conservative denominations toward restricting women's leadership roles and with the impact of the megachurch movement and its generally conservative views of male and female roles, gender issues remain an important topic.[7] Teaching at Asbury is different from working in many other evangelical schools because Asbury has had a commitment to training men and women for ministry since its founding. Nevertheless, from the 1960s to 1987, there were no women on the faculty in tenured positions (except the librarian), and when I came in 1989, I became the second woman to be on the faculty in a full-time, tenure-track position. Since then Asbury has added thirteen women to its tenured or tenure-track professors, changing the personal and institutional experience of women significantly. The reality of having more than token female presence is powerful. However, because I teach a course on "women in church and society," I have the opportunity to engage student views and experiences regularly.

HOW THIS PROJECT DEVELOPED

The idea for this project began one afternoon during a visit in Wilmore, Kentucky, when we realized that many of the women we had known in seminary in the mid 1980s had gone on to do Ph.D. studies. What was it, we wondered, that had made it plausible for such an unusual number of evangelical women in one cohort to pursue further academic work? What had prompted us to do it, and how had other women come to similar decisions? How had they fared? Did we all share similar experiences in finding jobs, raising families, fitting into churches? How had these women negotiated the experience of moving from evangelical environments to Ph.D. programs that were often much more liberal and sometimes feminist? What were they doing now?

---

[7]Several evangelical megachurches do hold more egalitarian views. See, for example, <www .willowcreek.org/SpiritualFormation/Membership/FAQs.asp#13>.

From these initial questions, and after reflecting more systematically on our own experiences, we decided to broaden our inquiry. What was it like more generally for evangelical women who pursued Ph.D.s in biblical and theological studies? What were their experiences as they taught and wrote, as they were mentored and became mentors? Who were their models? At some point, our casual summer conversation moved toward a decision to write a book together and then came to include a far reaching survey of as many evangelical women as we could find who would answer our questions.

The book is much more than a description of what we found in our survey, however. The women's responses to our questions provided us with rich material from which to draw insights and illuminate important issues. We were also interested in developing a fuller theological reflection on topics about which feminists and evangelicals often seem at odds. We have engaged much of the literature related to our interest in fostering a critical but cordial conversation among evangelicals and feminists.

Our survey of evangelical women. Over several years, we questioned academic women in the fields of theology, biblical studies, church history, ethics and missions who identify, or once identified, themselves as evangelicals. In an attempt to keep the numbers manageable, we restricted our focus primarily to women in these fields. We assumed that the tensions between evangelicalism and feminism would be posed more acutely in these disciplines than in English, physics or theater, for example. An evangelical seminary is an intensely confessional space, committed to the formation of its students, and it is often a place of close community. The transition to a theologically liberal graduate program, especially in the United States, can be lonely and difficult—a move to a world where assumptions and conversations are very different.

Our assumptions were not entirely borne out. Some of the women had studied in doctoral programs at evangelical institutions or under evangelical mentors, and others had never been to an evangelical seminary. A number of women in religious studies have avoided feminism, while some evangelical women in the humanities and social sciences have struggled deeply with the boundary. Nevertheless, there is a fairly consistent tension for women who teach and have authority in the area of religion. In no other academic discipline are theological concerns posed more acutely. Persons trained in theological and biblical studies are responsible for preparing the next generation of Christian thinkers and leaders, and questions of women's authority and legitimacy in the church are substantial.

While we did survey a few women in other related disciplines whose focus of scholarly work was theological, we largely limited our survey to the group described above. With regret, we also excluded the women who were trained at the Ph.D. level in Christian education and Christian counseling. Our assumption here was that the pool of women would have grown significantly, but also that these are areas of academic study that have been more traditionally open to evangelical women.

How we did the survey. Through a snowball approach of gathering names, we identified approximately two hundred women who seemed to fit our categories.[8] We sent out lengthy questionnaires (mostly via e-mail) to about 150 women, and approximately ninety were completed and returned. At the American Academy of Religion meetings in San Francisco and Boston in subsequent years we talked to approximately twenty-five women in additional face-to-face interviews. During the several years of the project we discovered other women who fit the categories, and some of them responded to the questionnaire. At the AAR meeting in Denver, Christine had a chance to reinterview a number of the women we first surveyed to gain a better sense of their ongoing experiences.

We asked them a wide range of questions, covering basic demographic data; their definition of *evangelical*; why they were, or were no longer, evangelicals; their experience of call; the significance of mentors and models; and the role of professional and friendship networks. They were asked what made them think they could do doctoral work and what their experience of the transition from seminary to doctoral program was like. We inquired about each woman's job searches, present academic institution, relation with faculty colleagues and students and role in the local church. There were also questions about family and about tensions between career and family responsibilities. The final questions covered more explicitly theological topics: their understandings of truth, definitions of evangelicalism, and key theological issues posed at the intersection of evangelicalism and feminism (e.g., authority of Scripture, sin, patriarchy and the transcendence of God). We also asked how they might have changed their minds over the years.

Responses ranged from very brief comments to chapter-long reflections. The group of women was quite diverse, and there was substantial variation in academic preparation and current location, as well as in evangelical identity and commitments. Because of the narrative and often informal nature of the responses, and the

---

[8]Because there is no available roster of evangelical women in religious studies, we were dependent on our own contacts and on those supplied by friends and acquaintances who suggested other names, who in turn suggested other women. This worked quite well, though occasionally we found women who were quite surprised to be included in the evangelical fold. They graciously declined to be interviewed.

sometimes incomplete data we collected, we are not claiming to offer the results of a formal qualitative study, though we have tried to be true to the emphases we discovered. We have understood our project to include describing and reflecting on a shared and previously uncharted landscape from the inside. Our findings are impressionistic, though our hope is that the final painting is as truthful as possible to what we learned. Because this is an important topic to each of us, both personally and professionally, we have included our own observations and experiences as part of the study and the book.[9]

The response of the participants. Most of the women enthusiastically described their journeys and were eager to participate. Cooperation was not universal, however. Some women were reluctant to respond because they had come to reject the evangelical label, did not want to rehearse old hurts or were suspicious or fearful of the intentions or implications of the study. A few women were concerned about the problems they might have with their conservative institutions if they were identified with the project. Nevertheless, most responded to the invitation positively, and for some, the survey and conversation offered opportunities to tell important personal stories and to share hard-earned insights.

We did not define evangelicalism in the survey because we were interested in the definitions the women themselves might suggest. The theological definitions, distinctive practices and institutional identifications the women offered generally fit the expectations one might draw from the literature on evangelicalism. However, we discovered that some women with very similar theological and spiritual commitments identified themselves differently. A significant number of women in the more conservative branches of the Wesleyan and Anabaptist traditions reject the label *evangelical,* as do many African American women, even when they are teaching at evangelical institutions.

If a woman did or did not define herself as evangelical, we wanted to know why. There was significant diversity in how women came to be evangelical, in the type of evangelicalism they embraced and in how and when that faith was challenged by feminism and liberalism. We discovered a Roman Catholic woman who had become an evangelical while attending a Methodist graduate school and other women for whom graduate school was a point of departure from an evangelical past. Some described the evangelical world as having been liberating at first and oppressive later. While a number of women found the more feminist academy a place to grow

---

[9]We assured the participants in the study that we would preserve their anonymity when we quoted them or made use of their responses. Therefore, we have not included any names, and occasionally we have had to modify minor details of a story.

and to explore alternative identities, numbers of other women found themselves and their concerns silenced there.

We found a wider range of experience and background than we initially anticipated. Among the women with whom we interacted, and based on the information we were able to collect, we found that approximately two-thirds of the women graduated from college between 1970 and 1985. Slightly under half had graduated from evangelical or conservative Christian colleges. The undergraduate background of the rest of the women was varied: Ivy League schools, large private universities, small private colleges and state schools.

Approximately half of the women said that they had had an evangelical or conservative Protestant upbringing. Of eighty-nine women we surveyed, sixty-six identified themselves as currently evangelical or neo-evangelical. Of these, some answered yes to the question of being evangelical and then went on to also identify themselves as Wesleyan, Reformed, Anglican, Presbyterian, Church of God, Anabaptist or Southern Baptist. Seventeen women said that they were not presently evangelicals but were Wesleyan, Anabaptist, Presbyterian, Anglican, Reformed, Lutheran or Church of God. Besides making it difficult to come up with clean categories, these responses exemplified the complex situation within evangelicalism today.

Among the women whose current denominational identity was clear, approximately half are in three denominations: Presbyterian Church USA, Anglican/Episcopal and United Methodist. The rest are scattered over mainline and conservative denominations: moderate Southern Baptists, Church of God, United Church of Christ, Lutheran, Mennonite, Evangelical Covenant, Free Methodist, Christian Reformed, Christian Missionary Alliance, Nazarene, Vineyard and so on. A number identified their churches as evangelical without providing any specific denominational identification. A large number of the women in mainline denominations identified their local church or pastor as evangelical.

One-third of the women we surveyed are ordained or licensed, and close to 20 percent had missions experience overseas. Most of the women had graduated from seminary, but the diversity of schools was noteworthy. Only Fuller and Gordon-Conwell seminaries stood out as producing a significant number of women who had gone on to doctoral work.

At the time we collected the survey information, fifty-six of the women had Ph.D.s (a few had Th.D.s), and thirty women had completed all doctoral work except their dissertation. Doctoral degrees were from a very wide range of institutions. Despite the fact that most of the women we surveyed were from the United States, almost a quarter of the doctoral degrees were from schools in England,

Scotland and Canada. Women studied at Fuller, Drew, Chicago, Yale, Duke, Southern Baptist, Emory, Garrett/Northwestern and many other schools. There was also wide variety in the schools where the respondents were teaching. Women were teaching at the undergraduate and graduate level in Christian colleges and seminaries, in missions settings and in religion departments of more secular colleges and universities. In only a few cases did we talk with more than one woman teaching at a particular school, and then it was rarely more than two women.

Of eighty-nine women, twenty-five were single, eleven were married with no children, six were divorced, and forty-two were married with children. More than half of the women who responded to the survey had children.

SITUATING OUR PROJECT
WITHIN A BURGEONING LITERATURE

Our sources for the book are the women we surveyed and interviewed, the growing bodies of literature about evangelicalism and about various types of feminism and women's experience, and our own experiences and insights. Because this is also a theological reflection on the experiences of women living on the boundary, we are not attempting to speak for hundreds of women, or even for the particular women in our survey. Rather, we are describing the boundary as we have found it, hoping to bring to light various insights from a diverse scattering of women. In addition, because the book involves a theological reflection on the boundaries themselves, the final chapters include a more systematic, constructive effort to further the theological conversation.

When we first imagined this project in 1996, there were almost no studies of evangelical women, except for those dealing indirectly with the situation James D. Hunter addressed in his culture-wars paradigm: evangelicalism and feminism can be understood as representatives of opposing cultures.[10] In addition, a few pioneering researchers had recovered the stories of evangelical women in the past, especially in the nineteenth century. But the limited attention has increased significantly in the last few years, and today there is quite a substantial literature on evangelical women, though not much on their experience in the academy. A notable exception is Elouise Renich Fraser's book in which she describes her life as one of the very first evangelical women to teach theology in a Baptist/evangelical context.[11]

Recent books have looked at women in evangelical and fundamentalist churches

---

[10] James Davison Hunter, *Culture Wars: The Struggle to Define America* (New York: BasicBooks, 1991).
[11] Elouise Renich Fraser, *Confessions of a Beginning Theologian* (Downers Grove, Ill.: InterVarsity Press, 1998).

and in parachurch organizations and have drawn out more ambiguity than had been previously associated with these communities. Although none of the women we interviewed would have identified herself as fundamentalist, many studies blur the distinction, and several important books have looked at the relationship between gender and fundamentalism. We have occasionally referred to these studies of fundamentalism and gender because some of their conclusions are relevant.

A substantial literature about evangelical identity and the role of evangelicalism in American culture has developed and continues to grow. Interestingly, few of these books give much attention to gender issues, despite the significant arguments about gender that go on in evangelical circles.[12] Dorrien, in *The Remaking of Evangelical Theology*, comments explicitly on this strange absence: "One sign that the progressive current within the larger postconservative trend is only in its beginning phase is the fact that it has spoken thus far almost entirely in a male voice."[13]

Among recent analyses, the book *Being There: Culture and Formation in Two Theological Schools* offers insight into the cultural, gender and ethos differences between an evangelical and a mainline Protestant seminary.[14] The findings of the study suggest that any student moving between an evangelical seminary and a more theologically liberal or feminist doctoral program would experience a jarring of cultures and changing frames of reference, often at a very personal level. Although both traditions are Christian, the differences in cultures are great, and rarely can one be comfortable in both or move between the two without spiritual and cognitive dissonance. *Being There* supports our claim that to engage both feminism and evangelicalism is to engage the boundary between well-defined maps.

Recent changes in emphasis in the Southern Baptist Convention and other conservative denominations have been closely tied to narrowing the roles of women,

---

[12]For example, Christian Smith's recent and important study of American evangelicalism has almost no discussion of gender, although he offers a fairly nuanced analysis of other sociocultural factors. Mark Noll's book *American Evangelical Christianity* includes only a small section on gender issues in contemporary evangelicalism. In Robert E. Webber's very interesting 2002 book, *The Younger Evangelicals*, women's voices are included but gender issues are nearly invisible. See Christian Smith, *American Evangelicalism: Embattled and Thriving* (Chicago: University of Chicago Press, 1998); Mark A. Noll, *American Evangelical Christianity: An Introduction* (Oxford: Blackwell, 2001); Robert E. Webber, *The Younger Evangelicals: Facing the Challenges of the New World* (Grand Rapids: Baker, 2002).

[13]Dorrien, *Remaking*, p. 203.

[14]The authors found that the evangelical seminary was characterized by discipline, theological orthodoxy and a generic Calvinism, while the mainline seminary was particularly sensitive to issues of inclusion, prejudice and language. The struggles in the mainline school focused on justice, exclusion and boundaries, while the struggles in the evangelical community were doctrinal. Moreover, the heroes in one were largely unknown and unacknowledged in the other. Jackson W. Carroll et al., *Being There: Culture and Formation in Two Theological Schools* (New York: Oxford University Press, 1997).

and these changes and their impact on women have also been studied. Experiences of women who teach in Christian colleges have been examined. Some challenges to the culture-wars paradigm, based on evangelical women's experiences, have been developed. Our work should also add to the various recent studies of women in the professions more generally and of women in the academy in particular.[15]

ENLARGING THE CONVERSATION

Although we previously identified our target audience for this book, we also hope that some of the material will be useful and of interest to people in other professions and communities. In general, we hope that this story will contribute to a more careful discussion of women, feminism and evangelicalism at the beginning of a new century. We realize that all of our experiences are not necessarily or entirely unique, and we expect that some of them will resonate with other populations. Women who identify with the historic Christian faith and evangelical women in other academic disciplines may find much in common with us. Seminary-trained evangelical women who are serving in pastorates and other clergy positions may also find much of the material true to their experiences. Some evangelical men may also identify with a number of the tensions we describe. Certainly some of the tensions will be recognizable to academics, whether male or female, who are involved in local churches.[16]

We hope that our reflections will add to the whole spectrum of feminist theology, now quite sensitive to differences in women's experience. Feminist theology written from the perspective of evangelical women has been largely absent. Giving voice to evangelical women's experience is thus a part of our academic and pastoral purpose. We hope to be able to show how these two movements, so often seemingly at odds with one another, can also be mutually helpful. In her book on the

---

[15] For example, see Lori G. Beaman, *Shared Beliefs, Different Lives: Women's Identities in Evangelical Context* (St. Louis: Chalice, 1999); Brenda E. Brasher, *Godly Women: Fundamentalism and Female Power* (New Brunswick, N.J.: Rutgers University Press, 1998); Sally K. Gallagher, *Evangelical Identity and Gendered Family Life* (New Brunswick, N.J.: Rutgers University Press, 2003); R. Marie Griffith, *God's Daughters: Evangelical Women and the Power of Submission* (Berkeley: University of California Press, 1997); Julie J. Ingersoll, *Evangelical Christian Women: War Stories in the Gender Battles* (New York: New York University Press, 2003); Christel J. Manning, *God Gave Us the Right: Conservative Catholic, Evangelical Protestant and Orthodox Jewish Women Grapple with Feminism* (New Brunswick, N.J.: Rutgers University Press, 1999). Interesting also is Marti Watson Garlett's "Waiting in the Wings: Women of God in the Evangelical Academy" (Ph.D. diss., Claremont Graduate School, 1997), examining gender inequities in Christian colleges.

[16] Because our study was not fundamentally comparative, we cannot state with certainty that each incident or experience is tied to gender. What we do argue throughout the book is that gender issues are extremely important in evangelicalism and, as a result, color and shape women's experiences in intense ways.

"changes in [mainline] theological education brought about by the presence of women and the emergence of feminist practices within theological education," Rebecca Chopp writes that "an interesting project would be to study what goes on for women in schools related to evangelical movements in the United States and for women in para-institutions of theological education."[17] In some small way, we hope that our work begins to meet this challenge.

Academic theology is done in the academy, and the academy, especially in theology, has been squarely on the liberal side of the cultural divide. Over the past decades, the analysts of evangelical theology have noted that there has been little dialogue across the liberal-evangelical border, and almost none has been initiated from liberal to evangelical communities.[18] In the past several years, however, this has been changing. With more attention to lived religion, to particular traditions and to Christian practices, new partnerships and conversations are developing.

While the potential for conversation across borders of evangelicalism, feminism and liberalism is promising because of the significant shared theological and epistemological histories, quick judgments and formidable cognitive boundaries make engagement difficult. When differences are transformed into bludgeons and political tools, the conversation ceases entirely. Thus we are seeking to carve out a space for discussion. A closer examination of women's lives will offer a more nuanced picture of the conflicts and should challenge the easy polarization of evangelicalism and feminism. Thus, in giving voice to our observations and experiences on the borders, we hope to encourage others who live there and to find companions along the way.

As already noted, for some of the women we surveyed, the encounter with feminism resulted in a move away from evangelicalism. And that, of course, solves the problem of living with the tensions and contradictions on the border. But for numbers of us, to relinquish an evangelical identity would be to give up a crucial part of our own stories and some deep intellectual commitments and alliances. Is it possible to be both evangelical and feminist? For some women, it is not possible to be either if to be one is to be defined out of line by the other. We discovered that the most fruitful insights into these tensions came from those who still struggle on the borders of evangelicalism or who live with difficulty but hope in its mainstream.

Many of the women with whom we spoke are finding ways to bridge multiple

---

[17]Rebecca S. Chopp, *Saving Work: Feminist Practices of Theological Education* (Louisville, Ky.: John Knox, 1995), pp. ix, xi.

[18]These dialogues and their absence are discussed in "Postconservative Evangelicalism: Dialogues in Search of a Generous Orthodoxy" in chap. 5 of Dorrien, *Remaking*.

theological, intellectual, ecclesiastical and academic worlds, seeking a place in environments that are at times quite polarized. Life on multiple margins brings insights that, however personally and institutionally troublesome, can provide starting points for larger conversations.

OUTLINE OF THE FOLLOWING CHAPTERS

In chapter two, we will examine questions of evangelical identity, privileging the voices of the women from the study. We consider various ways women are responding to feminism and to their experience within evangelical institutions. The chapter explores some of the strategies used to live with the deep tensions within evangelical identity. Chapter three further develops the discussion by addressing more general questions relating to gender and evangelical identity. In the fourth chapter, we examine questions of finding a voice, being mentored, studying and teaching. Chapter five delves more deeply into issues of community, call and church. The last two chapters examine theological issues on the boundary. We conclude by returning yet again to the questions Is evangelical feminism possible? and What is "unexpected and new" that might be found there?

| 2 |

THE VOICES AND THE STORIES

Staying and Leaving

—∎∎∎∎—

> It's my impression . . . that most people reared in the evangelical
> subculture either embrace it altogether or abandon it altogether.
> Either option strikes me as disingenuous, as an easy way around a tradition
> that is at once rich in theological insights and mired in contradictions.
>
> RANDALL BALMER, *Mine Eyes Have Seen the Glory*

Our efforts to make sense of the various ways women responded to our questions about evangelicalism and feminism eventually resulted in a typology within which to articulate identity and boundary issues. Some women had left evangelicalism, some challenged our assumptions about a boundary or denied that living on the boundary caused the kinds of tensions we suggested; others embraced an allied, more mainstream or ethnic Christian community; and a few ignored the boundary and with it feminism and all forms of liberalism. Most of the women we surveyed were working to find a richer spirituality, whether or not they maintained an evangelical identity, and many others were carving out a place for themselves within both worlds.

A closer look at what the women said and how they reacted to the tensions within evangelicalism and between evangelicalism and feminism illuminates some of the key issues related to the question Where are the good women? Women's choices and interpretations give a powerful picture of what it is like to try to find a place on one or several maps. An additional dimension of the issue is how feminism engages or fails to engage evangelicalism. This is another part of the story and will be considered at the end of chapter three. Here, however, we want to present the varying reactions to "the boundary" and the voices and stories of those who have persevered with life on multiple maps.

LEAVING EVANGELICALISM BEHIND

Mainstream evangelicalism is at odds [with]—and [is] often hostile to—the fullest emotional, spiritual and psychological development of gifted women. It is, in essence, a dysfunctional world which scapegoats intellectual women as "the other." Women who stay "inside" wind up making tremendous compromises in each of these areas, often to the detriment of their own health and life satisfaction. ❧

While for some women a demarcation from fundamentalism is sufficient to mark out an acceptable space for moderate evangelicalism, others have rejected any evangelical identity, or left it behind. For one former evangelical leader, there is no way to live in an evangelical feminist space with integrity; authenticity requires that one leave evangelicalism. For her and for several others, the label *evangelical* is too tainted to be acceptable. Indeed, some of those who consciously left evangelicalism had been hurt or ignored by the evangelical institutions that they had trusted or that had once nurtured them. Exploring this response helps us to understand some of the reasons academically gifted women no longer locate themselves within the evangelical world.

Diana Butler Bass, one of our Gordon-Conwell Seminary classmates, tells a story of departure in her book *Strength for the Journey: A Pilgrimage of Faith in Community*. For her, the abandonment of evangelicalism was a coming to self in the Anglican communion and to a recognition of God as love. She characterizes the evangelicalism she left as being in denial of feelings and emotion, encouraging only "scholastic Protestantism." "It was like a puzzle. Like math. Learn the formula, plug in the numbers."[1] Her critique is painfully true of academic theology as it has sometimes been taught in evangelical seminaries. While this model of theology has been challenged within parts of evangelicalism recently, it is also the cross-fertilization from outside the movement—interactions with postliberalism and narrative and liberation theologies—that has begun to break down the dominant modernist theological paradigm.

Departure appears to be easier if women have come into evangelicalism as adults, rather than having grown up within the culture. For such a woman, moving out and identifying with a related tradition seemed quite natural.

I grew up outside of the evangelical tradition, in an academic family—both my parents were university professors. When I entered the evangelical world, I always knew that this

---

[1] Diana Butler Bass, *Strength for the Journey: A Pilgrimage of Faith in Community* (San Francisco: Jossey-Bass, 2002), p. 168.

was only one way of seeing the world and not the only valid way. I felt constrained and controlled in many ways over the years among evangelicals—theologically, in terms of being a woman, cultural expectations, etc. . . . I went to graduate school because I wanted to broaden my horizons. In part I think it was a returning "home"; I came alive in my work there. ✍

For some women, however, the reasons for leaving or drifting actually parallel the criticisms expressed by others who nevertheless decided to persevere within the movement. "I don't like the word *evangelical* at all," said one. "At worst, I think it refers to a mindless, experiential and dogmatic form of religion." Identification and identity are very much the reasons for disconnecting from the tradition for this woman.

So it became a label I did not wish to own in nonevangelical circles for fear of being associated with what I was not. . . . I do not disown my evangelical roots and continue to value . . . them but choose to term myself differently. . . . Here I think the problem is not that I am now not evangelical in belief because I am something else, [but] rather that I feel evangelicalism, which after all grew in a specific historical time and circumstances, talks about itself and faith and God in ways that I do not wish to. Its very mindset is not the way I approach things any more. ✍

Another woman commented, "The closed spirit toward me as a woman in ministry began my reworking of my identity. Plus, I see in evangelicalism an arrogance that questions the validity of other Christians as truly 'Christian.' . . . I don't know where I fit anymore."

Specific theological concerns (e.g., understandings of hell, exclusivity and worries over Genesis) dominated for a few, though these were mentioned less often than the cultural reasons. One woman who no longer identifies with evangelicalism commented,

I do not believe many of the beliefs that I once thought were firm, i.e., the inerrancy of Scripture, the God-written nature of Scripture, the God-given role of submission of women to men, that God can be influenced by prayer in ways that contradict nature (healing of spinal cord injuries), that God leads and directs our lives in highly specific ways (marriage partners, protecting from accidents). Even within the faith my beliefs have changed, [have] become less magical. ✍

Another testified to theological changes that were associated with a new location.

I left evangelical circles because of their view and treatment of women, but as a result my entire theology has shifted. I see the evangelical treatment of women as symptomatic of [its]

entire theological approach to Scripture and Christian life. I think some women are able to be evangelical and feminists, but I don't think I'm one of them. ✍

One woman responded to these tensions by joining the Episcopal church, finding a place where she could worship when her "head and heart are feeling split." Another Anglican woman who had given up her previous evangelical identity added to her explanation, "I have retained enough of my evangelical identity so as to be rather nondenominational in outlook." She and others expressed their frustration at the anti-evangelical rhetoric they endured in their mainline churches. They still retained some remnants of their old piety and affiliation. One such woman said, for example,

I think my rage is around the feeling that the evangelical subculture excluded me when I became a feminist, even when much of my theology remained essentially orthodox and conservative. Many of my feminist professional friends, even the ones that teach Christian theology, consider themselves post-Christian and find me hopelessly orthodox, even if amusing and loveable. In Christian feminist terms, I am quite conservative. ✍

It is noteworthy that some women in this situation felt they had to define themselves against evangelicalism and others did not, and that some felt they could have a home of sorts within the evangelical world while others found it an increasingly barren place. Another former evangelical admitted,

I think a lot of it [not being evangelical anymore] is also sociological in my own life, that I just moved into different circles. . . .Which religious subculture am I going to have to learn to live with and deal with? . . . I have a picture of redressing myself as I applied for positions in first one tradition and then another. I've socialized myself out of the evangelical language. ✍

Not surprisingly, then, these women have rejected evangelical identity largely because the story within which they tried to live became too burdensome, hurtful, inauthentic or even pragmatically unhelpful, so much so that some questioned why any woman would choose to stay evangelical. Their reasons for leaving were quite diverse and often a mix of increasing theological, cultural, sociological and academic differences.

DENYING THE TENSION

Several women denied the notion of a boundary because they rejected the idea of tension between evangelicalism and feminism. "There is no border, only a choice," said one. "I don't deal on the boundaries between evangelicalism and feminism," commented another woman. "I'm not sure what you mean by that. Are you assuming that feminists are outside of evangelicalism?" Some of these comments came from self-identified feminist women who were writing on evangelicals or researching evangelical women, but whose personal attachments with evangelicalism were tenuous or whose past attachments were now severed. These women had not necessarily made an official break with evangelicalism, but they had become sufficiently removed from the institutional realities of the movement or from current and historical evangelical commitments that they did not experience or acknowledge a tension.

A similar reaction was expressed as discomfort with the language and grammar of boundaries of any sort. A few women maintained that all boundaries were constructed and harmful, and they worried that we were prolonging their existence by continuing to speak in those terms. Similarly, one respondent worried that this mentality was reflected in our questionnaire: "I think you have too much of the 'us vs. them' assumptions in your questions here. I think you need to rethink your basic parameters."

A couple of the women who disliked the survey questions, rejecting the very ground on which the questionnaire was based, equated evangelicalism with the drawing of membership boundaries. Having taken this view, they did not feel a pull in both directions. Even to ask questions surrounding evangelical identity was perceived as buying into the old evangelical culture of trying to decide who is in and who is out. While we found these reactions helpful and interesting in light of ongoing controversies over the nature of meaning and reality, for most women who live and work in evangelical institutions, denying the boundary does not dispel issues related to gender in those institutions.

Embracing an Alternative Identity

I define myself as evangelical, but sometimes I find it embarrassing because of the intolerance and tightness of evangelicalism—more like fundamentalism and self-righteousness —so it became a label I did not wish to own. . . . I do not disown my evangelical roots . . . but I have chosen to call myself a Christian.

Having been shaped by broad, transdenominational evangelical traditions, we did not at first realize how Reformed the evangelical world often is and how little other traditions identify with it, even when closely related in theology, ethical positions or practices. History, community, particular practices and culture make a great difference. Thus we found substantial diversity of opinion about who is included under the evangelical umbrella and who is not, and this affected very much who was willing to answer our questions and who was not. Some women would include most or all charismatics within evangelicalism, but some charismatics and Pentecostals do not see themselves as primarily evangelical.

At times, the label *evangelical* is understood over and against liberal or sacramental theologies, but there are a significant number of evangelical and charismatic Episcopal women. Reformed evangelicals tended to assume that Wesleyans and Arminians are subsumed in the evangelical camp, but many Wesleyan or Church of God women distinguished themselves from evangelicals or have only later come partially to own that label. An important group resisting the notion of a boundary between evangelicalism and feminism consisted of women from traditions that may or may not define themselves as evangelicals. For a number of Holiness, Wesleyan, Church of God, Mennonite and Nazarene women, personal and ecclesial identity involved some distinction from regular evangelicalism.

An Anabaptist woman teaching at an evangelical school said quite simply, "I'm not evangelical." A Chinese graduate student wrote, "I do not and did not identify myself as 'an evangelical.' . . . My American peers and professors label me so." For moderate Southern Baptist women, *evangelical* was at one stage a useful label, but it has subsequently become a much more ambiguous one for them because conservative Southern Baptists have self-consciously adopted the term *evangelical*. "I'm not evangelical," replied another woman. "That term is not understood apart from new terminology of reactionary right-wing Baptists now taking over the Southern Baptist Convention."

For many academic women, then, not only is there a move toward mainline denominations, but sometimes there is a move to own a particular tradition rather than the broad evangelical label, especially if institutional location allows or encourages an alternative identification. This is more evidence of the deeply ambivalent nature of evangelicalism for academic women. If there is another distinction available—Lutheran, Wesleyan, Anabaptist—it may be chosen as a first identity or as a cover against too openly having to own an evangelical identity. One woman working in a very liberal context, for example, came from a Baptist evangelical background, was ordained in a mainline denomination and still identified personally as evangelical. However, she also commented that she would never say so openly in her academic context. That environment was sufficiently difficult without adding the burden of such a label.

Another group to deny an evangelical identity, and thus the boundary, were African American women. Evangelicalism is overwhelmingly white in the United

States. Many conservative African-Americans affirm theological commitments similar to those of evangelicals, but they have their own ecclesial and institutional history, and in many ways evangelical categories and tensions are irrelevant to them. There are some African-American academics now being hired in evangelical schools, but very few. The response we generally received was that black and evangelical do not readily go together.

This does not mean that African-American churches are free of patriarchy or of the conservative-patriarchal combination that characterizes many evangelical and fundamentalist churches. Moreover, gender is equally important and equally hidden in many of these churches, but with very different dynamics. Serious concerns about alienated and powerless young men abound, and many churches and educational institutions take on a somewhat matriarchal character. Nevertheless, the very white nature of American evangelicalism is further evidence that evangelical is not defined by doctrinal position alone. Culture and a shared history are a large part of identity.

IGNORING FEMINISM

I am not engaged in any feminist issues. They are not my area of interest.

People on both sides of the discussion want me to take a strong stand either in favor of or against women's ordination, and I just don't find the topic compelling.

For a small but significant number of women, feminism remains a very marginal interest. This is partly a matter of choice, but much also depends on one's particular graduate school experience. Some women have never seen the compelling nature of feminism, or have rejected it.

I guess after reading feminist stuff for years, I simply cannot correlate some of the ideology with reality as I have experienced it, especially after the birth of my daughter. . . . [I am] more aware than ever of the importance of family bonding, relationships and eternity, and the relative unimportance of much that dominates life.

The sentiments expressed by this woman were rare. Nevertheless, many women would agree with the importance of family relationships and "eternity" and the way in which these are sometimes ignored and thus devalued in feminist circles.

Some women avoid, ignore or reject feminism because of its associations with the individuality-denying character of gender politics or because of fears of being co-opted by an ideology or a secular movement. In a related tension, some women resisted attempts on the part of the larger culture or their academic institutions to impose gender-consciousness as a defining aspect of their identity. In an article in

First Things, written while still in graduate school, Margaret Kim Peterson wondered whether she had become unemployable because she was female and an "independent" thinker.[2] These questions point, perhaps, to the difficulty most women experience in negotiating the rhetoric of gender.

STRUGGLING TO FIND A RICHER SPIRITUALITY

For almost all the women we surveyed, efforts to maintain an evangelical identity are at times accompanied by a sense of searching and even of anguish. Women who have experienced sustained struggles over their authority or their freedom to preach and live out their calling seek a regrounding in a spirituality less intimately bound to the common evangelical emphasis on cognitive exactitude. These women are weary and reluctant to engage boundaries, whether propositional or cultural. Evangelicalism, being very much a movement of words and Word, can feel liturgically and spiritually barren when words are used as bludgeons or slogans or when they do not square with experience.

One woman who has chosen a more independent and autonomous spirituality wrote, "I don't identify with any tradition now. . . . I do not have a sense of belonging to a church because I do not fit the mold. My faith has been renewed in the last two years through studying theology [and] through spiritual direction with an Anglican nun." Another noted her discomfort with "the lack of symbols and liturgy in . . . evangelical churches," finding that the corresponding absence of tradition, "particularly in the face of a church growth mentality, lends a certain blandness and superficiality to . . . evangelical worship."

A turn to some kind of Roman Catholic spirituality was not uncommon in women who had been through sustained battles in evangelical churches. Several spoke of their appreciation for contemplative and more inwardly spiritual approaches to faith, though for some this was combined with a continuing identity as an evangelical. When they moved toward Roman Catholicism, it was a selective appropriation that excluded the church's hierarchy. For others the evangelical labels had become unhelpful, and although they empathize with evangelical worship, they long to bring into it a wider theological framework.

I no longer use the word evangelical in describing myself (I prefer the term Christian*), but I am happy enough to be identified as having come from and lived within evangelicalism. I don't try to hide that now in "religious/church" contacts. I also value a lot of what evangelicalism has given me, including a love of Scripture and many of the tools for reading it. And*

---

[2]Margaret Kim Peterson, "What a Woman Ought to Think," *First Things* 82 (1998): 13-14.

in practice I worship and mix in evangelicalism most of the time! I am also happier in much evangelical worship in terms of style and approach than I would be perhaps in other modes— whether this is because it is familiar and therefore comforting rather than for other reasons is hard to say. . . . I think for me God has just become so much bigger than evangelicalism, or ecumenism, or liberalism or any other part of the spectrum. I am not threatened (any more) by people relating to God differently from myself. It does not undermine my attitude to and understanding of God; it simply reminds me that I don't have a monopoly on God. ✑

Aspects of evangelicalism remain important for many of these women, and they preserve a more ecumenical spirit than many of those who are now more firmly rooted in a particular tradition. Here there is no boundary either; rather there is an embracing of a spirituality that goes beyond the boundary and beyond the cognitive and cultural debates that often define it.

Even for those who stay within evangelicalism, however, there is a trend toward the contemplative and the liturgical, in keeping with the inclinations of the "younger evangelicals," as described by Robert E. Webber.[3] Some who acknowledge that every particular community brings with it strengths and promise as well as destructive and coercive tendencies remain grounded in evangelical identity while embracing a more inclusive spirituality and worship. In the following sections we examine the voices of those who have chosen this path.

ENGAGING BOTH WORLDS: LIFE ON THE BOUNDARIES

To engage both worlds or life-maps requires not only a fortuitous social and institutional location, but also some capacity to control, broaden or nuance the definitions of *evangelical* and *feminist*. In addition, it requires skills that allow persons to engage both communities in languages and styles that fit. The rest of this chapter is an exploration of the "type" of response most central to this book: responses from those who are living on the boundaries, on the maps of the evangelical and the feminist, the evangelical and the mainline, the evangelical and the confessional. Not only does this describe our journeys and the journeys of women who have chosen to live within the tension, but it is in part a story of evangelicalism itself, which, at least in some of its dimensions, is seeking a renewed center that is "catholic in vision."[4]

---

[3]Robert E. Webber, *The Younger Evangelicals: Facing the Challenges of the New World* (Grand Rapids: Baker, 2002).
[4]See Stanley Grenz, *Renewing the Center: Evangelical Theology in a Post-Theological Era* (Grand Rapids: Baker, 2000), p. 346.

Parts of the evangelical and academic world are opening up to new conversations across significant borders. Male evangelical academics are engaged in some important discussions about gender, and insights from the social sciences are increasingly prominent in these conversations. Most of the women who have chosen to live on the boundaries are critical realists, but an awareness of gender and of the social constructions of reality have also involved paradigm shifts in intellectual development. Coming to understand the social nature of our existence, the humanly constructed character of so much corporate living and the hidden workings of patriarchy and gender consciousness raise complex questions about identity. Understanding dynamics of power, oppression, perspective and collective identity affects theological interpretations and provides a window into richer readings of Scripture. This kind of reading of Scripture breaks open the mysteriously communal character of the biblical story that remains so obscured to individualistic modernists.

Nevertheless, issues of gender and the socially constructed aspects of our reality remain opaque in many evangelical—and indeed in many nonevangelical—circles. As a result, it is nearly impossible for academic women to live and work on this boundary without reflecting on identity—historically, theologically and spiritually. What is the inner experience, the value, the piety, the nature of the life that we are resolved not to give up? Why are the benefits and blessings of boundary living worth the price of remaining in what is often an uncomfortable position? Why has gender been such a key issue while being simultaneously so invisible?

The responses we received from most women who have chosen to live on the boundary were dense with the language of ambiguity. They were saying, I am evangelical, but with reservation. Said one woman,

> *I find valuable insights in both camps [evangelicalism and the liberal academy]. I have an orthodox Christian belief structure and a liberal social consciousness, and I am never truly at home in either camp. I have lived with my own contradictions for so long that paradox seems the norm. My resolution is to be reconciled to a certain amount of dissonance as "background noise" to what is worthwhile in evangelicalism and in academia.*

This woman described herself as a "parameter dweller."

Nuancing the definitions. Among the women we surveyed and among those who responded to the various presentations we have given over the last five years, we have discerned the desire to retain an evangelical identity while pushing beyond what appear to be constricting and restricting boundaries. There is a sense that, yes, I will own the evangelical label as long as I have some control over what that means. One evangelical woman's response captured some of the broadening impact of her encounter with feminism and liberalism: "The boundaries are now stretched, but I would give the same answer."

Some women respond by pressing on the boundaries of each world, seeking some integration that remains true to their deepest commitments in both arenas. Others identify the dilemma common to many evangelical women in the job market, that of not having an acceptable evangelical or liberal pedigree. "I guess I'll be too liberal for most evangelical institutions and too conservative for most mainline schools," said one woman in a sentiment reflected by many of the women in our sample.

Along with distinguishing evangelicalism from fundamentalism, there is a tendency to nuance evangelicalism so that it will function as a label more readily accepted and adopted. One woman explained, "I define myself as a contemplative evangelical: evangelical because I believe Jesus Christ was the Son of God, and contemplative because so much of evangelicalism is superficial and masks the real person of Christ." Another nuanced her definition by describing herself as

> *a liberal evangelical, or neo-evangelical. Some people think this is an oxymoron. I do not. I am an evangelical in the sense that the Reformers of the sixteenth century thought of themselves as evangelicals: i.e., there is no doctrine or institution that stands above the gospel of God's grace in Jesus Christ.* 🕮

As is evident from the above, a number of women have adopted modifiers to use with the term *evangelical*. "I still consider myself an evangelical, albeit a postconservative, postmodern one," said one woman in the survey. Another responded,

> *I resist the notion that the identification of myself as an evangelical inherently demands that I carry a specific set of political affiliations or agree to a few specific "shibboleths" in order to qualify as a "true" evangelical. I only accept the title of evangelical in its traditional sense or even in a broad sense as that discussed by such theologians as Donald Bloesch [and] Howard Synder.* 🕮

A respondent from a liturgical tradition said quite explicitly, "I am an evangelical and a feminist." She realizes that she has a lot of unpacking to do and acknowledges that she does not use the terms in quite the same way as her listeners usually do. But the ambiguity is intentional, and she sees it as part of her hearers' education. This willingness to live with and redeem the given categories may be due in part to the fact that we are educators, living and working with words and their repercussions. Said one teacher surveyed, "I'm a strong believer in the hermeneutics of retrieval. I'm not generally willing to abdicate a term because it is being misused. I'd rather get in there and say, This is being misused."

Jeffrey Bineham refers to this work of redeeming and reclaiming the evangelical heritage when he writes of Christian feminists empowering themselves "by decoding texts in ways that oppose established interpretations and interests. . . . Dominant readings have become 'commonsense' and are rendered easily; oppositional readings take work and require access to non-traditional codes that feminists can use in interpretation."[5] Academic evangelical women are well placed to do this work of recoding and redeeming the tradition, but such an enterprise is always fraught with difficulty in a largely conservative movement.

It is not easy to make understandings of evangelicalism more nuanced. The media often focus their attention on the evangelicalism of churches that are ahistorical, anti-intellectual bastions of patriarchy, all the more problematic because divine authority is regularly invoked. While most of the women we surveyed dwell in evangelical institutions that are more moderate and open, even in these places, gender issues, while less overt, are present in all aspects of life. In more moderate environments, the work of recoding, redeeming and nuancing continues.

The term evangelical *is problematic, but it best states my commitment to biblical authority. I use the term* infallible *rather than* inerrant *to define my hermeneutical commitment.*

I knew I was a feminist before I was an evangelical. . . . [This is] probably unusual in your survey? . . . It ended up making me fairly pig-headed, not able to be persuaded that there is anything wrong with women or that there are substantial differences [between genders]. I grew impatient with that way of thinking, screened out the foolishness, and went on my way; it seems to have been a pretty good strategy.

Another woman described a growing distaste for many expressions of evangelical popular culture: the jargon, praise choruses, and many evangelical books and magazines. Evangelical men who are academics are often similarly critical of evangelical popular religion, but their criticisms are usually articulated from a more comfortable situation in the academy. For academic women to endure anti-intellectual elements of the subculture and to be marginal in the academic culture is a difficult combination, but one that is often taken on as a call or a responsibility, as this woman suggested.

Being a [female] evangelical impacts my relationship with other evangelicals the most. They

---

[5]Jeffrey L. Bineham, "Theological Hegemony and Oppositional Interpretive Codes: The Case of Evangelical Christian Feminism," *Western Journal of Communication* 57, no. 4 (1993): 521.

are the people I live with, worship with and teach. My responsibility to them feels immense. Their needs are compelling to me, because they are also mine. . . . Granted, the anti-intellectual aspects of American evangelicalism can be frustrating, and the anti-woman bias has the potential to get on my last good nerve. However, my identification as an evangelical means that I cannot just abandon them whenever they annoy me. ✍

Ironically, such persistence can be the result of a fundamentalist or evangelical upbringing with all of its accompanying practice in resistance. One woman, for example, described how her fundamentalist background prepared her to stand against the world and thus to stay faithful to her call despite the setbacks. A stubborn resistance is built into the fabric of evangelical life, a characteristic that makes it possible to sustain long battles: "I grew up in a family steeped in evangelicalism. . . . I saw myself as strong—my life verse was Philippians 4:13—'I can do all things through [Christ] who strengthens me.' "[6]

Call and resistance are linked. A sense of call allows women to value themselves and their struggles despite a lack of clear valuation by organizations in which they serve. God's call is "my stronghold against adversity," said one woman.

However, persisting with one's call against a hostile "home" environment is troubling and exhausting. It is important to be quite sure that the battle is worth the effort, and women find themselves wondering at times whether they are staying for the right reasons. Is this tenacity a sign of steadfastness or of compliance with authority figures? Are we being faithful, even good, or are we participating in our own oppression? The answer is not always clear, and it depends very much on the individual's circumstances and the nature of the community within which she is located. Among a few women, call—which will be further explored in chapter five—undergirds a profound resistance, almost a defiance of institutions that will not let them serve. And the irony is not lost, as one woman put it, "that being a dissenting voice has been enabled by my evangelical upbringing."

The protean self. Women in many contexts have developed skills for taking on multiple roles and tasks simultaneously in order to be different people in different settings and to reconcile contradictions within the web of relationship. Circumstances, however, also impose this fluid identity. "I sometimes feel duplicitous when hanging out with liberal women because they think I fit," said one evangelical woman. "I work well in mainline situations because I know how to connect with many of the good parts of that world." Such a survival strategy can be helpful,

---

[6]S. Sue Horner, "The Wind Shifts," in *Rattling Those Dry Bones*, ed. June Steffensen Hagen (San Diego: LuraMedia, 1995), p. 69.

though difficult, because academic women must function in multiple worlds and because each community brings another aspect of ourselves to life or brings relief to parts of our lives where the other community is most oppressive.

Christel Manning takes up this idea of the "protean self" in examining how conservative women reconcile seemingly contradictory positions on gender issues. In her research, she encountered women who simultaneously affirmed the gender understandings of religious traditionalism while maintaining a feminist identity in the workplace. She quotes Robert Lifton, who first described the protean self, based on "Proteus, the Greek sea god of many forms."

> We are becoming fluid and many-sided. . . . Without quite realizing it, we have been evolving a sense of self appropriate to the restlessness and flux of our time. . . . Central to its function is a capacity for bringing together disparate and seemingly incompatible elements of identity and involvement . . . and for continuous transformation of those elements.[7]

While the protean aspect of evangelical women may worry some school administrators or theological departments, there is more strength than threat in this fluidity. Evangelical women often understand other traditions and would not be where they are had they not deliberately accepted the evangelical world with its strengths and weaknesses. Most administrators need faculty members who can talk across boundaries, act as catalysts of change and form links and networks outside the institution. One woman said, "I do this all the time. I act as an ambassador. . . . They know that I won't mess up, that I won't embarrass them."

This notion of a protean self was expressed by several women in the study: "I think women are used to thinking on multiple tracks at once, thinking creatively and laterally and practically," said one respondent. Another, teaching in an evangelical context, spoke of being "on the edge of everything" and therefore able to work in very diverse environments.

For another woman, the protean self was deliberate and subversive: "I think that my theology and faith profoundly shaped the direction and outcome of my Ph.D. thesis [in a hostile secular university], and the great thing was that the examiners didn't spot it." A common refrain is the idea that fitting in becomes an art in itself. One woman described her protean existence, which, while conflicted, also suggests significant multilingual ability: "What I do well is speak both religious 'languages'—evangelical and liberal." The protean self is evident also in this woman's

---

[7] Christel J. Manning, *God Gave Us the Right: Conservative Catholic, Evangelical Protestant and Orthodox Jewish Women Grapple with Feminism* (New Brunswick, N.J.: Rutgers University Press, 1999), pp. 156-57.

response: "My identification as an evangelical is strong when I 'hang around' loving and kind fellow-evangelicals; it weakens in the presence of meanness."

A similar idea stands behind the process of "bracketing." Women have the experience of leaving behind one self, or of bracketing one set of commitments, in order to live faithfully in another deeply valued community. One woman explained,

> *I'm probably most comfortable these days speaking and thinking in a more relativistic feminist framework and, most likely, I bracket all that when I go to church or talk about God with my children.*

Although some women find this practice to be internally dishonest, others use it to negotiate callings and situations that superficially, at least, seem profoundly at odds with one another.

This protean existence is not unique to feminist or academic evangelical women. It is a common experience for conservative women generally. Says Manning,

> Just as secular or liberal American women must juggle many different roles and do not adopt a consistently feminist identity, so religious conservatives are not consistently antifeminist and are frequently shifting between active, assertive, independent roles that are traditionally reserved to men to more passive, submissive, nurturing roles deemed appropriate for women.[8]

In researching gender identity in evangelical and fundamentalist women, several scholars have concluded that hierarchical gender relations in the home and church have a symbolic role. Women do not necessarily interpret these symbols in the way nonfundamentalists think they do, nor do all members of a community interpret them in the same way. Multiple interpretations of gender symbols are in place at any given moment.[9] Nor are American women in general as enthusiastic about feminism as might be expected. Many scholars have noted the general ambivalence regarding feminism in American society.

But for evangelical academic women the picture is a little different. Academic theology is now very feminist outside of evangelical institutions, and the differences and disjunctions are harder for academic women to ignore. Thus a reinterpretation and bracketing of some symbols and positions becomes important in certain contexts. As a result there is an urgent need to make a space on the boundary because there is so much of importance to be claimed and reclaimed in both communities and because there are many "solidarities" in spite of the significant oppositions.

---

[8]Ibid., p. 159.
[9]Ibid., pp. 159-60.

KEEPING THE QUESTIONS ALIVE
IN EVANGELICAL SPACE

The struggles of living on the boundary come partly from the clash of worldviews and theology and partly from the differing practices associated with each world. Additionally, practices and beliefs within a single worldview are not always consistent. Evangelical women living on the boundary are living out of several maps, looking in two or more directions at once, and the personal and the political are often confounded.

Practices in particular often inadvertently reflect and perpetuate earlier assumptions about gender roles far beyond the time when theological assumptions about women have been challenged. While relatively minor when they occur only occasionally, they can gradually add up to a strangely pervasive undermining of the commitment to live on the boundaries.

Conservative institutions are often very wary of political correctness or of PC language, a turn of phrase that tends to denigrate inclusiveness and to put the onus for justifying equality on the woman or minority. As noted earlier, there are times when concerns about political correctness can be oppressive, but the more frequent problem in evangelical contexts is insensitivity to issues of inclusion and justice. Even when evangelical women find themselves explaining to outsiders that a specific incident of insensitivity is not really characteristic of an environment that is generally undergirded by love, they are noting the tensions. They will be more conscious of blunders concerning gender and race when nonevangelicals are present because outsiders "don't know the bigger picture." However, this does mean that women are constantly aware of the contradictions; they are wondering, *Is this really how I am seen? Where do I belong in such an environment?* For women who live and work within the evangelical world, there is an ongoing, sometimes wrenching, internal conversation about their place within this space.

The forces holding academic women within evangelicalism are quite diverse. It may be deep theological commitments, a close-knit family, a vibrant local church or a parachurch organization like Evangelicals for Social Action or Christians for Biblical Equality. It may be a group of friends meeting to pray with a common expectation of answers and a common belief in what can only be called the supernatural. "I can put up with a lot in exchange for the knowledge that I can ask for prayer for my father," said one woman. Similarly, Brenda Brasher notes that for the women in her study, one reason they were willing to tolerate gender restrictions was the "longing for intense, convincing encounters with the transcendent."[10]

---

[10]Brenda E. Brasher, *Godly Women: Fundamentalism and Female Power* (New Brunswick, N.J.: Rutgers University Press, 1998), p. 5.

Other women remain in the evangelical world because questions about human origins, intelligent design and epistemology are addressed with vigor there. Friedrich Schleiermacher's words resonate: "I will always be a Herrnhuter . . . only of a higher order."[11] *Higher* here refers only to the sense that we, too, are a part of the "heretical imperative" and have had to choose, and that our believing will always be more critical than pure piety might demand. The piety, though, and the sense of God's presence will keep us identified as evangelicals in spite of some deep tensions and challenges.

For many evangelical women there is also the understanding that we are a part of a movement that is both changing and the life of the future.[12] Some mainline churches are taking steps toward certain evangelical emphases and practices. Some are beginning to search for a core of belief and a way of evangelizing in this new century. For example, one woman noted with hope, "I see the evangelical wing of my mainline church as the place where vitality and mission exist in ways that are less common in other places." And for many of us, the critical but believing engagement with culture occurs nowhere else. Where else can we find the serendipitous combining of the grammars of enquiry and the grammar of the scandal of the gospel?

CONCLUSION

The various responses to our questions about evangelical identity and its relationship to gender and to feminism are quite revealing of the ways in which women attempt to negotiate multiple worlds and of their reasons for staying within or leaving the evangelical world. Some respondents concluded that personal integrity required a choice between evangelicalism and feminism, but others were unwilling to use the language of boundary at all. A number of women chose to use a different label or to identify with a different tradition, and a few did not find feminism particularly interesting or compelling. For most women we surveyed, however, these questions involved a spiritual struggle. Life on the boundary involves ongoing reflection on identity and regular grappling with the complexity of gender assump-

---

[11] B. A. Gerrish, *A Prince of the Church: Schleiermacher and the Beginnings of Modern Theology* (London: SCM Press, 1984), p. 13.

[12] Perhaps some of the potential in the evangelical movement is best appreciated from outside. Gary Dorrien notes that "[George] Lindbeck rightly observes that the future of postliberal theology as a communal enterprise of the church lies primarily in the hands of evangelicals." Dorrien also reports that "near the end of his life, Hans Frei told Carl Henry that his deepest theological desire was to witness the emergence of 'a kind of generous orthodoxy' that blended and transcended elements of existing evangelicalism and liberalism." See Gary Dorrien, *The Remaking of Evangelical Theology* (Louisville, Ky.: Westminster John Knox, 1998), pp. 203, 209.

tions within evangelical institutions. Understandings of gender, though not explicitly part of most faith statements and creeds, are manifest in the practices, grammar and rhetoric of church and community.

Evangelical women teaching in theological disciplines encounter this boundary theologically, institutionally and personally. In recent years, questions about evangelical identity have been widely addressed, but until recently the academic conversation has often been strangely quiet on the role and significance of gender assumptions in the evangelical world.

In the next chapter, we examine some of the defining and paradoxical characteristics of evangelicalism that function alongside its theological commitments. The importance of practices, the role of experience and the centrality of gender conflict in evangelical identity are discussed. We describe how women navigate these paradoxes and why many continue to try to find a place and a voice on the boundaries of evangelicalism and feminism.

| 3 |

GENDER ISSUES AND CONTEMPORARY EVANGELICALISM

Critical Reflections from the Inside

—◄▥▥▥►—

Gathered for a small Christmas party in the home of a faculty member at a Christian college, a number of professors and their spouses are sharing a meal. The food is great, the conversation is congenial, and the people are very gracious. There is one new woman among the academics; the rest of the women at the party are wives of faculty members. When the host couple announces that it is time for the women to come to the kitchen, the new faculty woman is bewildered, but gathers herself together and follows the women out of the room, leaving behind her colleagues and the academic conversation. Being required to choose between one's gender and one's vocation is both embarrassing and painful, even when the tension is unnoticed by most of the group.

A complete response to the question Where are the good women? requires a closer look at evangelical culture and its interpretations of gender. Although evangelicals often define themselves in terms of theological commitments and statements of faith, other unstated factors like gender-consciousness, particular practices and distinctive artifacts may be equally important and defining of the subculture. While in theory there may not be a boundary between feminism and evangelicalism, in practice such a boundary is quite real and its negotiation is often difficult and demanding. In social practices as simple as calling all the women to the kitchen after dinner, academic women encounter awkwardness, embarrassment and a sense of institutional betrayal, together with conflict over which of several duties, identities and loyalties to act on. All this may happen under the eyes of men who are acting out the same drama without seeing the tension and the ambiguity that their female colleagues are experiencing.

Such ambiguity is made more troublesome by the larger definitional challenges. That evangelicalism can only be defined with difficulty is clear from the increasing number of articles and books devoted to this question. Few people struggle similarly over what it means to be Roman Catholic or Mennonite, identities more clearly defined by sacramental or denominational boundaries. From the outside, the evangelical world is a discordant collection comprising, for example, Chuck Colson, Stanley Grenz, Wayne Grudem, Clark Pinnock, Billy Graham, John Stott, Tim LaHaye and James Dobson. Among organizations, the evangelical label is applied to Fuller, Trinity, Gordon-Conwell, Asbury and Dallas Seminaries, Wheaton and Houghton Colleges, Liberty and Azusa Pacific Universities, Willow Creek Community Church, Women's Aglow, Promise Keepers, the Christian Coalition and Evangelicals for Social Action. Journals engaged by evangelicals include *Christianity Today, First Things* and *Sojourners.* Christians for Biblical Equality and the Council on Biblical Manhood and Womanhood reflect divergent, passionately held evangelical positions on gender.

All of these names evoke particular and often conflicting subcultures within the larger evangelical culture or on its edges. The looseness and the wideness of evangelicalism's definition is both a strength and a weakness. Evangelicalism is a remarkable mix: cultural, confessional, historical, institutional and denominational factors combine in a variety of ways. It has connections with Protestant fundamentalism and with prophetic social and cultural critique. Defining lines are also changing: Roman Catholicism, once viewed as a polar opposite or foil, is in some contexts and some senses an ally of evangelicalism, and more than a few women in the study were finding nurture in Catholic spirituality.[1]

Connections between evangelicals and Southern Baptists also have a complicated but illuminating history. Until the 1970s, neither lay nor academic people within the Southern Baptist Convention had much contact with the larger evangelical tradition. When denominational controversy began to break out in the 1970s, differences were structured in liberal versus fundamentalist terms and, in the 1980s, Southern Baptists on both sides began to pay much more attention to the broader evangelical world. There they discovered a parallel internal struggle within

---

[1]The journal *First Things* is an example of a forum for cultural engagement among conservative evangelical and Roman Catholic theological voices.

evangelicalism, and new alliances were formed across the two traditions. A decade-long battle ensued over which strand of Southern Baptist identity would prevail. Often this was dealt with at the level of hiring decisions in Southern Baptist seminaries. The litmus test question was very often a person's position on women's roles. Generally, the more conservative players have prevailed in the seminaries and in claiming the title of evangelical.

In the United States there is a significant historical connection between evangelicalism and fundamentalism and the Fundamentalist controversy of the 1920s. In England, however, evangelicalism is a long-standing Reformed division of the Church of England, differentiating it from the liberal demythologizers of the nineteenth and twentieth centuries and from high-church liturgizers. In Europe and in the European-derived denominations in the United States, evangelical is usually a label referring to a Reformation heritage rather than to the American or international evangelical movement.

Thus a significant difficulty in identifying oneself as an evangelical man or woman is that the term may resonate with groups, prejudices, practices, beliefs and historical identifications quite at odds with one's own. Women, however, find that the difficulty is compounded by the woman-defining nature of many of these sub-groups. Much of what is distinctive about some fundamentalist and conservative evangelical groups, for example, is their emphasis on male headship or on complementarian theologies of marriage.[2]

In spite of multiple institutional connections, evangelicalism has no particular church-based identity. There is no baptismal certificate or denominational membership that will guarantee evangelical orthodoxy or identity. Thus, critiquing evangelicalism from the inside is difficult and sometimes risky, and unless you are extremely well placed institutionally, or very famous, your critique may simply define you out, especially if you are a woman. Nevertheless, the ferment of discussion now surrounding evangelical definition opens up the possibility of more substantive critique from the inside.

Complex gender assumptions create a contested space for women within evangelicalism, which in turn affects women's perceptions of the movement, their willingness to stay and work within its institutions and their sense of well-being. To understand the issues more fully, we will now consider the mixed set of variables normally assigned to evangelical identity: propositions, experience, culture and institutions. How

---

[2]This has been particularly emphasized in Sally Gallagher's latest research on the evangelical family. Sally K. Gallagher, *Evangelical Identity and Gendered Family Life* (New Brunswick, N.J.: Rutgers University Press, 2003).

do women relate to the cognitive dimensions of evangelicalism, and how does evangelical culture work to maintain or disguise gender consciousness?

COGNITIVE BOUNDARIES AND
THE AMBIGUOUS PLACE OF EXPERIENCE

When I cringe at the term [evangelical], it is because of literalistic inerrantists. ◢

The word evangelical was liberating originally; it provided a larger worldview. Later it became unliberating. When rehabilitating a hyper-Calvinism, it became a bludgeon. ◢

Symbol systems and icons have shifted and left no room for me. I have been battered by the word evangelical *and a sense of double betrayal.* ◢

> Neither children of the Enlightenment nor children of the church,
> most evangelicals put their confidence in *sola scriptura* and their
> own subjective experience in determining how God wants them to live.
> SALLY GALLAGHER, *Evangelical Identity and Gendered Family Life*

When asked to define what it means to be evangelical, the women in the survey, like evangelicals generally, first answered in terms of theological commitments. Affirmations of the orthodox creedal statements of the historic church—that Christ really lived, died and rose again—and a high view of Scripture are central. As is the case in the larger evangelical community, evangelical academic women are convinced that we live in a religious world that is neither entirely constructed nor materialistic. On the whole, the women articulated a critical realist epistemology, believing that although the world of discourse is a partially constructed space, there is, nevertheless, a reality out there and within us to which our language refers. The supernatural and miracles have a place in this reality, whether within a supernaturalist naturalism or a frank supernaturalist framework. Questions of truth, origins and relations to other faith claims are vitally important, as are questions of salvation.

In popular imagination, in George Lindbeck's taxonomy of theological method and in some self-definitions, evangelicalism *is* its cognitive boundaries, and these locate evangelicalism very close to fundamentalism, with which it largely shares a doctrinal core.[3] Often, people assume that evangelicals are just more *open* funda-

---

[3]George Lindbeck divides the theological world into three parts: the cognitive/propositionalists, the experiential/expressivists and his own preferred mediating category, the cultural/linguists. George A. Lindbeck, *The Nature of Doctrine: Religion and Theology in a Postliberal Age* (Philadelphia: Westminster Press, 1984).

mentalists or "fundies" with an interest in culture. Yet among the women we surveyed, most were adamant that they could accept and embrace the evangelical but not the fundamentalist label. One woman with deep evangelical commitments noted that she was finding it increasingly difficult to claim an evangelical identity or theology because "there seem to be so many litmus tests that are hair-splitting in nature and intent," a tendency she associated with fundamentalism.

In fact, many of the cognitive boundaries surrounding and defining evangelicalism serve an important symbolic function. As a case in point, very few teachers at evangelical seminaries accept the doctrine of inerrancy without some nuancing, even where it is an official statement. Nevertheless, cognitive boundaries serve to modify the direction of questioning at the institution and provide a deep structure to the grammar of the discourse. Headship, too, in evangelical families is more proclaimed than really lived out in all areas of life. "Headship," writes Sally Gallagher,

> plays a strategically important yet largely symbolic role in the lives of ordinary evangelicals. While husbands retain the status of head of the household, the roles of evangelical men and women in decision making, parenting, and employment demonstrate that, for the most part, evangelical family life reflects the pragmatic egalitarianism of biblical feminists while retaining the symbolic hierarchy of gender-essentialist evangelicals.[4]

Cognitive boundaries, then, may act to keep notions of truth and commitment prominent, but they do not always dictate meaning in quite the way they appear to do from the outside. Evangelical academic women on the whole have very little issue with the central tenets of faith. But cognitive and propositional emphases can also obscure other dimensions of faith and silence conversation in particular areas, especially about gender. Furthermore, to argue that certain cognitive boundaries serve a symbolic function is not to suggest that they have minor implications; disagreements over male headship and biblical inerrancy have cost a number of academics their jobs.

Today, important theological questions are being raised within certain evangelical schools and in much of evangelical academic literature. Experimentation with narrative and with more multifaceted definitions of Christian belief is quite common. There is also an increased openness to giving attention to the world-defining and experiential aspects of faith. Developments in the "emerging church" movement and within missions theory—where Christian faith is understood in terms of direction rather than boundaries (centered instead of bounded "sets")—also re-

---

[4]Gallagher, *Evangelical Identity,* p. 84.

flect this trend.[5] While one might think that this widening of theological discussion would automatically be accompanied by a loosening of gender tension, this has not necessarily been the case.

As evangelicalism has engaged postmodernism, the strict propositionalism of previous generations has been tempered. Nancey Murphy, for example, in her book *Beyond Liberalism and Fundamentalism*, sets forth a new postmodern understanding of truth that includes and transcends both traditions.[6] Thus while there are multiple streams within American evangelicalism, including the recent megachurch movement (and the churches and denominations that look back to a purer theological orthodoxy inherited from the first-century, Reformation or Puritan churches), there is also a much looser association of reformist and postconservative evangelicals who engage contemporary culture more fully and more critically and who interact more regularly with theological voices from other Christian traditions.

Many of the women we interviewed who continue to accept the label evangelical would locate themselves in this last group. "Evidence is growing," says Roger Olson, "that some theologians who insist on wearing the label 'evangelical' (or cannot escape it even when they try) are shedding theological conservatism. A new mood, if not movement, in North American evangelical theology can be described as 'postconservative.' "[7] Many of these evangelicals, as Olson discusses, have grown up on mythopoeic literature and take an incarnational or narrative approach to theology and Scripture.[8] These developments may contribute to a more hospitable environment in which evangelical women can more fully explore feminist analyses and concerns and bring distinctive gifts and insights to the movement.

Indeed, while a commitment to a critical realism and a respect for truth are central to the evangelical endeavor, the conversation is often much more nuanced in academic circles than it is in the wider evangelical world. Stanley Grenz speaks of the importance of being a "pietist with a Ph.D.," and the Wesleyan and more con-

[5]Paul G. Hiebert, "Sets and Structures: A Study of Church Patterns," in *New Horizons in World Mission: Evangelicals and the Christian Mission in the 1980s, Papers Prepared for the Consultation on Theology and Mission*, ed. David J. Hesselgrave (Grand Rapids: Baker, 1979).

[6]Nancey Murphy, *Beyond Liberalism and Fundamentalism: How Modern and Postmodern Philosophy Set the Theological Agenda* (Valley Forge, Penn.: Trinity Press International, 1996).

[7]Roger E. Olson, "Postconservative Evangelicals Greet the Postmodern Age," *The Christian Century* 112, no. 15 (1995): 480.

[8]Robert E. Webber also discusses the emphasis by "younger" evangelicals on embodiment and "incarnational ecclesiology." See chap. 6 of Robert E. Webber, *The Younger Evangelicals: Facing the Challenges of the New World* (Grand Rapids: Baker, 2002).

versionist strands of evangelicalism are being more fully appreciated.[9] Several women made comments that reflected the new mood evidenced in some parts of the movement. "While still very much an evangelical," one woman noted, "all the hard lines I was raised with are softer now." Another spoke of believing in the same things, but in a broader and deeper way.

This broadening and deepening within a conservative framework should allow for fresh theological insights and useful dialogue on the boundary between evangelicalism and feminism. The broadening, however, does not necessarily yield a place for women or for full discussion of the deep paradoxes between experience and propositional beliefs in evangelical life. Gary Dorrien comments directly on this issue when he writes, "Some postconservative evangelicals are clearly much less committed to gender equality than to narrative hermeneutics or epistemological nonfoundationalism."[10] The conversation that continues around the edges does not necessarily reach the center of evangelicalism. Furthermore, while missions theory might experiment with new paradigms, systematic theology often remains untouched. Evangelical systematic theology and missions theory are themselves somewhat different "maps." And as one woman who regularly works in both disciplines noted, there is little dialogue between the two.

The evidence that new intellectual approaches do not necessarily provide a safe space for gender discussion is perhaps most apparent in the tension between the place of propositional beliefs and experience in evangelical circles. The experience of conversion is central in evangelical culture. Much language and song in evangelical life speaks of, anticipates or remembers the conversion moment or the salvation experience. Not surprisingly, an experience of conversion was important to many of the women surveyed. For some, this involved a childhood camp or youth-group experience; for others there was a later experience in the evangelical world. "I did define myself as evangelical because of an evangelical conversion at fifteen years [old] and because I was deeply involved in evangelical communities," said one woman. Another woman included both experiential and conversionist themes:

I think of evangelicals as Christians who want to talk about a particular experience of grace they have encountered in the church, or who focus on a personal relationship with Christ, and who highly value the normative authority of Scripture.

---

[9] Stanley J. Grenz, "Concerns of a Pietist with a Ph.D." (address at an additional session of the American Academy of Religion, Toronto, Ontario, November 23, 2002). Available on the Web at <http://www.stanleyjgrenz.com/articles/pietist.html>.

[10] Gary Dorrien, *The Remaking of Evangelical Theology* (Louisville, Ky.: Westminster John Knox, 1998), p. 204.

Such definitions are the marks of a distinctive language and grammar among evangelicals. Teaching, scholarship, witnessing, praising God and praying all occur against a background of shared experience and assume some kind of personal relationship with God.

This emphasis on a definitive conversion experience or, alternatively, on an evangelical upbringing suggests that evangelicals are as interested in religious experience as are liberals, albeit a different kind of experience. This has been and remains one of the profound ironies of evangelical life. "I could not refute the power of my personal experience in Christ, the dynamic relationship I had with the Holy Spirit. . . . These things kept grounding me in my evangelicalism," wrote one woman. When the conversion experience is in an evangelical setting, it is interpreted within a worldview defined by evangelical theological discourse and scriptural hermeneutics. Because experience per se is a suspect category for many evangelicals, the fact that experience is actually central to conversion stories is often overlooked. Experience and dogma, then, are mixed in evangelicalism, though in discussions about gender, the interaction between experience and Scripture is largely overlooked.

Certainly there are ways in which evangelicalism's emphasis on the Word seems to justify ambivalences about women that are not necessarily scripturally derived. The inerrancy debates, which have "run like a fault line through evangelicalism," (to borrow a phrase used by a younger male evangelical sympathetic to gender equality in the church), tend to obscure how thoroughly related they are to concerns about women's authority. As one woman noted, "Inerrancy is masking a deep ambivalence and hostility to women. It is an acceptable shield to take cover from the issue of women." Dorrien argues similarly that

> the lack of a developed feminist perspective in progressive evangelical theology is undoubtedly symptomatic of the serious difficulties that attend any attempt to reconcile feminist egalitarianism with a theological perspective that affirms the divinely secured infallibility of scriptural teaching.[11]

Susan Shaw and Tisa Lewis continue in the same vein, observing that although the debate at Southern Baptist Seminary centered on inerrancy, "the academic debates that raged around issues such as biblical inerrancy were secondary to the very personal effects of controversy around women's right to participate in ministry."[12]

---

[11]Dorrien, *Remaking*, p. 203.
[12]Susan M. Shaw and Tisa Lewis, " 'Once There Was a Camelot': Women Doctoral Graduates of the Southern Baptist Theological Seminary, 1982-1992, Talk About the Seminary, the Fundamentalist Takeover and Their Lives Since S.B.T.S.," *Review and Expositor* 95, no. 3 (1998): 404.

Thus women may find themselves addressing cognitive assumptions that obscure underlying prejudices about gender. Even after the theological conversation has opened up, surprising ambivalence about gender sometimes remains, and the movement's selective valuing of experience complicates the picture for many evangelical women. Although women's experiences of conversion, of intimacy with Jesus and of a calling to ministry are just as strong as those for male evangelicals, women's experiences in these areas do not fit as neatly with certain traditional interpretations of Scripture. Little attention is paid to this contradiction, leaving some women wounded, confused and alienated from existing church institutions.

While *sola scriptura* continues to be the stated authority for evangelicals, this glosses over considerable ambiguities related to how authority functions in most evangelical circles. It overlooks the significant role of feelings and of an individual's understanding of God's direction that so characterize popular evangelicalism. For a woman, the tension between the propositional nature of evangelical faith and a wellspring of experiential faith becomes more obvious when her call to ministry is dismissed by dogmatic pronouncements and theological arguments that appear to disregard fuller understandings of faith. Thus for women there is often a disturbing disjunction between the subjective and the objective forms of knowing.[13] While the recent broadening of the theological enterprise in dialogue with missions and postmodernity can be helpful, it certainly does not ensure that egalitarian impulses will emerge. It is important that women be able to bring their experience of God, calling and empowerment to the theological discussion, insisting that these experiential aspects of faith not be silenced by selective hermeneutical judgments.

INDIVIDUALISM AND INSTITUTIONAL CONNECTIONS

I think there are people in a variety of Christian traditions and churches who may make the same theological claims that are typically associated with evangelicalism, but it is the institutional connections and awareness of the importance of certain institutions that form the subcultural connections that somehow define evangelicals. [These connections] may not be shared by those who do not identify themselves as evangelicals. ✐

As a broad transdenominational movement, evangelicalism has an ambiguous

---

[13]Cynthia Crysdale warns about the danger of this conflict where the "reification of truth and value . . . [can] lead to personal and communal disjunction in which the best of the human spirit (its desire for intelligibility, truth, and value) is deemed to be the enemy of human authenticity." Cynthia S. W. Crysdale, "Reason, Faith and Authentic Religion," in *The Struggle Over the Past: Religious Fundamentalism in the Modern World*, ed. W. M. Shea (Lanham, Md.: University Press of America, 1993), p. 179.

relation to religious institutions. Evangelical identity depends heavily on an individual relationship with Christ; any broader categories and identifications are sometimes suspended. Evangelical "spirituality is individualistic even though church participation is important," observed one woman. Evangelicals are often less aware than other Christians of denominational boundaries and of the history and strengths of particular traditions. But despite its individualistic mindset, evangelicalism is more institutionally linked than many other movements. Much of its strength is found in parachurch youth organizations and coalitions of nondenominational churches. Evangelicals believe in the *church* but collectively do not have a strong ecclesiology.[14] Church attendance and membership are considered crucial, but the importance and priority of the historic church and its nature as a corporate body are often underappreciated. Evangelicals, as much as any other group in society, are likely to think of the church as a voluntary society and to treat it as a "lifestyle enclave."[15]

Evangelicalism is closely linked to a number of key organizations and schools. Wheaton, Gordon-Conwell, Fuller, Bethel, Trinity and Eastern seminaries and most of the members of the Coalition of Christian Colleges and Universities, for example, are self-consciously training evangelical leaders for the future, as are a few key Wesleyan institutions like Asbury Theological Seminary. Centrally important also are parachurch organizations on state and private college campuses. Many of the women we surveyed were initially shaped either by an evangelical upbringing or by parachurch organizations: evangelical conferences, healing and evangelistic meetings, summer camps, evangelical missionary societies, Youth for Christ, Inter-Varsity, Youth with a Mission, Operation Mobilization, L'Abri or Tear Fund. For many women, intimate relationships were nurtured and faith became an identity in some small group within a larger organization—a campus fellowship, cell group or house church.

Although being institutionally located is not necessarily part of the definition of evangelical identity, evangelical organizations—especially parachurch ones—are uniquely influential in evangelical lives. Within the evangelical academy, graduation from an evangelical college or seminary quite often functions as an important indicator of evangelical identity. Among the very few women teaching theology in evangelical schools, a number have graduated from the school at which they are

---

[14]See Stanley Grenz, *Renewing the Center: Evangelical Theology in a Post-Theological Era* (Grand Rapids: Baker, 2000), pp. 288-300.

[15]"Lifestyle enclave" is a key term used in Robert N. Bellah et al., *Habits of the Heart: Individualism and Commitment in American Life* (New York: Harper & Row, 1985).

teaching or an allied institution and have an evangelical pedigree. Although the significance of institutional affiliation is often underplayed, identity as an evangelical becomes strained when we are separated from all such communities or when we have been rejected by particular institutions, especially on issues related to gender.

Some groups like Evangelicals for Social Action and Christians for Biblical Equality attempt to carve out a space between several worlds, while locating themselves squarely within the evangelical subculture. In these border institutions, social justice and feminist issues are consistently addressed within evangelicalism. By explicitly situating itself within evangelical theological commitments and communities, CBE's arguments about egalitarianism can be heard in fairly moderate circles. In this way it can raise many of the issues that feminism raises but reframe them as hermeneutical or biblical questions.

We find, then, a very mixed picture. At one level, institutions do not matter very much. The heart of the Reformation, after all, was the individual's going directly to God without any human mediation or intervention. But at another level, institutions do matter; they matter a great deal. Without formation in a major evangelical school and without the backing and trust of key evangelical organizations and leaders, evangelical identity in the academy is often strained. When women attempt to speak out in evangelical settings, then, they often do so in institutions that have nurtured and formed them. Institutional attachment is not a defining characteristic of evangelicalism, but in practice it is one of the key elements of being evangelical. This is another paradox of evangelical life that tempers any criticism from inside the movement, especially on matters of gender.

The deep individualism and individualistic interpretive emphasis that characterize much evangelicalism add to the difficulty of doing social analysis and offering any internal critique. Individualistic approaches obscure the workings of power and privilege and the importance of social roles and expectations within institutions. The complex ways in which institutions both shape and are shaped by human beings are often overlooked.[16] An individualistic lens makes it very hard to understand issues of voice and power as being larger than a particular woman's "problem." If, in fact, the cognitive commitments of evangelicalism are largely present within Christian orthodoxy more generally, then evangelical women who critique evangelical culture are potentially threatening not to theological commitments, but to institutional power and structures.

---

[16]See the very helpful discussion of the general lack of understanding of the significance of institutions in the United States in Robert N. Bellah et al., *The Good Society* (New York: Alfred A. Knopf, 1991), pp. 5, 10-12, 40, 49, 290, 303.

GENDER: CENTRAL AND OFTEN INVISIBLE

Someone once asked me if there was a split within evangelicalism over the role of women. I replied that there couldn't really be a split because the issue was not even on the agenda.

Evangelicals and fundamentalists are often known for their strident public image and their absolutist stands on particular ethical and theological issues. While evangelicalism may appear to the outsider to be propositionally based and defined by cognitive boundaries, as discussed above, this outward appearance belies the centrality of gender issues. In her work on Protestant fundamentalism, Margaret Lamberts Bendroth has described the progressive shift in attitude toward women as Christianity became feminized, especially in the early twentieth century, when liberalism and fundamentalism divided. She observes that while women flourished in many sectarian churches at the end of the nineteenth and the beginning of the twentieth centuries, by mid-century, women were nearly absent from positions of ecclesial authority.[17]

Fundamentalism and its legacy within evangelicalism have been constituted, in part, by certain understandings of gender hierarchy that are religiously legitimated and, in some cases at least, defining of the group. Betty DeBerg argues,

> To understand fundamentalism as a widely popular movement in early twentieth-century America, we must look to causative factors beyond scholarly discourse and denominational meetings. . . . A historian of fundamentalism must reject a purely theological or intellectual approach to interpreting popular fundamentalism, because fundamentalism at that level was primarily a reaction to social change and conditions external to it and to religion in general. . . . But probably none of these social factors could affect as many Americans and in such an intimate and intense way as the vast changes in gender roles that also occurred during the period. Yet this flux in cultural symbols and norms relating to gender has not been a factor in most social analyses of fundamentalism. . . .
>
> Popular fundamentalist rhetoric contained frequent references to gender-related social conventions and beliefs. Close analysis of such rhetoric reveals that conservative evangelical Protestants perceived and reacted to the disruptions in the dominant gender ideology and in social behavior that were occurring all around them.[18]

Indeed, the fundamentalist and evangelical movements, in attempts to be dis-

---

[17]Margaret Lamberts Bendroth, *Fundamentalism and Gender, 1875 to the Present* (New Haven, Conn.: Yale University Press, 1993).

[18]Betty A. DeBerg, *Ungodly Women: Gender and the First Wave of American Fundamentalism* (Minneapolis: Fortress, 1990), pp. 6-7, 12.

tinctive, have adopted the so-called traditional family as an icon.[19] Women then bear the burden of exhibiting the difference between the true evangelical Christian and the nominal or liberal Christian or secular person, usually exemplified by a stay-at-home mother and the headship of the husband. In practice, there are ways in which this image is complexly subverted, as Brenda Brasher, R. Marie Griffith, Christel Manning and Sally Gallagher have all shown.[20] Nevertheless, every woman must, in some sense, contend with the associated expectations and limitations.

In different ways, Julie Ingersoll and Betty DeBerg have defended the thesis that gender issues, differences and conflicts are central to fundamentalist and often evangelical identity. Embedded in their definitions is an opposition to feminism.[21] Gallagher similarly concludes from her research that "ideas of gender hierarchy and difference persist among evangelicals because they are *the* central metaphor for the ontological world view of this particular religious subculture."[22]

Even if this thesis is only partially correct, it is certainly not surprising to find deep tensions in life on the boundary between feminism and evangelicalism and in being a theologically educated evangelical woman. The space in which we attempt to find an authoritative voice is particularly primed to gendered conflict. And yet, as several women have noted, it is rarely talked about openly.

While we agree with DeBerg and Ingersoll that gender is often the "elephant" in the evangelical living room, we would want to stop well short of a reductionism that defines the whole movement in these terms. Indeed we are persuaded that women, in spite of the depths of gender conflict, also discern things of perennial

---

[19]Gallagher has studied the complexities of the current manifestations of these arguments and the high stakes that hold them in place. She writes, "Maintaining the idea that the husband is the head of the family, even if that headship is largely symbolic—provides a dramatic contrast to the nominal egalitarianism of the culture. In doing so, it supports evangelicals' sense of being faithful to their mandate to be both in but not of the world. . . . For gender essentialists, abandoning the notion of husbands' headship threatens to undermine not only the authority of the Bible but also basic ideas about the nature of God and human beings. When ideas about gender hierarchy and authority are so closely linked to basic ontological understandings of existence and being, it is no surprise that conservative evangelicals find the prospect of abandoning the notion of husbands' headship so threatening" (Gallagher, *Evangelical Identity*, pp. 170, 173).

[20]One very noticeable tension for the traditional models is that even as they are affirmed, most of the women being interviewed are working outside the home.

[21]See DeBerg, *Ungodly Women*, and Julie J. Ingersoll, "Engendered Conflict: Feminism and Traditionalism in Late Twentieth-Century Conservative Protestantism (Fundamentalism)" (Ph.D. diss., University of California, 1997), p. 32. See also Christel J. Manning, *God Gave Us the Right: Conservative Catholic, Evangelical Protestant and Orthodox Jewish Women Grapple with Feminism* (New Brunswick, N.J.: Rutgers University Press, 1999), p. 52.

[22]Gallagher, *Evangelical Identity*, p. 174.

value in the evangelical community, including its shared understandings of transcendent reality and cultural critique.

Several nonevangelicals have attempted in various ways to answer the question Why then would any woman claim an evangelical identity? Brasher, Griffith and Manning have done close studies of women in conservative Christian congregations and parachurch organizations. Brasher, for example, notes that

> in addition to the . . . religious beliefs that make up the sacred canopy covering each fundamentalist congregation, gender functions as a sacred partition that literally bifurcates the congregation in two, establishing parallel religious worlds. . . . Women-only activities and events create and sustain a special symbolic world, parallel to the general one but empowering to fundamentalist women.[23]

Griffith studied women in the interdenominational, international charismatic fellowship of Women's Aglow, and Manning looked at women in conservative congregations, including evangelical ones. These authors observed that women carve out for themselves, within the divided sacred canopy, a space with considerable power and influence. This power, however, depends on a certain naiveté regarding the dynamics of gender and power in relationships and a willingness to work within the system for the greater good of the church at large. The influence is also somewhat subversive, and relies on women not drawing attention to their status, certainly not using the language of feminism and not presenting themselves as particularly well-educated in theology.

For academic women trained in theology and equipped to recognize and reflect on patriarchy, the issues play out quite differently. Having been taught to be attentive to gender and power dynamics in language, social life and texts, it is difficult not to see them. While women in other disciplines may never find themselves forced to a decision about women's voice and power, women in theological disciplines are more likely to notice the language and institutions of patriarchy and to be in positions in which conscious choices must be made regarding a relationship to feminism and to the patriarchal aspects of culture.[24] Often, however, significant gender reflection must be suppressed in church, in talking with one's children and in relating to students and even colleagues. This bracketing is both strategic—not wanting to fall afoul of institutions and friendships—and pastoral, addressing people where they are. Hence these issues for academic

---

[23]Brenda E. Brasher, *Godly Women: Fundamentalism and Female Power* (New Brunswick, N.J.: Rutgers University Press, 1998), pp. 4-5.
[24]For a minority of women, as noted in chapter two, the choice is made to ignore feminism.

women in theological studies will be both complex and entangled.

But why is gender so important to evangelicals? The answer is undoubtedly multifaceted. Gender issues arise in most conflicts over power, and sacred space is among the most contested space in America, notes Robert Wuthnow.[25] Important also is what Linda McKinnish Bridges calls the "Lydia Phase." Although institutions born in revivals (as are many evangelical churches) often begin with women in positions of leadership, these same institutions tend later to relegate women to secondary roles to gain cultural legitimacy and to diminish the feminizing effect of women's leadership.[26]

We would suggest that there are also theological reasons for the centrality of gender; evangelicals take the first chapters of Genesis very seriously and work hard to honor the integrity and intent of the material. Reconciling the literary character of Genesis and its truthfulness is not easy within the evangelical world. These chapters cannot simply be "dealt with," ignored or rendered an archetypal dilemma. Because they are so important, gender consciousness not only is politically or socially derived, but emerges from the primal theological story of the monotheistic religions. For evangelicals, careful interpretations of the creation of man and woman and of the Fall and its consequences are deeply important for understanding the nature of God, human beings and gender relationships.

Additionally, several difficult New Testament passages must be addressed.[27] These verses have taken on a life of their own and shape much conservative evangelical thinking about gender roles. Despite the availability of careful exegesis and historical examination of these texts since the nineteenth century and often conflicting evidence in the biblical text itself, evangelical churches seem to examine the passages anew in every generation. Particular forms of scholastic theological method and biblical hermeneutics within the evangelical world continue to support ahistorical readings of several New Testament passages. Although some of the arguments that counter these readings are as old as the sixteenth century, were well rehearsed in the nineteenth century and were rediscovered in the late twentieth century, parts of evangelicalism continue to bring to these difficult texts a highly gender-differentiated and hierarchical worldview. Rather than dismiss these texts as irrelevant to contemporary life as many nonevangelicals do, evangelical men and women struggle with them and take seriously the conclusions they reach. This is

---

[25]Robert Wuthnow, *The Struggle for America's Soul: Evangelicals, Liberals and Secularism* (Grand Rapids: Eerdmans, 1989).

[26]Linda McKinnish Bridges, "Women in Church Leadership," *Review and Expositor* 95, no. 3 (1998).

[27]See I Cor 11:2-16; 14:34-40; Eph 5:21—6:9; I Tim 2:8—3:16; I Pet 3:1-7.

the case whether the interpretations support a hierarchical or a more egalitarian view of gender relations.[28]

EVANGELICALISM AND SOCIAL, RELIGIOUS AND CULTURAL PRACTICES

Evangelical is not just a label for many of us.
It is an emotive word that evokes powerful memories and
deep-seated feelings of sawdust floors in open-sided tent meetings,
moments with God and his people around altars and bonfires,
sanctuaries and classrooms with preachers and teachers steeped in Scripture
and soaked in the Spirit, and participation in Billy Graham crusades,
Youth for Christ, Campus Crusade for Christ, and InterVarsity Christian
Fellowship. This is our story. This is our song. This is our family.
ROGER E. OLSON, "A Forum: The Future of Evangelical Theology"

We may not have all experienced the bonfires, sawdust or tent meetings, but we have all experienced the powerful corporate worship in classrooms, small groups, churches or parachurch organizations. Olson goes on to describe evangelicalism primarily as a theological movement rather than as a cultural one and, in some ways, we would agree. But the central theological tenets of evangelicalism are not uniquely held by evangelicals, and theology is embodied in a language, story and song that, in turn, form the theology and its expression. This embodiment is often experienced differently by men and by women. Women in positions of leadership are more likely than men to notice evangelicalism's tendency to use exclusive language, the importance of men's prayer breakfasts where significant work is accomplished and valued relationships are forged, and the absence of women on many organizational and conference platforms. Despite treasured moments in evangelical community and worship, women are ambivalent about aspects of its culture.

I no longer consider myself to be an evangelical after coming to a different view of the Bible.
I developed a distaste for evangelical exclusivism and experienced overkill with regard to
evangelical choruses, jargon and the various features of evangelical sub-culture. . . . Atti-
tudes toward women would prevent me from going back into the evangelical world, though

---

[28]See books by the following evangelicals for an egalitarian interpretation of the biblical record: Gilbert Bilezikian, Mary Evans, Stanley Grenz, Craig S. Keener, Catherine Clark Kroeger, Alvera Mickelsen and Aida Besançon Spencer. See also the discussion of gender in chap. 4 of Miroslav Volf, *Exclusion and Embrace: A Theological Exploration of Identity, Otherness and Reconciliation* (Nashville: Abingdon, 1996).

I don't think they were among my main reasons for leaving. ✍

I think "evangelicalism" in this century is primarily a social movement rather than a theological stance. ✍

When we asked women to define the nature of evangelicalism, we received, as noted earlier, a diversity of definitions, but they included the cognitive/belief aspect and a cultural component—"at least half culture," said one woman. This has certainly been borne out by our research. Cognitive commitments are always included; a high view of Scripture, a high Christology and belief in the resurrection are almost givens. But most women who have reflected on evangelical identity would also agree that a significant part of that definition—the particular mix of shared "language," evangelical worship, personal piety and relation to Christ, corporate prayer and community, and commitment to missions—is cultural: "a story, a song, a family." While to leave would mean abandoning part of ourselves and our family, living within evangelicalism can sometimes feel like being invisible among difficult and uncooperative family members.

One woman described this feeling and her associated way of coping within evangelical organizations: "I do not exist; I am not here," she says to herself when she is ignored by colleagues or subordinates in everyday social and academic settings. Naming the marginalization is her only defense against it. Yet she also acknowledges that she thinks better of the overall evangelical tradition than she does of her local church and is convinced that prayer brings men and women together in an eschatological sense, in spite of almost irreconcilable differences in the here and now. This is a remarkable insight, because it both expresses the intense alienation women can feel in evangelical academic circles and also identifies the uniquely evangelical response—prayer, the tradition as it transcends the moment and its eschatological hope.

Some of the women we surveyed identify themselves with denominations that are explicitly evangelical, but the majority have joined the evangelical minority within certain mainline denominations. As noted previously, changes in the Southern Baptist denomination have further complicated the task of definition; as the denomination has become more conservative and more closed to women in ministry, it has also quite self-consciously adopted the label evangelical. This has pushed some women who previously identified themselves as evangelical to repudiate that identity.

The nature of evangelical culture, then, is still a puzzle. How does one recognize it? Evangelicals, along with fundamentalists, are often seen as reactionaries and obscurantists, as behind the times and longing for some lost ideal time like the Victorian age or the 1950s when "proper" relationships between human beings and society, human beings and God, and man and woman were briefly realized. Despite megachurch models, cutting-edge technology and contemporary music, certain cultural assumptions in many churches reflect a former era.

But there is another sense in which evangelicalism and to some extent fundamentalism can be seen as countercultural. People are attracted to these religious communities precisely because they critique the larger culture. Manning notes this in her study of conservative women who had come to evangelical churches as adults. These women saw themselves as resisting mainstream culture and rediscovering something of value.[29] She finds that women are able to live with seeming contradictions—having feminist notions about equality at work and submissive attitudes at church. Again, women are seen trading one benefit for another and living within a social context that sees ambiguity in feminism even while aspiring to equality.[30] Similarly, Bendroth notes in *Fundamentalism and Gender* that one of the reasons women were attracted to fundamentalism was because of its "language of cultural critique."[31]

This inclination toward cultural critique can manifest itself in a brand of evangelicalism that is self-consciously outward looking, intent on engaging culture rather than reacting to it. But even fundamentalists may feel that they are critiquing the dominant culture more than they are preserving or conserving an older one. Thus the fundamentalist/evangelical world looks very different depending on the location from which it is observed. What appears triumphalistic to the liberal, feminist or secular onlooker may be an expression of prophetic witness from inside.

The authors of *Being There* suggest that the whole style and culture of doing theology in evangelical circles is quite different from the mainline or liberal world. Evangelical seminary education is formative in several ways. It shapes students toward different concerns and commitments than they would get in a mainline school, and it also pulls them away from the culture of popular evangelicalism.

> The religious culture of the students who enter [a mainline seminary] consists mostly of general ideas and attitudes. The Evangelical students have practices—manners, prayers, forms, approved dress styles, and a vast inventory of songs—as well as a network of organizations with which many are still in touch.[32]

---

[29]Manning, *God Gave Us*. See esp. chap. 7, "Understanding Inconsistency."
[30]Ibid., p. 159.
[31]Bendroth, *Fundamentalism and Gender*, p. 11.
[32]Jackson W. Carroll et al., *Being There: Culture and Formation in Two Theological Schools* (New York: Oxford University Press, 1997), p. 237.

Although liberals and evangelicals know of the other, they often know very little of the ideas, cultures and stories across the boundary. But in an interesting twist, evangelical students find internal cultural conflict from the beginning of their time at seminary, where the academic faculty are pushing for a more cognitive approach and where the students are attempting to maintain the practices and culture with which they entered seminary. This is evidence of the considerable tension in evangelicalism among its cognitive, scriptural, pneumatic and cultural dimensions.[33] Students at an evangelical seminary may experience a great deal of cognitive debate around issues liberal seminarians never touch, but they also may find themselves attempting to maintain a cultural evangelicalism not encouraged by the faculty. Evangelical theological training, therefore, can create a significant gulf, for both men and women, between those who have and those who have not attended seminary.

SOCIOMORAL ISSUES AS LITMUS TESTS

Adding to the conflicted and paradoxical nature of this space are the boundary conversations and ethical issues that, like gender, often silently undergird it. Few particular issues in contemporary American society define the alternative maps evangelicals live on more than the issues of homosexuality and abortion. The terms and grammar of these conversations in mainline churches and in the guild are completely at odds with those in evangelical organizations. The debates are structured by both communities in such a way that it is very difficult to hold a contrary position and be defined as a member in good standing. To attempt to do so often means that all of one's loyalties will be questioned.

And yet for many women in our study there are commitments in both directions—to the evangelical community and also to the mainline church and the guild conversation. Attempts to define the issues and opponents in more careful ways often make women "untrustworthy" to both camps. Many of the women surveyed want more careful reflection and thoughtful listening on both sides, and some would want to frame the issues differently. A few would prefer to agree to disagree, focusing their energies on other pressing social questions.

---

[33]Some of this tension is manifested in the conflict (described in ibid., p. 236) between incoming evangelical students and their evangelical professors. The authors observe that students "learn right away that the school's view of things is in fact very different from their own." The importance of discipline, hard work, restraint and "the primacy of reason over feeling" are strongly emphasized. Students often bring with them a "piety tuned exactly to their immediate feelings and needs." Most faculty value "an orthodox sermon on a biblical text, to which theologically correct prayers and dignified hymns can be added." Students arrive "averse 'to hearing another lecture' in chapel . . . and accustomed to filling the interval of worship with fervent testimonies and religious love songs."

In both worlds—evangelical and feminist—the language of community, solidarity and care are powerful, but both movements are capable of demonizing the
opponent, and both require positions on issues that then become tests of loyalty.
While these issues have a deep theological significance and resonance, there is
some irony that certain contemporary moral conclusions should be the *theological*
litmus test for any church community. Other social and bioethical positions do
not define the difference between maps and are thus often not given the attention
they deserve. Issues like pornography and abuse, where feminists and evangelicals
would share common ground, are not emphasized and rarely generate a base for
unified action.

The way these worlds have been carved up is somewhat paradoxical. It is remarkable that feminists are not protesting against selective abortion for gender.
This kind of ideological commitment to abortion makes evangelicals cynical about
feminist blind spots. Evangelicals often express frustration that the grief associated
with abortion is silenced in feminist circles and moral costs are never acknowledged. But in evangelical circles, concerns about abortion are rarely linked to other
prolife causes like the abolition of the death penalty. The tendency among evangelicals to support war and the death penalty makes prolife positions on abortion appear very peculiar to feminists. So women are left perplexed that what they view as
a consistent prolife stance fits into few defined packages.[34]

Similarly, differences regarding homosexuality are far more complex than either
side usually allows. Evangelical women might ask why the postmodern constructed
world becomes very essentialist on the issue of homosexuality. Why is the ambiguity of sexual response in adolescence or the need to avoid hasty conclusions regarding sexual identity not discussed more openly? Some evangelical women would also
want reflections on homosexuality opened to complementary sources of input—
the social sciences, mental health and neurobiology, for example.

Women, then, often define themselves as evangelical or feminist for reasons
that are different from the emphases others within these groups regard as litmus
tests for membership. As some evangelical communities move toward imposing
more explicit boundaries on particular issues and as a number of mainline denominations move toward being more accepting of disputed practices, churches are becoming increasingly polarized and the space for careful discussion and ongoing
research is shrinking.

---

[34]Sometimes, a more consistently prolife ethic is present in evangelical left, Anabaptist and Roman
Catholic views.

POSTURE IN RELATION TO THE OTHER

Deep in the grammar of evangelicalism is the notion of being separate and other, being different from nominal or liberal believers—an *us* and *them* mentality. While few evangelical academic women would now articulate their understandings this way, it has been a significant part of the culture. Said one woman who had been converted into evangelicalism and has since given up most of her evangelical identity, "I came to carve up the theological and Christian world in the way that evangelicals do: for example, nominal versus real Christians; those who accept the ultimate authority of Scripture versus those who don't."

Ironically, while this drawing of boundaries has characterized generations of evangelicals and continues in evangelical institutions in various forms, it has been and is being challenged within parts of evangelicalism. For example, postmodern evangelicalism, or the evangelicalism of the younger evangelicals described by Robert Webber, emphasizes an incarnational ecclesiology and an ecumenical and open style and identity, while nevertheless operating out of distinctly evangelical commitments and communities.

In identity discussions among many evangelical leaders, it is possible to discern significant divisions. Often the evangelical world is split between what Olson calls traditionalist and reformist coalitions or parties. He notes that while both "embrace the basic evangelical paradigm and work out of it," they hold different views on a number of issues including "theological boundaries, the nature of doctrine, progress in theology, and relating to nonevangelical theologies and culture in general."[35] For many more traditional evangelicals, the culture wars continue, and liberalism and feminism provide central foils against which to define and unite evangelical commitments. Evidence for deep antagonism toward the "other culture" is found in James Davison Hunter's research.[36] Daniel Alvarez, writing in *Theology Today*, commented on the agenda for theology drawn up by several leading evangelical men. He observed that "words like 'weapon' and 'invade' reinforce our skepticism about the authors' commitment to engage contemporary thought and culture substantively and fairly."[37] Discomfort with a too-close engagement with the "other" has surfaced when influential voices, like Clark Pinnock, begin to dialogue openly with people from the "other" side, like John Cobb.[38]

---

[35]Roger E. Olson, "A Forum: The Future of Evangelical Theology," *Christianity Today* 42, no. 2 (1998): 41.

[36]James Davison Hunter, *Culture Wars: The Struggle to Define America* (New York: BasicBooks, 1991).

[37]Daniel Raul Alvarez, "On the Possibility of an Evangelical Theology," *Theology Today* 55, no. 2 (1998): 183.

[38]See Clark H. Pinnock and John B. Cobb Jr., eds., *Searching for an Adequate God: A Dialogue Between Process and Free Will Theists* (Grand Rapids: Eerdmans, 2000).

Fueling the sense of *us* and *them* has been a bias toward the here and now of many evangelicals and an associated lack of appreciation for church history and tradition. However, this too is being challenged in deliberately postmodern churches, where an emphasis on recovering ancient practices, worship and liturgy is being combined with evangelical piety.[39] And it is precisely this us versus them distinction that is broken down by a wider exposure in graduate school to the broader theological world. This is especially true for women, whose delineations of us and them become more muddy as they become more educated and as their identity within the evangelical world becomes suspect.

Some women more closely associated with confessional traditions, whether Reformed or Wesleyan/Holiness, draw more of their identity from these traditions than from evangelicalism. Their sense of historical continuity mitigates some of the polarization within contemporary evangelicalism. Connection with a confessional tradition also provides a wider frame of reference and modifies the individualistic and ahistorical character of much contemporary evangelicalism.

Even within the broad nonconfessional evangelical movement there have been efforts to address the polarization of us and them. Both Wheaton and Messiah colleges have hosted conferences with themes related to this divergence, and dialogue was opened up. Wheaton College has also run theology conferences that intend conversation with allied movements like postliberalism. And there are theologians, also, working toward a more catholic understanding of evangelical faith. Additionally, a narrative approach has been appropriated as an evangelical tool by many theologians. At Fuller Seminary, Murphy has postulated that Anglo-American postmodernism can be a *useful* corrective to old foundationalism in both liberalism and fundamentalism, thus opening up new ways of crossing boundaries. And Miroslav Volf, formerly at Fuller and now located at Yale, has an innovative and creative egalitarian voice that reaches well beyond evangelical confines.[40]

THE RHETORIC OF THE FEMINIST "OTHER"
IN EVANGELICAL CIRCLES

I was the top candidate for the job, but I was not chosen because my dissertation topic was "too dangerous."

Some of the strongest expressions of us-them distinctions are evident in evan-

---

[39]Weber, *Younger Evangelicals*, pp. 71-82.
[40]See, e.g., William C. Placher, *Unapologetic Theology: A Christian Voice in a Pluralistic Conversation* (Louisville, Ky.: John Knox, 1995); Murphy, *Beyond Liberalism*; Volf, *Exclusion and Embrace*.

gelical characterizations of feminism. That evangelicals regard feminism with suspicion and are unaware of its diversity and fearful of its influence is not hard to discern. If Ingersoll, Gallagher and DeBerg are right, the contemporary evangelical movement is characterized, at least partially, by a cluster of conservative positions on gender and by a suspicion of feminist or egalitarian concerns. An example of the intensity of these suspicions was the response to the carefully and conservatively prepared inclusive language edition of the New International Version of the Bible during the 1990s.[41] The Council on Biblical Manhood and Womanhood has reiterated male headship and the playing out of divinely ordained separate roles. Conservative movements and authorities have won significant support from grassroots conservative Christians.

The existence and continuing need for an organization like Christians for Biblical Equality—and the extent to which it is always a minority voice—underscores the underlying uneasiness many evangelicals feel about women in positions of leadership and about gender equality in the church. While the mainline church engages quite radical feminist theology, the evangelical community continues a different struggle for basic equality in home and church. This struggle, and the work of organizations like CBE, is largely unknown and unheeded in the larger feminist world, but is important in a movement that encounters gender issues on a very different cultural and theological level from mainline Protestants. There are men and women within evangelicalism, noted one woman in the survey, "who continue the work of bringing an egalitarian vision to populations long since abandoned by traditional feminism."

Antagonism toward feminism sometimes takes the form of open hostility to women in academic positions in theology and biblical studies in evangelical schools. In recent years, the antagonism is more likely to come from students than from other faculty.[42] Women can find themselves so battle weary and pressed that the old responses seem empty. Defenses of their authority based in Scripture can seem reactionary, as one woman noted: "I was once so armed with a backpack of responses. But as I became more aware of my place as a daughter of God these words [of defense] became awfully uncomfortable." For this woman the years of hostility she had experienced in pursuit of her call left her reluctant to engage in the rationalistic, re-

---

[41]See, e.g., Vern S. Poythress and Wayne A. Grudem, *The Gender Neutral Bible Controversy: Muting the Masculinity of God's Words* (Nashville: Broadman & Holman, 2000). See also <http://www .keepthe faith.org>.

[42]A number of female professors have recently observed an increase in the number of male and female college students who are embracing a very traditional understanding of gender roles and questioning women's authority in the theological classroom.

peated arguments over the difficult passages in the New Testament epistles.

Rebecca Merrill Groothuis describes the instant and passionate reactions in some evangelical circles toward any thinking that moves beyond traditional boundaries. She notes that such responses are often couched in contradictions and in mistaken understandings of history, and they beg many questions. *Feminist* becomes an antifamily code word, and feminists (or any movement outside of certain boundaries) become the focus of an opposition whose intention is the salvaging of civilization and religion itself.[43]

This deeply felt polarity between feminism and evangelicalism is ironic, however, given the history of feminism and its roots in the nineteenth-century revivals. Women were very active in those revivals and in the debates around slavery, women's suffrage and women's ordination, although even at that time there was considerable difference of opinion about "the woman question."[44] Charles Finney, the great revivalist, was also one of the great champions of women. Antoinette Brown, the first woman to be ordained in the United States, was a graduate of his college, Oberlin, and was for much of her life evangelical.[45] Esther Bruland concludes, however, that "despite its role as a fountainhead for feminism . . . evangelical religion gave women mixed messages."[46] On the one hand women were esteemed for their piety, and on the other hand they were feared for their moral influence.

Nevertheless, in spite of the significant tensions, there are, as Bruland pointed out fifteen years ago, "complex solidarities" between feminism and evangelicalism. They share a history, both place a high value on relationship, and both are suspicious of any method that relies exclusively on reason. At varying stages in their histories, both have emphasized the need for structural justice.[47] However, Bruland also acknowledges the differences—different sources of authority and different understandings of sin, different emphases on the Word and different spiritualities. These loom larger than the similarities, and "only rarely do we see coalitions of evangelicals and feminists forming" to address shared concerns.[48] Furthermore, mainline feminists rarely acknowledge the evangelical roots of feminism.

---

[43]Rebecca Merrill Groothuis, *Women Caught in Conflict: The Culture War Between Traditionalism and Feminism* (Grand Rapids: Baker, 1994), p. 179.

[44]See Nancy A. Hardesty, *Your Daughters Shall Prophesy: Revivalism and Feminism in the Age of Finney* (Brooklyn: Carlson, 1991). See also Donald Dayton, *Discovering an Evangelical Heritage* (Peabody, Mass.: Hendrickson, 1988).

[45]She later turned to Unitarianism after struggling with pastoral implications of extreme Calvinism.

[46]Esther Byle Bruland, "Evangelical and Feminist Ethics: Complex Solidarities," *The Journal of Religious Ethics* 17, no. 2 (1989): 141-42.

[47]Ibid., pp. 147-48.

[48]Ibid., pp. 149-51.

Evangelical women, then, find themselves in positions where they may have sympathies for aspects of the feminist movement, even identifying with it quite strongly; but in evangelical circles this movement is little understood in its complexities, subtleties and historical connections. Instead, it is often feared and caricatured. Despite rational reasons why there could be a much more constructive engagement, the lived reality is decidedly hostile.

How Feminists Regard Evangelicalism and Fundamentalism

Born and bred in a land of patriarchy, the Bible abounds in male imagery
and language. For centuries interpreters have explored and exploited
this male language to articulate theology: to shape the contours and content of
the Church, synagogue and academy. . . . So harmonious has seemed this
association of Scripture with sexism, of faith with culture, that
only a few have even questioned it.

PHYLLIS TRIBLE,
"Feminist Hermeneutics and Biblical Studies," in *Feminist Theology: A Reader*

It will be clear, then, that there is nothing intrinsically incompatible
between being a feminist and conceiving of oneself as a religious person. . . .
There is, however, I believe, an incompatibility between
being feminist and Christian.

DAPHNE HAMPSON,
"Luther on the Self: A Feminist Critique," in *Feminist Theology: A Reader*

In the picture of the king-redeemer, individuals are condemned
who rebel against the power and the glory of the monarch,
assigning to themselves the status that only the king deserves.
The king judges the guilty and metes out punishment, or as the Christian story
happily concludes, takes the punishment upon himself and thus absolves
those condemned. In the picture of the mother-creator, however,
the goal is neither the condemnation nor the rescue of the guilty but the just
ordering of the cosmic household in a fashion beneficial to all. . . . She is
concerned with establishing justice now, not with condemning in the future.

SALLIE MCFAGUE,
"The Ethic of God as Mother, Lover and Friend," in *Feminist Theology: A Reader*

Contemporary writings within theological feminism rarely, if ever, refer to evangelicalism per se. Many of the early third-wave feminists were Roman Catholic, but in almost all cases their foil has been traditional church interpretations of the last two thousand years. Nevertheless, while evangelicalism is not mentioned as "other" by feminists in the way that "feminism" is by evangelicals, the topics and theological discussions among feminists are in themselves indirect attacks on or red flags to the evangelical world. Feminism takes for granted the "hermeneutics of suspicion," the deep patriarchy and androcentrism of the Bible and tradition and the need for reimagining God-symbols. It challenges the central metaphors of substitution in atonement theory and reconsiders the meaning of sin in women's experience. The Fatherhood of God is questioned and replaced. As an obvious representative of patriarchal interpretations and practices, evangelicalism needs no special mention, at least in print. Often it is dismissed a priori; in large part, it is simply excluded from the world of academic discourse.

In feminist classrooms, however, a number of the women we surveyed had experienced explicit mention of fundamentalists and evangelicals as "other" or had encountered incomprehension in response to their allegiances. One woman described her otherwise positive experience in a graduate school very influenced by feminist thinking.

> *I did hear much negativity toward evangelicalism, which people mostly interpreted as fundamentalism and right-wing conservatism. I did find myself confronting unexamined perceptions of evangelicalism on a number of occasions. In one of my classes we were studying the urban revival movement in the United States. At one point I commented that what was interesting about the discussion was the way in which the class was talking about my tradition. One student looked at me in disbelief that I could even remotely claim to be an evangelical and said, "Really? But you're so warm and accepting!"*

The particular project of contemporary theological feminism has been to rediscover the role of women in the church, to find or imagine lost voices and to name and condemn the persistent, religiously legitimated patriarchy—if not misogyny—in Scripture and church life. For such feminists, redemption has most often been cast not in terms of redeeming or reclaiming a flawed tradition, but in terms of re-creating religion. "Woman Church" and new images of God and persons have often been portrayed as the only hope for a patriarchal tradition.

Moreover, women's complicity in patriarchal arrangements has been strongly critiqued. Hence feminists have assumed that there is a problem in the Christian tradition and that women suffer from this problem even when women in conservative congregations claim that this is not the case. Feminists argue that patriarchy runs so deep, and women are so inclined to cooperate with its demands, that only as feminists can women come out from under it and see the reality of their situation.

Thus all conservative and evangelical women are under suspicion of cooperating in some sense with the "enemy," and questions are raised about integrity and authenticity. This is rarely said openly, but it follows logically from the arguments against patriarchy and is very much the subtext in many feminist groups and classrooms. Feminist theologians, at least those who define the feminist core—those with whom academics interact—draw the lines strongly in identifying conservative religion as the enemy.[49] Evangelical women familiar with the negative evangelical rhetoric about feminism and liberalism notice the similarly hostile rhetoric in feminist theology classes in graduate school.

A number of the women in our sample who had gone from an evangelical seminary to a liberal graduate school expressed their frustration with feminist theology classes, feeling that it was not their experience that was being universalized and feeling patronized by women who assumed that others less radical than themselves were merely at a lower level of consciousness. Even in friendships among evangelical, mainline and feminist women, there is sometimes a level of condescension toward evangelicalism and its assumptions that can be quite disconcerting.

Feminism is now, of course, much more open to the plurality of women's experiences, especially in the Two-Thirds World. But these insights are rarely turned to the evangelical woman's experience, and the particular coupling of identities in opposition makes any sensitivity to evangelicalism more problematic and the dialogue more urgent.

Groothuis suggests how complex these efforts at dialogue will be. While she is critical of the evangelical propensity to misuse the word *feminist*, as discussed above, she notes the similar situation on the other side. She argues that the polarity that so entangles evangelicals and feminists is reinforced when people like Hunter describe the phenomenon of the "two cultures." His model assumes one is either progressive, denying traditional authorities, or orthodox and thus committed to external, definable and transcendent authority. If a person is in between or lines up on one side for some issues and on the other for different issues, he or she is viewed

---

[49]The so-called three waves of feminism are not entirely distinct, nor do they necessarily apply similarly in the secular and theological worlds. The first wave of feminism coincided with efforts for women's suffrage in many places around the world. In the U.S., women were also fighting for black emancipation. The second wave identifies the early women's liberation movement of the 1960s and 1970s. The third wave is contemporary feminisms of diverse kinds. The major theological feminist core, however, is mostly post-second wave feminism—works from the late seventies to 1980s. More recently the theological feminist world has also become more diverse and has incorporated voices of women from the Two-Thirds World.

as morally confused and inconsistent. Groothuis argues that the

> assumption on which Hunter bases his analysis of the culture war in secular society
> is precisely the assumption that fuels the culture war in the evangelical church. It is
> . . . the conviction that the positions taken by today's conservative and radical groups
> can only be based on the orthodox and progressivist views of moral authority, re-
> spectively, and that someone in the middle ground is therefore confused about what
> ought to be the basis of moral authority.[50]

The structuring of the analysis and the taken-for-granted mapping of the terrain continues to make alternative interpretations and more fruitful conversations difficult.

CONCLUSION

In this chapter we have described many of the tensions surrounding gender in evangelical identity, institutions and commitment in order to situate our discussion of life on the boundary within the larger evangelical world. Evangelical culture contains a number of complex paradoxes, some hidden and some quite obvious. Cognitive commitments and boundaries are given priority over experiential factors, but assigning significant value to certain experiences is a central part of evangelical life. Gender assumptions are mostly hidden but are of great importance in maintaining symbolic and actual identity. The significance of institutional connections is not emphasized but is very important to having a voice within evangelical circles.

While various theological commitments might be described as defining characteristics of evangelicalism, gender-related practices and beliefs have a very important role. Evangelical women live within these paradoxes and attempt to carve out places for themselves and niches of influence. Academically trained evangelical women face particular challenges in trying to work within this gendered space.

Both evangelicalism and feminism have viewed one another with deep suspicion, and the rhetoric of the "other" has been employed by both sides. These positions have made it very difficult to address gender issues within evangelicalism and to find a place where the strengths of both views are affirmed. In the next chapter we look more closely at the academic environment and the experiences of women as students and teachers. In addition, we describe the tensions and the opportunities within the larger guild and academy.

---

[50]Groothuis, *Women Caught*, p. 179.

| 4 |

PASSING THE TABLE, FINDING A VOICE

Students, Mentors and Teaching

———

*I remember when I was studying for my Ph.D.—I would bypass the table of women . . .
to get to the table of men where I felt they were talking real stuff. And I have thought about
that so many times, and I have felt ashamed, and I have wished I could do that better. . . .
But part of coming back home to myself is being able to say, I don't ever want to pass that
table again. In my own experience, to bypass the table is to bypass a part of who I am.* ⬿

Looking back on graduate school experience, on the challenges of finding a job and
on the complex dynamics of being accepted in any academic setting, a woman can
feel that her previous selves are somewhat distant and disconnected. Or, as the sce-
nario above suggests, a woman may repent of her previous associations and sensitivities as she "composed a self" in a male-dominated environment.[1] This is perhaps doubly true of women attempting to carve out new niches in evangelical
institutions or to walk down paths that others have not walked down before.

In this chapter we look at how we became who we are, our mentors and models,
our experiences in school as students and later as teachers and our relationships
with the guild. At each stage of the journey, we find that we are composing ourselves anew while simultaneously striving for a deep integrity. We learn by acting
out our roles, examining our identities and priorities, confronting sometimes-alien

---

[1]This image is richly developed in Mary Catherine Bateson's book, *Composing a Life* (New York: Plume,
1989).

graduate school environments, sorting our loyalties and liminal experiences and organizing strategies for teaching. To understand what it means to be formed as a theological educator who is faithful to the gospel, a closer look at these dimensions of women's stories is important.

Women in any area of public life who eventually develop a feminist consciousness often acknowledge that there had been a period of time when they had internalized the belief that women were less important than men, and when they had made choices based on that assumption. For evangelical academic women, the pressures in this direction can be greater and, at the same time, more obscured. An evangelical seminary, even one that is open to women, can be a place where traditional women and traditional perceptions of femininity are approved and rewarded, often in subtle ways, and where any suggestions of feminist strength can make most people uncomfortable. "When I speak my mind directly I am considered a 'pushy broad,' " one respondent noted in her survey. In some environments, it is almost impossible for a woman to express her views in a straightforward manner without being perceived as inappropriately aggressive and assertive. Several women spoke of the social forces within evangelicalism that discourage women from "growing up" or taking on roles of responsibility and leadership in which they function as full adults.

In some evangelical institutions, women are strangely invisible. This peculiar phenomenon is evident in regular complaints, such as, "We can't find evangelical women to participate in this conference" or "There aren't any good evangelical women to hire for this department." As we noted at the beginning of the book, the reality behind these complaints is complex. In part they are true. The evangelical subculture has not been particularly friendly to academic women who want to pursue advanced theological studies.[2] But in some cases the complaints are misleading because the women who are present are overlooked and their sometimes-different styles are not viewed as equally valid. In a telling incident, a female graduate had returned to speak at her theological school's commencement exercises. The president had enthusiastically applauded her for her insights, accomplishments and presentation. Afterward one of the women on faculty suggested to the president that he might invite her to speak at the upcoming leadership conference for which he had found no women speakers. "Ah," he said, genuinely perplexed, "but what would she say?"

---

[2]In fact, a quick survey of seminary and college websites was illuminating regarding the number of full-time female faculty members at evangelical schools. At several well-known evangelical seminaries, the number of women in relation to the total faculty was between 4 and 13 percent. Only at Fuller and Asbury were percentages a little higher. In reviewing several Bible and religion departments at evangelical colleges, the numbers ranged between 7 and 14 percent. Of the schools surveyed, only Calvin College's percentages were significantly higher.

In this context it is difficult, even for women, to learn to value women, and some of us can remember "passing the table," as in the description noted above. We passed by the table full of women in the cafeteria to go and sit with men because we thought they were more interesting and more theological than the women students, who we too suspected were only playing at the whole academic enterprise. Thus, women learn to appreciate and respect the academic competence of other women only with effort, perhaps especially in evangelical schools, where commitments to male leadership still echo quite loudly and where there are few female professors to model vigorous intellectual engagement.

THE ROLE OF ACADEMIC MENTORS AND MODELS

Very few women or men survive in the academic world without some positive mentoring. This was true of the women we surveyed and, interestingly, their mentors were almost always male. One woman observed that mentors were important in pursuing further study because they "provided challenge and support along the way, opened my horizons, gave encouragement." Another commented on how much she appreciated the deep respect with which her teacher/mentor treated her and his encouragement to go on in studies.

A respondent noted with gratitude how one of her male professors in graduate school

> took my academic goals seriously and encouraged them but also invested in me as a person, showing concern for me spiritually, emotionally and so forth. Though he encouraged my academic visions, he also warned me of the toll they would take upon the rest of my life, a warning I have found only too true. Furthermore, he made it clear that letters after one's name do not make one a better or more important person, though many assume the contrary. I appreciated his realism and his immense concern for me as an individual, whether or not I went on to study for my doctorate. Like my parents, [he] was no "feminist." However, I could not have received greater interest or care from any prof[essor and,] later, friend. ✍

For many of the women, a combination of challenge and support was crucial in a mentor. But so also was an integrity of faith, intellect and life. Mentors who could demonstrate an integration of the "intellectual, family, work and community parts of their lives" were particularly valued.

Women noted that it was especially helpful when mentors provided opportunities to coauthor articles. "This," as one woman noted, "gave me much confidence and was instrumental in helping me believe that I could actually write something that could be published." Other mentors were particularly treasured because they made the subject area both "existentially and intellectually exciting."

Although a few women had female mentors, the dominance of men in the areas of theology, biblical studies, church history and ethics meant that most academic mentors were male. This, in itself, brought a certain ambiguity to the task of carving out a career or a calling as an evangelical woman. "[My adviser] had an enormous impact on me," one woman noted. "He was excellent in his field. He took my work seriously and made it possible for me to imagine going on to doctoral studies." In seeking to offer helpful guidance, however, he advised his female student not to get distracted by women's studies but rather to stay in the center of the tradition. Such comments are not meant to undermine, but it can take years to challenge the assumptions that research and writing on or about women, or studies that take gender seriously, are somehow not important scholarship.

Some mentors were helpful in modeling to women how they could do academic work and retain evangelical commitments, while others challenged or helped to broaden those commitments.

> [Dr. ————] helped me decide to go on for the Ph.D. He also challenged my identity as an evangelical. . . . He offered hope that one could remain part of the broad evangelical movement without subscribing to the most conservative segment of the movement.

Another woman credited her mentors with encouraging her to be both evangelical and open. She wrote, "My identity was birthed through their seeing me in ways I could not have comprehended. . . . Their intellectual integrity and social concern allows me to be a progressive sort in the evangelical camp."

Sometimes women in evangelical circles have a very strong sense of calling but lack confidence in their ability to pursue further study, even when there is no doubt that they can handle the academic demands. Mentors, whether male or female, can make an enormous difference in whether a woman moves toward further study. Encouragement does not always have to be direct. The following account is one woman's story of seeing a former mentor several years after she had finished undergraduate school. The connection between mentor and model blurs in the encounter.

> I thought maybe I should go on and do a doctorate. . . . As I was pondering these things, there was one Sunday morning when I was really distraught and I went to church and out of the blue [Dr. ————] came in and sat a few pews in front of me. And I just started crying and I thought, "Okay, I can do it." Just the fact that she came to church was like a word from God: "Yeah, it's okay—you can do it." Just the fact of her existence as

a bright Christian woman with a doctorate—that said to me, "You can do it, go ahead, and give it a shot." I always took that as a kind of sign. ✍

Serendipitous models, words of encouragement and mentoring were invaluable in the lives of almost all the women we surveyed, but often, careers and study paths were pieced together without a great deal of assistance. One woman, for example, mentioned the encouragement she had received from teachers, but said also that it was never linked to career counseling. The sentiment suggested was, Yes, your essays are good, and perhaps you should study for a further degree, but why would you want to become an academic? Her teachers found it hard to imagine her in the role they themselves held.

Some women found that they needed to take all the initiative in forging ahead with academic work or in taking a teaching path. One respondent describes eloquently the ambiguities sometimes present in mentoring.

> *In the academic realm, my primary experience regarding mentors was one of confusion. It seems that the male world has a clear-cut idea of what a mentor-protégé relationship is supposed to look like—a certain number of lunches, introductions and recommendations—but the male-female world has no such paradigm. In my experience, I found the mentor-protégé relationship very confusing. There seemed to be much more verbal than practical support. I always had to initiate; I never knew when I was asking too much or too little. I was often overlooked for opportunities that I was clearly most qualified for simply because I wasn't at the right lunch table at the right time.* ✍

She was convinced that much of the confusion was connected to taboos regarding Christian men and their relationships with women, especially younger women. In these contexts, rather than attempting to find ways to transcend difficulties, some men choose a heightened professional distance that inadvertently closes doors on women's opportunities to move forward. Given the current concerns about sexual harassment, men are sometimes very wary of mentoring relationships with female students. Nevertheless, the importance of mentoring suggests that it is crucial for faculty members to identify settings and practices that allow appropriate mentoring relationships to develop.

Several women described their own uncertainty in mentoring male or female students because as students they had themselves experienced such inadequate direction. Ironically, it has affected their ability to mentor female students who come to them for guidance. "I . . . have been approached by women wanting to be mentored—and I'm not sure what to do in an active mentoring relationship since most of my mentoring was passive (and all by men)," said one woman.

Mentoring relationships can also become complex when a woman's attempt to move beyond the confines of the evangelical world into more diverse settings is discouraged. Sometimes there is subtle pressure from mentors "to be a 'good girl' and not rock the boat." As this same woman observed, "this puts pressure on my own identity as an independent thinker."

For some women, there was little formal mentoring from anyone. One woman wrote, "I'm very tempted to say I had none. In some ways fundamentalism taught me very well to be a loner, as did my parents." Another woman who had gone through doctoral work quite a few years ago wrote,

> *There are probably few women my age who had female mentors in academia. But friendships with fellow graduate students (who are now professors), friendships with teaching colleagues and friendships with other professors in my field have all been very important to me in maintaining my commitments.* ✍

The evangelical tendency to value group identity while simultaneously maintaining a piety that is highly individualistic may have a distinctive impact on women. There is something deep in the evangelical psyche that expects to be able to get by alone—just God and me. This can be an extraordinary strength in difficult circumstances, and women can move doggedly forward without much support. But this individualistic approach also obscures the many social and cultural dynamics and structures at work in every community.

The inbuilt trajectories that have existed for men in the academic system are much less predictably present for women. Many female academics who have survived this system are determined to make it better for the women coming after them and are committed to giving female students more positive and proactive encouragement.

Whether or not women had significant experiences of being mentored, many could identify *models* who inspired and shaped their lives and, in some cases, their academic identity. Interestingly, for a number of the women we interviewed, stories of women from the past were the most powerful models. Some identified specific nineteenth-century holiness women who were preachers, evangelists and teachers as powerful sources of inspiration.

Others described specific missionary women whose courage and fortitude challenged them to press on to live out their own callings. One woman described a missionary she had known who had never been "reined in by missions; she never compromised on one thing in her life." Stories of women whose faithfulness to a difficult but life-giving call provided strong support for contemporary evangelicals in the academy.

Other female models were noted with deep appreciation: mothers who had a "strong sense of community obligation and a well-developed moral sense" as well as a gracious humility, missionaries who had been guests in their homes when they were children and contemporary evangelical academic women, like Mary Stewart Van Leeuwen. Only occasionally did we hear about other faculty women who were models, largely, we would assume, because they had been so rare in students' experience.

However, there were a handful of women who responded quite differently. One wrote, "I have never had people whose lives I consciously wanted to emulate." Another woman said that she could "think of women that I don't want to be like. Not that these women aren't OK or even wonderful people, but I don't want to relate to men like they do . . . or 'apologize' for my views like some women seem to do."

TRANSITIONS TO GRADUATE SCHOOL

There are a number of junctures at which evangelical women (and men) can find it difficult to move forward toward work within the theological academy. The transition from an evangelical seminary to a doctoral program is one such juncture and, in their responses to survey questions, women described widely different reactions to graduate school. A number thrived in the more open and critical milieu of the graduate school seminar; for the first time they felt free to examine ideas without confessional bias. A few others completed a Ph.D. within an evangelical institution. But the majority experienced some difficulty, as is indicated in the following accounts.

> *It was a big culture shock to go from my seminary experience to graduate study at [————] University. I felt judged to be a (and you must understand, these are "cuss" words) right-wing, fundamentalist, Republican, narrow-minded, ignorant person. I found myself inadvertently saying things that offended others. Sometimes I couldn't even figure out what the offensive element was. I found that faith issues were frequently treated with a mutually understood humor and scorn which was rarely explained. I felt out of place and denigrated.* ✑

> *My initiation into the academy as it exists outside my own [evangelical] tradition was quite a shock. In my first graduate level class the lecture was on how theologians cannot speak of sin, evil or resurrection—too politically incorrect. It really traumatized my head and heart to hear that.* ✑

I have been confronted by people who feel my perspectives are narrow and close-minded. My morality has been challenged. . . . My system has been turned on its ear. I listen more, say less. Sometimes I am mute. ✑

Beginning doctoral work felt like going back to first grade. Overnight I felt like a naïve, sheltered, simple-minded believer whose chief redeeming features were commitment to women and to doing my homework.[3]

Faculty members in religion departments of prestigious universities who openly dismiss the church and faith commitments can be especially trying. A woman who had done her doctoral studies in an Ivy League school, described her professors as advocating atheism. In departments like these evangelical women suffer. "I had several professors who had had bad life experiences with the church," said one woman, "and several seemed committed to making my life a living hell in order to heal their own pain." In some particularly puzzling cases, one may have cause to wonder whether some men were projecting onto female students and colleagues the feelings they had toward other women in their lives.[4] Problems with transference are not limited to women or evangelicals, but insofar as the academic theological world includes numbers of men who once held more conservative beliefs and have had unhappy experiences within that context, it is not surprising to find occurrences there.

Particularly hard for an evangelical are the cynicism and reductionism of a great deal of graduate school discourse in very liberal—but respected—institutions. This is especially true when church experience is denigrated. One woman remembered:

The first two years were hell. . . . Professors favored the local students and dismissed any talk of church life as irrelevant to the classroom. . . . I entered an environment where I seemed to fit nowhere. ✑

This particular woman persevered, worked as a pastor, mothered small children and eventually found a voice as she moved into the role of a teaching assistant and began to develop personal relationships with faculty and other students. Another woman in a similar school, however, was critical of the warnings she had received from her evangelical seminary professors about such doctoral programs.

I think I would have done better just going and being an evangelical than going and think-

---

[3]Elouise Renich Fraser, *Confessions of a Beginning Theologian* (Downers Grove, Ill.: InterVarsity Press, 1998), pp. 39-40.
[4]Penny Jamieson, the first diocesan bishop in the Anglican communion, notes the significance of projection and transference in her book *Living at the Edge: Sacrament and Solidarity in Leadership* (London: Mowbray, 1997), pp. 59-63.

ing that I had to hide my evangelicalism while maintaining my commitments. This feeling that I was somehow a "secret agent" made for stupid and unnecessary challenges in certain personal and professional relationships. Moreover, it seemed to exacerbate the paranoia that many of my more "liberal" colleagues had regarding evangelicals' social and ideological commitments. ✍

She now advises her own students to go into such settings and be more openly evangelical, thus not causing the dysfunction that she had experienced. It may be that this openness is helped by the current academic climate that gives more respectful attention to particularity and difference.

In graduate school settings that are more diverse and in which students and faculty represent a wide spectrum of theological opinion, evangelical women's experience of fitting nowhere can still be quite intense:

In some ways graduate school made me feel like someone with multiple personalities. To the men, particularly my evangelical male classmates, I was an outspoken feminist and they didn't understand my desire to uncover "women's history." To a great number of the women professors and students, I was a backward traditionalist and they couldn't fathom why I would study evangelicalism. I had no classmates who understood this dilemma and am indebted to my husband for helping me remember that I was sane. ✍

One woman who had not attended any evangelical schools described the tensions between her evangelical faith and the more liberal academy as remaining "unresolved while in graduate school." She wrote that the dichotomy resulted in "depression and reduced capacity for work." For other women, there was a slow, personal and private working out of differences, accompanied by a broadening and widening of faith's boundaries. One woman noted that certain professors "showed me that the horizons of Christian thought and history are much broader than those of evangelicalism." Another commented, "The dissolving of the tension between evangelicalism and feminism was a gradual and mostly private experience. I didn't talk much to others about it."

Achieving a doctorate is exhausting work, and where students and faculty operate out of conflicting paradigms, the level of pressure is much greater. One woman described the challenge she had faced:

I worked hard to get as good in their paradigm as I was in mine. Then I attempted to separate their evidence from their paradigm, pass that evidence through my paradigm and come to my own conclusions. This was a lot of work. It also got me into trouble with professors who wanted things parroted to them in their own terms. But I think this is the key to evangelicals surviving in the academy and evangelicalism surviving in the modern world. ❧

Filtering material through multiple paradigms is certainly an experience many of us can remember, and to a large extent, the process continues as we engage multiple boundaries and diverse communities. Elouise Renich Fraser captures this experience powerfully when she writes,

> Beginning with my family of origin, every Christian community in which I have lived, worked and worshiped has produced garments for me to wear, sometimes hand-me-downs, sometimes new. Labels abounded. . . . Some always fit; some always didn't. And even garments that fit always seemed to clash with each other. How could this be?[5]

Garments. Labels. Yes, women have many garments—or identities—in our wardrobes, and we are not always sure which ones to put on, which one will fit this occasion but not another. Will this constituency be offended or that one? Because one is never "just doing theology," evangelical women are often conscious of the labels we are asked to wear and increasingly conscious also of the potential clashes. Many women took up theology intent on studying and knowing God. Our focus was almost completely outward and upward. Only slowly, and often painfully, did we begin to grasp the powerful cultural, social and political realities that accompany theology and theological reflection.

Despite some difficulty in adjusting to the ethos of doctoral programs, a number of women commented that they had had very strong academic preparation at the seminary level. Many evangelical seminary programs had required academic rigor. While some women noted that they had not been adequately prepared for the critical thinking required in doctoral programs, others acknowledged that they had been very well prepared in biblical studies.

Some women found themselves silenced in their doctoral programs, unprepared for the intense academic sparring that is part of many graduate school classes. Sometimes the silence came from being unsure of how to situate themselves in the arguments, and other times it was because the environment itself, either liberal or feminist, was not open to the particular contributions or concerns of those who came with somewhat different perspectives. But other women reported little trouble in finding a voice. They had reputations as "feisty debaters." One woman remarked, "I have my arguments ready and articulate them very well. Also, I don't mind losing a fight. Intellectual battle was my favorite thing about graduate

---

[5]Fraser, *Confessions,* p. 40.

school—next to the library." Another commented, "I got into it with my postmodern buddies/classmates all the time. They still loved me—even though they were somewhat condescending about my beliefs."

But one woman's story is particularly important because it demonstrates how a single faculty person can affect a woman's educational experience. After studying with very affirming professors and taking undergraduate honors at a Christian college, the attitude of one professor at the master's level in another school had very destructive results. The woman explained that in her master's program she had had no difficulty articulating her views until, for the first time in her life, she ran into

> *a completely chauvinistic professor. His treatment of me in his class (e.g., not allowing me to speak, allowing only the male seminarians to speak) and his remarks to me after my comprehensive exams effectively silenced me for my first two years [in my Ph.D. program]. I simply could not speak in public or to my professors. This was the first time in my life that this happened. I was not aware of his effect until after I regained my "voice," toward the end of my second year [in doctoral studies].* ✐

WOMEN IN THE TEACHING ENVIRONMENT

Evangelical women go into teaching because they love their field of study and value opportunities to bring it to life with students. To be able to teach theology, biblical studies, church history or ethics is a great privilege, and to open the treasures of Scripture and tradition to each class of students is an amazing gift. Helping students grasp some of the complexity and wonder of the Christian faith, engaging some of the difficulties and distortions, reflecting on faith in the context of contemporary life, and training a generation of leaders for the church are opportunities and responsibilities none of us takes lightly.

Nevertheless, the teaching endeavor is also a complex and multifaceted opportunity for women. Issues of style and authority pop up everywhere. Collegial and student expectations can be quite disconcerting. One woman described her pedagogical style.

> *I think my style is more relational than my colleagues'. . . . My approach to any class is that we are co-learners; the students will teach me and I will teach them. . . . I think the difference in my teaching style has a great deal to do with being a woman. I relate to students as people with issues other than passing my class. . . . My classes are very conversational, with a lot of student interaction with one another and with me. I "listen" to students as carefully as I can, trying to hear what they are really saying.* ✐

This approach to teaching can conflict with many traditional notions of authority. Sometimes women's choices in pedagogical approaches collide with their ability to maintain an authoritative presence in the classroom. The disappointment in this experienced teacher's story is palpable.

> *Until a few years ago, I thought that I had the ability to relate to men well, especially those male students from conservative backgrounds. However, in recent years, I have received evaluations that devalued my teaching role, stating that I was too nurturing in class, my lectures were not authoritative enough, and I cared too much for class discussion and practical applications. . . . Is this backlash? Have I found my feminist voice and claimed my own style, rather than the traditional voice of the academy, and now I am receiving the criticisms against it? I am not sure what has happened. But it has taken a lot of energy to stand up against the onslaught, particularly in an environment that I thought would be different.*

She went to the administration of her school looking for help, but they offered little. They did not see that the issue might be gender related and, instead, simply encouraged her to give more formal lectures and to reduce the amount of application. She might have been able to resist the criticisms of the vocal male students and to pursue her particular teaching style had the administration been more supportive. But they did not value a more collegial approach to teaching either, and she was left feeling discouraged and less than competent.

A woman's attempt to find her own voice almost always involves differences and changes in teaching style, thereby challenging the expectations of some students. Experiments in pedagogy by teachers whose authority is also somewhat contested can result in difficult evaluations. Students criticize lectures, style and reading choices.

Fraser describes her experience of student criticism and administrative response:

> A year earlier, students had lodged serious complaints against me. They were reported to me anonymously at the end of the semester: several pages, single-spaced and typed. I was devastated. The seminary president requested a meeting with my dean and me. . . . The meeting was long and difficult. I couldn't believe this was happening to me. My request to meet with concerned students was denied.[6]

What makes this more than just a teacher's depressing story is the systematic disempowerment that it represents. Women often begin their work in evangelical

---

[6]Ibid., pp. 131-32.

institutions at a considerable disadvantage. Because they usually enter somewhat contested space, they find themselves "on trial" in ways that male faculty members usually do not. When women also attempt to use pedagogical approaches that respect adult learners, this can intersect with both their lack of stature and their more tentative voices in ways that undermine authority. Students comfortable with a lecture model can be extremely critical of alternative pedagogical styles, assuming that if the material is not presented in a lecture format, they are not learning.

Maintaining a distinctive voice and speaking with authority is a learned skill, as many women have noted.

> Learning to speak in my own voice has been and still is the most challenging part of becoming a theologian. It has taken decades. Ever since childhood my female voice has been shamed, overlooked, disbelieved, punished and silenced more times than I care to admit. There haven't been many women around to show me the way.[7]

How can women teach with integrity in conservative institutions while also attempting to make changes and adaptations? In schools where the approach to gender issues tends to be mostly silence, women sometimes find that they can make progress best by not directly engaging gender concerns. If one simply presses on, does one's work and does not fuss too much about injustices, it is sometimes possible to be in leadership without generating a great deal of overt resistance. However, the unacknowledged gender injustices must then be absorbed by the women themselves.

Women frequently observed that they needed to appear "safer" than their male colleagues. Even when not wanting to be adversarial, women find that if they want to raise issues of feminism they become doubly suspect in an evangelical world. Worries about what "women are up to" surface in unexpected ways. When women students or faculty congregate together, people ask, with surprising frequency, what they are "plotting." But in settings in which women are a real minority, friendships among women become very important, even when the women themselves are quite different from one another. In minority situations, female faculty and students often forge important friendships that would be unusual in more gender-equal settings.

Female faculty members also face other kinds of hurdles in the academic environment. The fatherly or patronizing senior faculty member or administrator

---

[7]Ibid., p. 109.

can pose a particular sort of problem when he subtly affirms or rewards silence or childishness that is hard to confront and hard to ignore. Female students pose another challenge. Some women resist looking at gender issues and dismiss any attempt to do so as representing feminist anger. Among younger women especially, there is sometimes an assumption that the issues have been settled, that the playing field is now equal and that gender dynamics are irrelevant to their lives. Sometimes the resistance masks a fear of looking too closely at previous hurts and exclusions, and sometimes it is tied to an unwillingness to reflect on the implications of one's female identity for ministry, vocation or responsibility.

An additional problem for women teaching in evangelical schools emerges in relation to issues of power. Most evangelical organizations are deeply resistant to paying attention to power dynamics because such categories sully the image of close community and moral uprightness. Such a posture makes it very difficult for anyone to name the powers at work in gender relationships without being seen as cynical or disloyal. There is significant pressure on women in these contexts to demonstrate their commitment to the community by tempering their criticisms and concerns about justice and equality.

Teaching in nonevangelical universities and seminaries also imposes a certain marginality. In many mainline, liberal or secular schools, evangelicalism is completely misunderstood. For example, in the early days of working on this book at a college in the southern United States, Nicola found that few faculty members knew or cared who evangelicals were or how women fared in their midst. While these same people would have been very sympathetic to the plight of a homosexual or an African-American minority, evangelicalism was, in their minds, too closely allied with moralistic posturing and imperialistic politics. Another set of difficulties can arise for evangelical women on secular campuses. In some cases, otherwise "liberal" people regularly use exclusive language and engage in gendered politics. Thus, evangelical women sometimes find themselves fighting the feminist battle on the other front—sometimes as the only ones who are sensitive to language and gender issues on nonevangelical campuses.

THE GUILD AND THE LARGER ACADEMIC WORLD

The guild presents another forum within which to form and test both an evangelical and an academic identity. Women who are from evangelical backgrounds or who represent evangelical values and theology are quite disconcerting to liberal institutions such as the American Academy of Religion, the Society of Biblical Literature and the various organizations related to academic specialties. Evangelical women are sometimes seen as naive, as not yet having come to "consciousness" or as betraying essential feminist values. By virtue of being evangelical, female and academic, we challenge the academy's assumed images of women and evangelicals. We are working on multiple maps, representing to ourselves the truths from several positions, a very postmodern situation.

The sense of camaraderie and solidarity that other women might achieve in such settings is often absent for evangelical women. Dealing with assumptions can be complex, as when entering mainline or liberal conversations with appreciation for some concerns represented there and then finding that evangelical beliefs or practices are simultaneously ridiculed. Liberal academics often assume evangelical women are speaking out of one conversation, as are they, rather than several. For them it is nearly incomprehensible that a thinking person, much less a thinking woman, would be evangelical. In guild meetings and other gatherings across the theological spectrum, evangelical women often find themselves interacting on multiple maps, engaging writers from various perspectives and involved in conversations that bridge multiple theological worlds. In spite of this, the mainstream academy does not often interact with evangelical thinkers.[8]

A setting such as the AAR or one of the various specialized academic societies can be alienating in another way. Within many of these guild meetings are evangelical interest groups that meet annually. It is rare to find more than a few women at these meetings. Often these groups are attended by progressive evangelical men, and their programs are increasingly popular. But the intensified minority status of women in such groups reinforces a sense of difference and aloneness, even as it provides an important community within the larger academy. For example, for a number of years, Christine was often the only woman at the Evangelical Ethics interest group at the Society of Christian Ethics. While welcomed warmly by her male evangelical colleagues, and while serving for several years as co-chair, the absence of any other women was a very disturbing and alienating experience. These men are most of her closest friends at the SCE, but her identity as both an evangelical and a woman in these settings feels very divided.

The overwhelmingly male identity of evangelical academics reminds evangelical women that they are a very small minority. Only when the topic of a session in these meetings concerns gender is there a more equal distribution of men and

---

[8]See Gary Dorrien, *The Remaking of Evangelical Theology* (Louisville, Ky.: Westminster John Knox, 1998), pp. 185-86.

women, as men are sometimes less likely to attend and as nonevangelical or formerly evangelical women who might be interested in evangelicalism or gender deliberately participate.[9]

Hiring has received a great deal of attention recently in all aspects of academic life, especially as jobs become scarcer and the academic world harsher. Even well-endowed institutions are struggling. The hiring of women can become a particularly political space. The women we surveyed found employment in a variety of ways. Some, of course, went through "regular" hiring channels of responding to job openings, application, interview and so on. A few women within specific denominations found employment quickly within a denominational school. A number were hired by their undergraduate college or seminary, occasionally being put on a retainer before they had finished graduate school; this represents a deliberate and proactive attempt to increase the number of evangelical women available for teaching positions. By maintaining the connections, this approach also helps to keep evangelical women situated within evangelicalism, even as they encounter the broader theological world.

Evangelical academic women are also vulnerable to wider guild or denominational publicity and politics. Denominational splits over issues like homosexuality are worrisome for a number of reasons, but also because it is not clear what posture the sides will take on women's issues. In a post-split church, evangelicals with egalitarian or feminist commitments may find no home. And when the more extreme feminist stances get the headlines—Sophia, goddess worship and women-church—this sets the entire discussion back for evangelical women. Conservative men then feel justified in fearing that when women get into positions of leadership and responsibility, the church is on the slippery slope to idolatry and disorder.

Much of the academic world, including religious studies and theology, is quite divorced from the church. This is extremely problematic for anyone committed to the church and to the nurturing of local congregations of believers. One place where rich dialogue is currently underway is within projects funded

---

[9]In recent years, many evangelicals within academia have moved closer to the mainstream while continuing to insist that they have something distinctive to contribute. For example, for a number of years, the Evangelical Theological Society has met before the annual meetings of the American Academy of Religion and the Society of Biblical Literature, and some of its members also participated in the larger and more diverse conference. Now the Evangelical Theology Group *within* the AAR is gaining widespread support, both in evangelical circles and in terms of the larger meeting itself. Other groups such as the Christian Theological Research Fellowship are hosting vigorous and well-attended "additional" sessions at the AAR/SBL.

or sponsored by the Lilly Endowment that encourage conversation among academics who also have deep commitments to the church.[10] Opportunities to bring together theology, ethics, church history and contemporary concerns in discussions of Christian practices and lived theology have allowed academics from quite different positions on the theological spectrum to develop friendships and to enrich conversations. A commitment to the church and an appreciation for the historic Christian tradition provide a foundation on which evangelical and mainline academics and practitioners can hold important conversations and forge promising alliances.

Mary Catherine Bateson's book *Composing a Life* makes it clear that struggles in the academy are not unique to evangelical women or to evangelical educational institutions. She identifies a number of reasons why women who show great promise sometimes fail at jumping academic hurdles, including tenure. Certain strengths are also vulnerabilities.

> This subversion [leading to failure] was accomplished by taking advantage of two kinds of vulnerability that women raised in our society tend to have. The first is the quality of self-sacrifice, a learned willingness to set their own interests aside and be used and even used up by the community. Many women at Amherst ended up investing vast amounts of time in needed public-service activities, committee work, and teaching nondepartmental courses. Since these activities were not weighed significantly in promotion decisions, they were self-destructive.
>
> The second kind of vulnerability trained into women is a readiness to believe messages of disdain and derogation. Even women who arrived at Amherst full of confidence gradually became vulnerable to distorted visions of themselves, no longer secure that their sense of who they were matched the perceptions of others.[11]

Bateson herself describes how easily she fell into the trap of believing derogatory comments made to her by an incoming president, even after she had achieved considerable academic success and had held the position of dean at Amherst through troubled years. These stories of struggle from outside the confines of evangelicalism are both disturbing and encouraging; the institutional forces women encounter are far more widespread than the difficult gender dynamics within particular schools and seminaries. Her account suggests a number of reasons why it remains difficult to find "good women" in the academy, whether evangelical or not.

---

[10]The Templeton Foundation exerts a similar impact on discussions and interactions across the liberal-evangelical boundary, but it has less influence on women because the topics have engaged fewer female scholars.

[11]Bateson, *Composing a Life*, p. 54.

VOICES OF DISCONFIRMATION

Women hear numerous voices of disconfirmation, but some are more persistent than others in the evangelical world. It is a common assumption that if women are teaching in theological schools, they are doing so in the fields of Christian education or music (subject areas generally perceived as appropriate for gifted women). The mistakes made by new students and visitors in assuming that a faculty woman—even when her office is filled with books—is a secretary to other faculty members are surprisingly frequent. Minor incidents are not important unless they pile up and subtly disconfirm academic identity or reinforce a sense of being an imposter.[12] In many cases, a woman will choose to avoid embarrassing the person who has made a mistake, but such mistakes do take a toll. When calls come from other countries requesting seminary professors for intensive courses but a woman has learned to ask whether they will take a female professor, a woman's sense of estrangement from her own tradition is heightened. To complain about specific experiences often seems petty, but the cumulative impact can be quite trying.

Additional disconfirmations can come from the liberal academy. Several women noted that they had encountered assumptions that if a person was teaching at a denominational or an evangelical school with rich theological connections and commitments, he or she could not be a serious scholar. The men at evangelical institutions are also aware of these prejudices, and this can make them averse to experimentation and innovations in pedagogy that might seem to further undermine academic legitimacy.[13]

EVANGELICAL INSTITUTIONS
IN SEARCH OF LEGITIMACY

Because evangelical scholarship has not been taken seriously in much of the larger academic world, concerns about legitimacy and respectability are often heightened in evangelical institutions. Women and women's concerns have historically been undervalued, and therefore, legitimacy issues interact with gender in complex ways. Evangelical women's scholarship is sometimes overlooked by evangelical institutions that are in search of wider academic credibility. Evangelical women can find

---

[12]Female faculty members in evangelical schools are still sometimes asked whether they have a "real" Ph.D. Female academics are often addressed as "Mrs." when the male faculty members are routinely addressed as "Dr." Even in fairly egalitarian settings, female faculty and students sometimes endure chapel services where the only references to women are negative or the source of humor and where language about pastoral practice is exclusively male.

[13]There is an irony in this response, however, given that innovation is currently being encouraged in many liberal and secular schools.

themselves caught between the battles over what counts as valued scholarship in both worlds. Evangelicals may be less willing to take on certain methodologies and topics not only because these methodologies and topics are associated with feminism, but also because they represent approaches with less prestige than others. When women's academic work is recognized by the evangelical world, it is often work done by women who are orthodox but outside the evangelical community—providing another form of legitimacy.[14]

One result of giving a high profile to theologically orthodox women outside evangelicalism is that it can be used to de-legitimate concerns about the recognition of women within evangelical institutions and about the difficulty women have in finding a voice within those schools. Well-known women speakers can sometimes provide a replacement for gender analysis and criticism. Nevertheless these women do become models of excellent scholarship and, presumably, their presence subtly changes the evangelical ethos. Evangelical women scholars, however, working within the evangelical subculture do not often have the status in the guild that lends credibility to their voices in the evangelical world.

CHOOSING STRATEGIES THAT WORK

Women find strategies for working within these confines. One respondent explained that she talks about feminist concerns without naming them as feminist and is conscientious about including women authors in her reading assignments. Nobody in particular might notice this, though there are always some students who enthusiastically embrace the inclusion.

Other strategies include anticipating student reactions and challenging them from the outset. Some women name the tensions publicly and have procedures in place for coping with instances of passive or active hostility.

> *I should note that there is almost always at least one male student in the semester who will feel it necessary to challenge my position of authority. Because I know that this is part of the territory, I "patrol the borders" by insisting on respect in the classroom from the outset. At the first open challenge, I usually ignore it. If the problem occurs again, we have a "discussion" after class. So far, no one has dared a third offense.* ✍

---

[14]Ellen Charry, who can be characterized as a "friendly fellow traveler," was featured in a *Christianity Today* article on promising "new" theologians. She is theologically orthodox, teaches at Princeton, but has no evangelical background and does not claim an evangelical identity. See Tim Stafford, "The New Theologians: These Top Scholars Are Believers Who Want to Speak to the Church," *Christianity Today*, February 8, 1999, pp. 30-31, 47, 49.

One of the strengths and treasures of evangelicalism is the love for Scripture and the authoritative place of the Bible in evangelical thinking. By rooting their work and their concerns in the Scriptures, evangelical women are able to introduce students to new ideas and to overcome some of the resistance students might have to notions that conflict with their previous reading of the tradition.

Several women mentioned how important it was to them to make the teaching environment different from what they had experienced. One woman noted that she always remembers to offer praise; she has chosen to establish a more nurturing classroom environment than any she had been used to. When grading papers and especially in working with women students, she is careful to combine affirmation and criticism.

> *I would always say something positive as well as critique their work. I remember how important praise was (and still is, if I'm honest) to me in knowing I had done something well. I was also aware of how difficult some of these women found writing essays—a good number were lacking in confidence even if actually very capable.* ♆

Another talked about the competitive and alienating environment of her own seminary experience and how she hoped to make her class a more cooperative community experience. Other women were determined to create a classroom in which every student would find freedom to speak and would learn to respect classmates and their contributions to the discussion.

Several women were particularly wary of the behavior they had seen rewarded at seminary. One woman wrote,

> *When I reflect on my own seminary experience, it seems that somehow the human element, or the spiritual element perhaps, was lost. I knew guys who would live in the library . . . despite the fact that they had families. . . . At the end of the year . . . some of them were given awards as promising leaders.* ♆

As a woman who anticipated raising a family, she found it very disturbing to think about male students and faculty who put inordinate amounts of time in libraries and study sessions and left their wives alone to deal with small children. That such practices are rewarded by evangelical communities that simultaneously proclaim the importance of strong families seemed deeply inconsistent. Women with children are very conscious of the complex accountabilities to mothering, teaching and collegial relationships.

> *I take very seriously Paul's New Testament admonishments about the accountability of those who teach (and preach). In the midst of the practical juggling act that career and*

mothering demands, I am careful to consider how much (or little) preparation [or] reflection will allow me to teach with integrity on any given day. ❧

Because gender is so often the hidden variable in the evangelical equation, a few women have found that they must teach male and female students how to work and study together, challenging their distorted views of women's and men's roles. One woman mentioned her concern with the ways in which Carol Gilligan's work has been used to reinforce gender stereotyping.[15] She observed that Gilligan's conclusions regarding differences in how women and men think about moral concerns can sometimes lead to a heightened differentiation of men's and women's roles and gifts, especially if taken uncritically or out of context. She further noted that Gilligan's work had been used to reinforce the nurturing role of women so much so that they become seen as "mothers" in the church rather than as "partners in ministry." The result of "genderizing gifts, talents . . . or communication and leadership styles" is a truncated vision of what God can do through people.

Being Liminal

Evangelical institutions themselves often operate on the boundary of several cultures. With obvious connections to contemporary American culture and academia, most also draw from conservative and religiously legitimated hierarchical traditions. In these institutions especially, women can feel liminal, betwixt and between, permanently on the margin. One woman's story captures an intense expression of liminality.

> *At a gathering that included faculty and their spouses, a special program had been developed for female spouses. At a certain point in the program, the male faculty member in charge invited faculty members to go into an adjacent room and invited the "ladies" to remain behind for another program. When one faculty woman looked bewildered, a male faculty friend who caught the tension responded, "Oh, please, come with us." But when the tension was brought to the attention of the faculty spouse leading the "ladies session," she responded regarding the female faculty members: "Oh, they're not ladies, they're faculty—you know, neither male nor female."* ❧

Many of the women we surveyed did not sense that they were treated differently in social contexts than in academic ones. But others, especially those in close-knit communities, found that social occasions around academic life could include pain-

---

[15]Carol Gilligan, *In a Different Voice: Psychological Theory and Women's Development* (Cambridge, Mass.: Harvard University Press, 1982).

fully awkward moments. This can also be true for female seminary students.

> *I remember, while I was at [seminary], going to advisee-group get-togethers. I think I was*
> *the only single woman in the group. Most of the students were married men. Their wives*
> *would congregate in the kitchen and talk about babies. The men sat in the living room and*
> *discussed theology. Although the men's discussion was where my interests lay, I tried to*
> *spend some time in the kitchen because I felt uncomfortable . . . spending all the time with*
> *the men. I don't dislike babies; I just didn't have one to talk about.* ✍

While gender relations and interactions may have been sorted out in the work environment, uncertainties and older practices sometimes surface in social settings. Men get caught in dilemmas, wondering, *Should I stand when my female colleague walks into a social gathering? If I stand am I reinforcing nonegalitarian patterns? Am I being rude if I stand up or remain seated? Is my colleague a woman or something else—neither male nor female?* Academic life can be treated as time out of time, but in social settings the roles can be confusing. Some women then feel that they become a spectacle, their sexuality simultaneously invisible and a burden. In those settings, it often becomes easier for a woman simply to act out the traditional gender role and absorb the confusion and ambiguity into herself. Although these encounters can be quite painful and disconcerting, it is almost always quite clear that no malice is intended.

Single women are particularly vulnerable to this marginalization. While there is a rich history in evangelicalism of extraordinary women who have gone off to be missionaries, communities of evangelicals still seem quite perplexed regarding what to do with single faculty members and how to relate to their sexual and gender identity. This is clear in a remark made by a retired faculty member who was giving a lecture on the founding faculty at an evangelical seminary. He spoke of the single female professors in the first years of the school as "God's unclaimed blessings" and clearly intended to identify the current female faculty—all single—with these founding women.

One woman expressed her discomfort this way: "As a single divorcee, I find that I am often a forgotten person, both in the church and in the academy. Not rejected. They just forget to realize I'm there." Another said, similarly, "Being a single woman is something of a pain, in the sense that wonderful and godly male colleagues sometimes clearly wish to 'build a fence around the Torah' with respect to hypothetical temptations."

Liminality for married evangelical women is generally similar to that experienced by women in secular academic institutions. The authors of *Women of Academe*, for example, describe the confusion regarding roles of many women in secular colleges in the 1980s.[16] Either one is a married woman or an academic, but it is very difficult to be both and to be taken seriously. Being pregnant and teaching is particularly problematic; one's seriousness about both roles is called into question.

A few women respondents said that their institutions had deliberately given them the freedom to build their day around their children's needs, but more common were stories of significant tension in juggling children and career, not because they were incompatible, but because institutions did not easily acknowledge a woman's motherly role in the academic setting. Married women with children worked different roles and donned a variety of hats in any given day, but they had to change their identities as they moved from one setting to another, rather than integrating them. None of this is distinctive to evangelical communities, except that the tensions are played out within a larger evangelical culture of uncertainty about women who work and suspicion of women who live out multiple roles.

Although liminality and marginality are difficult, they are locations from which important insights can be generated. But a sustained outsider status can finally be quite destructive, as Fraser suggests.

> I needed a way of identifying myself theologically. How would I connect myself to the Christian tradition that ran like a thread through *all* these theological approaches? I drew on a survival skill nurtured in me from childhood and modeled at every stage of my so-called higher education: I developed the fine art of belonging on the outside. No matter where I found myself, I took up a position on the outside, withholding myself from full membership. I became a critical presence, owning my relationship to Christianity by way of *dis*owning its many failures and limitations....
>
> But somewhere along the way, in my desire to speak for truth and against falsehood, I forgot I was a part of the system. I had discovered how to keep showing up without actually belonging. I was lost.[17]

Through identity struggles in graduate school, coinciding as they do with rigorous intellectual effort, and finding themselves to be liminal within the evangelical teaching environment, women are searching for a voice, an integrity and a space within which to be whole and to be faithful to a calling.

CONCLUSION

This chapter has examined complex issues of selfhood and scholarly identity and the ways in which evangelical women struggle and persevere in academic environ-

---

[16] Nadya Aisenberg and Mona Harrington, *Women of Academe: Outsiders in the Sacred Grove* (Amherst: University of Massachusetts Press, 1988).

[17] Fraser, *Confessions*, pp. 41-42.

ments—through grace, stubborn resistance and liminality. Women cherish the few
mentors and models available and hold on to a call that is sometimes undermined.
In this and previous chapters we have named some of the tensions and paradoxes
within which women live. Ultimately, however, this is not a solitary journey. Call is
located within a space, and that space is the community, the church, the people of
God. How do we reconcile the inner and outer selves, the parallel lines of story, the
multiple "garments" of our constructed lives with the common story in which we
live? In the next chapter we examine these issues of collective identity by reflecting
on the family, the church and the larger community.

| 5 |

SHAPING THE GOOD WOMAN

Call, Church and Community

I felt called by God to missions at a young age. I shared that information with my pastor. I planned to go to college to train as a missions teacher. I took Spanish in high school rather than French, feeling I was called to Latin America. . . . But in my last year or so of high school, as my pastor would introduce me as a potential missionary to visiting missionaries, they all said the same weird thing to me: "When you get married, we'll be happy to have you on the field." . . . Why did the missionaries seemingly discount my own call by God to serve?

When, as a young woman, I was seeking the blessing of the church for missionary service, my pastor said, "When will you ever get it through your thick skull that when the church says no, God says no."

> Even where no strict injustice is perpetrated against women, they are
> often plagued by a vague but persistent sense of homelessness.
> The social world which they inhabit is not constructed according to
> "their measure"; it is a male world and they often feel as aliens in it.
> MIROSLAV VOLF, *Exclusion and Embrace*

In the previous chapter, we examined evangelical identity and the academic context. Our lives, however, are also embedded within communities, churches and families. A sense of calling is shaped, tested, confirmed or disconfirmed within these networks. The first woman quoted above, for example, discovered that her inner sense of call, though taken seriously by her pastor, was disconfirmed by the missionaries she encountered. Her inner religious yearnings took her into the contested domain and the gender politics of conservative religious life. She has persevered although her life's work and calling have taken her down a different path.

The second woman quoted has also found her home in the academy, but her experience highlights how closely tied call and community can be. In general, an evangelical woman with deep religious and academic inclinations still struggles with the gap between her perception of call and the usual expectations regarding women's roles and gifts. This can leave women with a sense of "homelessness," as Miroslav Volf recognizes. In this chapter, we consider our callings and our communities and their implications for living on the boundaries and for making choices to serve within the academy.

CALL

I would define my call to teach as a very certain and deep awareness that God has gifted me in certain areas with a unique purpose in mind and that I am responsible for the use of those gifts.

The sense of God's call has been the only thing that has helped me persevere. If it hadn't been for a very clear sense of call, I would have thrown in the towel a long time ago.

Call is a central, though problematic, category in many religious traditions, and its importance is often strongly emphasized within evangelical communities. The scriptural narrative is replete with stories of men and women who have heard and responded to God's call, sometimes against all odds. A sense of God's call on our lives can empower us for extraordinary tasks and can sustain us in our labors over long periods of time.[1] It can help us to pursue opportunities for service and ministry even when human support is limited. As one woman wrote,

My awareness of God's call, and my certainty that to disobey God's leading would be worse than anything that I went through in the process of following it, is precisely what kept and keeps me going when things have been difficult in the academy.

Call and resistance, as we noted in chapter two, are closely linked. Another woman said, "Call has helped me persist in the face of often painful resistance from colleagues." Such strength is crucial in the church and the academy, and the significance of call was notable in the responses of almost all of the women we surveyed. But especially when call is contested within our most important communities, we find ourselves examining and re-examining our paths; call must be discerned and tested within community.

---

[1] Of course, there are also occasional but frightening examples of religious fanaticism that find their legitimation and justification in some notion of God's direct leading or call.

Often a woman's concern about the stewardship of her gifts accompanied comments about calling. A sense of call enables women and men to name the conviction that their lives are not entirely their own and that the work they do is as much a response to God's inner workings as it is a personal or pragmatic decision. In understandings of call and vocation, Christians recognize that they are responsible to others and to the larger good. Men and women who feel called will often persevere through almost impossible circumstances, aware of the faithfulness of biblical and historical models who have gone before them.

Evangelical women who pursue theological studies often point to theological interests and sensitivities from a young age. They describe themselves as "driven by theological curiosity," propelled "by curiosity about God" and by a yearning to "serve the church" with their minds. As one woman put it, "I enjoy the exchange of thoughts and ideas with others. In moments of honest intellectual engagement with others, I often have a strong sense of God's presence and benediction." A number of other women noted, however, that initial callings were to pastoral or missionary work, and when those doors were closed, they found opportunities for service and even a fresh sense of call to work within the academy. While several women denied having any experience of a specific call to academic work, most were quite emphatic about its role in their decisions, persistence and sense of fulfillment.

Because the evangelical world is a complex combination of individualistic piety and institutional connections, call is experienced and interpreted in distinctive ways, as the following comment indicates. "I am gifted, called, sent and available because of a direct relation of accountability to God. If others reject or misunderstand my gifts, it's sad, but I look to God for direction, opportunity, comfort and pacing." Or, as another woman put it, "Recalcitrant Southern Baptists can't thwart God's will for me."

Part of what keeps women within the evangelical world are its close-knit communities of prayer, support and worship, as well as its deep conviction that a person's work in the world matters for eternity. Yet as women pursue theological education, their communities sometimes become quite ambivalent about, and less affirming of, the new woman that is emerging. The gulf between church and academy widens, doors close and women's gifts are overlooked within their own churches.

The church's affirmation is more immediate and more consistent when it is young men who are called to ministry or theological education. Because for most men there is less conflict between subjective experience and evangelical institutions, there are also fewer tensions between the demands of God and the community and less pressure to reflect on the dynamics of authority. But for women, call can become the point at which subjective experience and authoritative institutions come into painful conflict. Evangelical authorities may bluntly reject, subtly challenge or silently ignore a call. Because a woman's commitment to be faithful to a call can be quite strong, there is often a sense of betrayal, especially when her openness to God's call has been nurtured by those very authorities. In response, some women move toward communities and authorities more supportive of such callings.

From women's responses to our questions, we can make several observations about call or vocation. Women may be quite hesitant to claim a direct call from God in the form of a spoken word or sign. Nevertheless, they will appeal to the fruits of their ministry and to the historic fruits of other women's calls and work, hoping to temper the frequent resort to debates about the hard passages on women's leadership and authority in the New Testament Epistles. For women in the Wesleyan tradition, the strong precedent of John Wesley's affirmation—albeit reluctant—of the fruit of women's ministry provides strength for the journey. Wesleyan women can locate their call to pastoral ministry, preaching and teaching within the practices of early Methodism. Women in the branches of evangelicalism most influenced by Reformed or Baptist traditions often face more opposition, have more new ground to cover and are pushed into defending their experience of call against selective biblical arguments to the contrary.

While call is an important category, the life anticipated is sufficiently alien that call is often tentatively recognized, especially at first. Opportunities are taken as they are presented. Some women take time to come to a sort of inner cognitive approval of what they are doing. Within the "doing" comes the confidence. Women's tendency to proceed step by step, combined with the community's ambivalence about women in ministry, often prolongs the process of discerning a call. Furthermore, women are more likely to doubt the inner voice that presents itself as call in part because they are more likely to take seriously the voices of the community and the relationships around them. It is also harder to recognize the validity of a call if there are no models. The young girl who is drawn to pastoral ministry but finds no examples in her tradition might ignore the call or find other avenues for being faithful.

A call to academic work, however, is even harder to define within the tradition. For men and women, the call is often first to ministry, and academic work unfolds subsequently as a possible avenue for service. This is evident from the large number of graduate students in theological disciplines that have obtained a seminary degree prior to their beginning doctoral studies. Some of the women surveyed clearly differentiated a call from a particular career: "I am not so much interested in having a career as much as doing that work that God has called me to do." Nevertheless, many expressed gratitude for the surprising ways that doors had opened and saw this as a work of God in their lives.

Even in religious cultures that exclude women from leadership, teaching or authority, there is often a category for the "exceptional woman." One woman who teaches at the seminary level but is a member of a very conservative denomination explained that her denomination still thinks of her as an exception. This category has been particularly important as an opening through which gifted single women have been able to move forward in ministry and in teaching. This avenue, however, is ambiguous because while it provides opportunities for the individual woman, it can also alienate her from other women because of her distinctive status. While a woman might find it powerfully affirming to be considered exceptional, she may also unwittingly reinforce the basic hierarchy by transcending it.

A sense of call and stewardship sometimes also mediates the awkwardness women might feel in academic circles when standing up for their rights or asking to be recognized for the valuable work they are doing. Academia does not, on the whole, encourage humility, yet humility is a Christian virtue. Where a woman might have difficulty saying, "I am the best person for this job," she might be more able to acknowledge, "I am called by God to do this work." While hesitant to bring attention to her own accomplishments, a woman might sense a responsibility to other women or to the kingdom to make sure her work is recognized.

Call also allows women to persevere despite a sense of academic inadequacy or struggles with the "imposter syndrome."[2] Several women described uncertainty about their scholarly ability, but women often learn their way into roles they could never have imagined filling. Because call and God's will are tied closely together, it can become nearly unthinkable to abandon the call even when the tasks are difficult. One woman said, "I have had many doubts about my ability but have persisted because I felt led to go through the program."

How then is call discerned and recognized? Should we expect to be raised from our beds like Samuel and to hear the word of God speaking to us? While some women have received a supernatural call of some sort—a voice, a Scripture passage or a word of knowledge—for others it is a path encouraged by models or mentors, or an inner direction that is affirmed by people they trust. Some women have ex-

---

[2]The "imposter syndrome" is most common among successful professionals, especially women, who imagine that they have "fooled" people or the system into thinking they are more intelligent or gifted than is actually the case. Despite significant and often obvious achievements and capacity, they worry about being frauds or "being found out."

amined their talents and interests and interpret these as evidence of God's call. "Calling is tricky. Part gifts, part confirmed from outside, part 'this is where I am peaceful,' " said one woman. For other women there is simply the awareness that teaching, mentoring and ministering are sources of joy, fulfillment and peace.

A sense of call also develops in dialogue with the biblical narrative, and narrative hermeneutics, as we shall describe in chapter six, has been a crucial link between feminist, postliberal and evangelical communities. Call can be affirmed by discerning patterns of life and their biblical character or by recognizing that we live within the biblical story. Those who experience interminable waiting might identify with Sarah or Abraham; for those called to a ministry of healing or rebuilding, it might be Nehemiah or Daniel. The pattern of the story and the dynamics of waiting on God, in spite of adversity, become the fabric of resistance and persistence.

This kind of call is sometimes less specific in its vocational object. Few women suggested that they were called to a particular job. Indeed, for those who have survived crises or severance from an evangelical environment, an overall vocation allows and enables them to be flexible in the manner in which they seek to live faithfully. This woman articulated the flexibility inherent in call.

> I would define my call to teach as a very certain and deep awareness that God has gifted me in certain areas with a unique purpose in mind and that I am responsible for the use of those gifts. On other occasions I have said that my calling has been to Christ, and I could have done any number of things (vocationally) without having stepped outside of that "calling."

Call is also helpful in remaining centered, in keeping priorities straight and in providing the bigger picture, motivation, goal or reason for studies. This was explained by one of our respondents: "A sense of calling has helped me persevere in the academy, largely because it helps me keep sacrifices and petty indignities in perspective." Another wrote, "I consider my scholarly work and teaching my mission field. This sense of call helps me to persevere when I feel frustrated with politics, alienated because of my religious beliefs and discouraged with my students' academic abilities or motivation."

THE IMPORTANCE OF STORIES IN SHAPING THE "GOOD" WOMAN

> I think there's plenty of historical precedent for evangelical women being called to ministry beyond their homes and families. The call to follow Jesus has to ultimately supercede commitment to home and family.

Stories about female missionaries and church leaders from the past are a surprisingly significant source of inspiration for evangelical women (especially for those who grew up in the tradition). One woman remembers that she "determined as a child to be single and a teacher, from missionary books." Such accounts and biographies, sometimes more than live models, inspired an initial sense of calling, even if that call was subsequently redirected when theological education was acquired.

Missionary tales, kept alive in evangelical homes and institutions, are heroic religious stories in which women—even more than men—against all odds, take the gospel to the world. They usually include some sort of supernatural call; missionary women took significant risks and often defied institutions. They were ultimately vindicated by the telling of their story, a finished narrative that, whatever the complexity and messiness of the life, made sense in the end.

Missionary stories, like biblical narratives, provide patterns within which we can read our own lives, and they give a vision of what can be done in a world where prayer and faith are primary. These stories have helped women endure the small everyday frustrations of patriarchal institutions, knowing that such difficulties are much less grave than the miseries other women have lived through. In these stories women often find some form of solidarity. Such stories and models provide the discipline to stand back from indignities and frustrations and say, "In the kingdom, does this matter?" Stories are sources of encouragement when women's lives appear to contain only unfinished ends and complex hurts.

For male and female academics from Wesleyan backgrounds there is often another significant resource of stories about women in leadership; they can remember "preaching" grandmothers, mothers and great aunts. They describe experiences of sitting under powerful women preachers and learning from compelling missionary teachers. One male professor at a Wesleyan school remembered his great aunts as fine preachers and church planters. He noted that he had never felt it strange to have women in the classroom because women had provided most of his significant early theological formation. In the 1960s, such roles were delegitimated, and few Wesleyan men or women acknowledged the work of their foremothers. But today, that legacy is more deeply appreciated and eagerly owned. A number of Wesleyans we talked with acknowledged that they had grown up with many female models for ministry. This is particularly true in the smaller holiness sects whose histories incorporate an unusual mix of strict dress codes, high behavioral boundaries and women's authority.

Missionaries' stories and missional concerns about the kingdom can subtly shift contemporary evangelical women's orientation to feminist concerns. On the one hand, these missionaries and leaders are models of forthright and assertive women who have fearlessly stood up to patriarchal institutions. On the other hand, they challenge feminist approaches to theology by insisting that the gospel can never be defined by the well-being of women alone. It is always bigger. Women's needs cannot be understood as entirely separate from the needs of other persons or from God's purposes in the world.

Some of the female pioneers in evangelical institutions have been fed and nurtured by these stories, and they use these resources in overcoming the difficult institutional hurdles encountered in breaking new ground. As women steeped in the missionary ethos, they are, from an organization's point of view, sometimes also seen as safe because of their willingness to make personal sacrifices for the sake of the larger endeavor. Missionary stories can feed the subtle pressure on evangelical women to sacrifice themselves before they have a sense of self or clear direction. This willingness to serve releases great energy and giftedness for the community, but it can come at significant cost to the woman's well-being and distinct academic contribution.

In any case, identifying with such stories can give a backbone or sturdiness to evangelical women such that they are less inclined toward fussing over small difficulties and despairing over minor inconveniences. Utopian expectations are tempered by recognizing that ultimate fulfillment will not come in this life and that incompleteness, longing for wholeness and aching for reconciliation are part of human existence pointing toward heaven.

CALLING AND CONSTRUCTING A LIFE

While a woman's experience of call can be very strong, much that is involved in working out a call, or in discerning God's leading, is experienced as gradually "constructing a life," in Mary Catherine Bateson's definition. Women's lives often do not come all of a piece, dedicated to one job or profession for a lifetime. We do our work while nurturing children, caring for aging parents, applying for jobs and making a living "in the meantime." We create our lives little by little, much as a sculptor finds life in a stone or as a bricoleur creates beauty from an odd assortment of objects. This piecemeal approach to academic as well as ordinary life can leave women feeling quite insecure and appearing to be somewhat unfocused. Nothing is ever done completely: we have not published as much as we would have liked; we are less present to our families than we want to be.

Many women struggle with a sense that numerous parts of life are out of control. We wonder how it will be possible to write a dissertation while our toddler is in "mother's morning out." Will daycare workers be able to contact us in the library? How will it be possible to complete the semester when unexpected family illnesses beckon us to another part of the country? There is no adequate script. In all of this women may feel we are indeed "constructing" our lives. Bateson says, for example,

> Each of us constructs a life that is her own central metaphor for thinking about the world. But of course these lives do not look like parables or allegories. Mostly they look like ongoing improvisations, quite ordinary sequences of day-to-day events. They continue to unfold.[3]

Bateson's metaphor works well for the kind of patched-together existence that women often feel characterizes their lives. Nevertheless, women construct their lives by discerning deep currents of continuity amidst the surface chaos. On looking back, the incoherence of identity and experience is eclipsed by a deeper, persistent theological interest and commitment. However, the unevenness and the multiple foci of women's lives can give the false impression of a lack of serious commitment to the academic enterprise.

Because, as evangelicals, we construct our lives through call, "construction" will always include an important element of being led by God or of following Christ. This touches the deep tension in Christian, and especially in evangelical, theology between understandings of human freedom and divine sovereignty. A richer and more complex understanding of this tension would be helpful in enabling faithful women and men to articulate a coherent account of the constructed and called elements of our lives.

A helpful consequence of understanding our lives as constructed under the call of a loving God is that we are enabled to hold certain commitments more loosely and can be less fearful of letting go of situations and positions that are harmful and hurtful. Because of the high levels of uncertainty and change in contemporary society, women and men can tend to "hold on to the continuity we have however profoundly it is flawed," Bateson writes.[4] Perhaps, as she further suggests, we should take some opportunity

> to explore the creative potential of interrupted and conflicted lives, where energies are not narrowly focused or permanently pointed toward a single ambition. These are not lives without commitment, but rather lives in which commitments are continually refocused and redefined.[5]

---

[3] Mary Catherine Bateson, *Composing a Life* (New York: Plume, 1989), p. 241.
[4] Ibid., p. 8.
[5] Ibid., p. 9.

Learning how to live into a combination of fidelity and freedom is both necessary and important. For women it is crucial to find or to form small communities that will help in discerning when and how long to remain committed to particular forms of service. Communities are also important during times of transition and in providing support through periods when a person is sure that sustained commitment, though difficult, is necessary.

FAMILY

I do not believe that evangelical women scholars experience tensions between career and family any differently than other professional women. Given the difficulties that face women in the workplace and the nearly impossible task of maintaining a family and a career, generic tension soon fills every possible space in any woman's life. ✐

There is more pressure within evangelical circles for a woman to be the traditional "Becky-homecky." In sermons, in evangelical publications, in Christian bookstores and certainly on the airwaves, the message comes through that a woman's highest callings are to build up a man and to raise children, which translates into staying at home with the kids. . . . Even some of the prominent women in evangelical circles who have active public ministries lambaste that very activity. ✐

For all the promise of a new society in which men and women might equally share the joys and burdens of work and family, working women still encounter social and cultural difficulties. Women today have fewer children and more freedom than did women in previous generations, but the politics surrounding childcare and religion remain highly charged. Individual decisions to stay at home or to work outside the home are often moralized, with associated judgments rendered on those women who follow a different path by choice or necessity. Academic women experience certain challenges because while working hours in academia are more flexible than in many other fields, it is also important for academics to stay connected to their profession without taking any extended breaks. Additionally, many women have begun professional work later in life—both because preparation for theological studies requires a significant time investment and because they have chosen to try to blend motherhood and scholarship.

Not surprisingly then, the women in our survey admitted that they were torn between family and academia. One woman wrote, "I have felt that I had to choose between career and family. We will probably not have children." Another is postponing plans to have children until after tenure review when, she admits somewhat poignantly, "I may be too old." Those who do have children tell stories of varying degrees of desperation and fulfillment within family and academy.

> *I have had both (career and family), mostly because I've worked my rear end off and sacrificed by doing part-time work, but I'm very satisfied with the amount of time I have with my kids, and my career has not suffered ultimate loss either.* ✍

Again, this situation is certainly not unique to evangelicals, but the stress occurs against a backdrop that is not necessarily very open to women who attempt to combine both tasks. One woman noted,

> *Perhaps [evangelical women] carry more baggage in terms of traditional expectations. At the same time they may be more accustomed to talking through precisely these issues, since evangelical churches focus so intently on them. Evangelical women have been strongly directed toward self-sacrifice and feel this to be in tension with holding a career, but so have and do all women. I think much depends on particular personalities, including the expectations of particular husbands.* ✍

For many of the married women we surveyed, the responses of their husbands were extremely significant. A number of women described themselves as fortunate to have husbands who have "always been very supportive and an encouragement." One respondent described her husband as "long-suffering" and another as "amazing." Acknowledging that her husband's support had developed gradually, another woman wrote, "I cannot imagine doing this with a spouse who was not as respectful of my vocation as I am of his." For a few, their husbands also served as some of their most important mentors. In several cases, the kinds of work or types of careers in which the husbands were engaged made it easier or more difficult for them to be helpful.

Where the relationship was more difficult between a husband and wife, however, the impact of the marriage on the woman's ability to combine career and family was quite apparent. One woman explained that, in the "bad moments," in arguments over childcare arrangements and finances, she heard the clear message, "If you weren't doing this nonsense our children would be just fine." She explained that she never "got from him the headship kind of thing. . . . It was more subtle than that. It was more 'our children won't come up right if you don't give more attention to the family.'" Another woman articulated what seems to have been a fairly common experience: her doctoral program saw her as "super-domestic, my husband thought I neglected him and the children somewhat, and I thought I had it about right."

Reducing the tension by giving up one or the other task is not appealing; it is a process of continual negotiation. The loneliness that women often express as theo-

logians is exacerbated during periods of extended separation from academic conversations. One woman commented, "I have always, since my children were born,
been active in either ministry, other work or studying. For myself and for the good
of my children, I need the academic/intellectual work."

Most of the women we surveyed replied that, although evangelical women
might feel the tension between the family and the academy more, it was difficult
for all women in academia and probably for all women who work outside the home.
However hard it is to judge the relative difficulties, there is consistent testimony
among evangelical women to "playing old tapes" about the place of women in the
home, even when women have long since given up explicitly believing them. If it is
the case that gender issues are central to evangelical identity, then the problems will
be more acute for evangelical women, and there will be fewer support systems to
help. The old tapes are so internalized that one hardly needs external pressures to
keep ambivalences in place. This is especially the case if women find themselves
with any major difficulty in childrearing or family relationships. In a very realistic
way, the following quote expresses the ambiguity inherent in many women's lives
and suggests how important it is to be aware of the interplay of sin and grace.

> Since American culture in general condemns women who both work and parent (at least
> whenever the balance is the teeniest bit problematic), I think the tensions are similar for all
> women. But evangelical women see this tension as a faith issue in which their ultimate
> responsibility is to God. I certainly see my career-family balance in that light, with all the
> overtones of sin, repentance and grace that such an orientation implies.

The scarcity of married women in evangelical seminaries and in religion and
theology departments in colleges further underlines the problem of combining
family and career. Evangelical schools appear to have more single than married
women on their full-time faculties, and the jury is still out on why this may be the
case. Does married status clash even more with evangelical sensibilities than does
singleness in the workplace? Do fewer evangelical married women ever get to graduate school? Do more married women choose to stay away from full-time tenure-
track positions while their children are young? Are women more acceptable as
Christian educators if their sexuality, especially their pregnancy, is bracketed? For
the few married women who are pregnant and teaching, there are additional
stresses. One woman in the survey recently discovered that her pregnancy became
the occasion for her school's forging of its first policies on maternity leave for faculty members.

Despite the additional challenges of juggling family responsibilities along with academic tasks, married women sometimes find that their marital status makes them seem "safer" to male colleagues, while it also leaves less time for interacting with those colleagues at a social level. Being married may function as an expression of normalcy in evangelical contexts. Some women find, however, that evangelical organizations (especially some missions agencies) limit the teaching opportunities of married women. One observed, "I have not always been allowed to do what I was capable of doing because I was a married woman."

For many evangelicals, traditional notions of male headship and complementary roles for men and women have become sufficiently flexible to accommodate the increasing need for women to work outside the home for family income. While headship is affirmed, there is simultaneously room for men and women to live fairly egalitarian lives in the workplace.[6] But traditional notions of hierarchy are much less flexible if the workplace is the theological academy, if evangelical women are in positions of religious leadership and authority, or if women are working because of giftings or calling, rather than financial necessity.

All of these tensions occur against the backdrop of an increasingly demanding profession in which even single women find themselves consumed with work that never ends and tasks that are never done. "I have not accomplished what I would have liked in my writing and research because of my commitment to my family. But I live with the frustration by trying to let go of those things I cannot accomplish." "I have to do everything in interrupted pieces because of family and household demands," wrote another woman. Blaming the promises of feminism for her mistaken notion that she could do everything, a woman observed, "I can 'have it all' if I do not need to sleep. I have become increasingly disillusioned by what I now believe to be a feminist myth."

The comments of another woman reflect the difficult pressures many women experience when they try to combine academic work and family. This woman, who has had a distinguished writing and teaching career and is raising several children, wrote,

It finally dawned on me a couple of years ago that there are three major components of my life. One is home and one is the teaching and one is the research. And the simple fact of the matter is I really can't do all three. It simply is a fact. One of them falls off. . . . They really are three totally different personas, or three different tasks. . . . It's sort of like I'm living a triple life or something. And then of course in the midst of all of that, there's just plain old me.

---

[6]Sally K. Gallagher and Christian Smith, "Symbolic Traditionalism and Pragmatic Egalitarianism: Contemporary Evangelicals, Families and Gender," *Gender and Society* 13, no. 2 (1999): 211.

Other women agreed that the combination was possible, though difficult. One noted simply, "I have very little free or discretionary time." "You can have both," said another, "if husband and wife as a team with community support handle both childrearing and housework. Also, the institution needs to be flexible." As the authors of *Women of Academe* concluded, when a woman succeeded in combining her personal and professional life, there was usually something extra: more financial or human resources—a supportive husband or mother, helpful colleagues and no disasters.[7]

Several single women described family pressures that came from a different direction. One woman wrote, "During the time I cared for sick and aging parents, there was lots of conflict. . . . The conflict and labor of school and caring for my mother was terrible." A woman's responsibilities toward her parents, especially when they are living in a different part of the country, can pose both acute and chronic tensions for any kind of career. But in evangelical contexts in which family responsibilities are so strongly affirmed, it is particularly painful when schools are not sympathetically aware of the effect that such family ties can have on a woman's time for research and publishing. With general increases in longevity and mobility, this challenge will surely increase not only for single women, but also for anyone who takes family responsibilities seriously.

A number of women noted the important roles their parents—mothers and fathers—had played in helping them to see themselves in a particular academic career. One woman wrote, "My parents always taught us that we could do anything we set our minds to do, so when I sensed God's calling, there was no question in my mind about whether I could do it or not—only who was going to pay for it." Another commented, "Dad has always encouraged me to do anything I wanted. He taught me that I am accountable to God to use my gifts and talents to the best of my ability." For several women, their mother's interest in reading and engaging their dissertations was deeply important. One said that it was crucial that "my parents have believed in me and my projects . . . and known I could do it." Another woman's father, who had worked hard for his entire life in blue-collar jobs, was a deep inspiration for her to see all work as noble and was her model for faithfulness to a task.

Parents were important in another way for several women. Those who thought going on for doctoral studies was a natural, "of course" kind of response had mostly grown up in academic homes, with one or both parents as professors. For

[7]Nadya Aisenberg and Mona Harrington, *Women of Academe: Outsiders in the Sacred Grove* (Amherst: University of Massachusetts Press, 1988), p. 129.

these women, the academic world was not foreign, study was highly valued, and their own theological interests were sometimes affirmed. They had much less difficulty "imagining" themselves as academics than did some of the other women. As one woman wrote, "I sometimes think I went on to graduate work the first time because it was the only world I knew. My parents were college teachers."

CHURCH AND COMMUNITY

I remember thinking (during a visit to a Celtic worship center), "God, I want to be safe, safe within my relationship with you, and to be embraced by you, but also safe from the bitterness and the hostility of all those years of injustice."

Mom and many of the people from my home church are concerned about my struggles with God and the Christian faith. They "hold onto" me with their concern, but also bind me. I feel like if I lose my faith, I will lose them. It is a terrible feeling.

Pioneers don't tend to have large cheering sections. Often more people are standing by— shaking their heads—than encouraging and cheering one on. And as for me, I've found it often necessary to stop and rest, gauge the territory, try to get some perspective, gather my energies and my will to go on. The work often seems so demanding and the rewards so slim.

For most of the women we surveyed, a love for Christ and the church and a desire to serve God and God's people stand behind much academic effort. Ours is rarely disembodied academic work; it is work for the church and for God's reign. Thus personal experience within the local church is highly charged and very significant. Recognizing the importance of church and Christian community, most of the women were involved in a local congregation. But often their experience was difficult, and sometimes there was evidence of a deep alienation and loneliness.[8]

Evangelicals do not generally have a very high or well-developed ecclesiology, but they do have a high commitment to church and high expectations of particular churches and church life. Evangelicals care about community and value coherent and prayerful corporate life. When vibrant worship is combined with rigorous intellectual life and loving community, the resulting environment can be wonderfully life giving.

In response to the question of why she continued to define herself as an evangelical, one woman wrote,

---

[8]The authors of *Defecting in Place* report a similar finding in their study. See Miriam Therese Winter, Adair Lummis and Allison Stokes, *Defecting in Place: Women Claiming Responsibility for Their Own Spiritual Lives* (New York: Crossroad, 1994), pp. 196-97.

My first reaction is that I can't get away from it. Having grown up in an evangelical house I have been formed by this conversionist strain of Protestantism. Now my political commitments, and in some significant ways, my worldview differ from "mainstream evangelicalism" as expressed in Christian media, and yet here I am pastoring in an evangelical church. I guess it's the drive to know God in loving relationship that aligns me with evangelicals.

A strong sense of responsibility and stewardship undergirded many women's reflections on their roles in church and community. Women who knew that they had received gifts and opportunities also knew that they were responsible for using them well for the sake of the church. While pouring themselves into teaching students and doing research and writing, they also recognized the significance of church involvement.

Thus, most of the women we surveyed were moderately to highly involved in a local church. Their contributions ranged from preaching and Sunday school teaching to diaconal and district-wide responsibilities. As noted earlier, more than half of the women were involved in mainline denominations, but usually the local church was evangelical in character. In such churches, they often found communal and missional vitality. Certainly, there are interesting possibilities if the vigor and energy of evangelicalism are infused into mainline churches. As one senior woman put it, "This shows that God has a sense of humor; the women rejected by evangelical churches may be the ones who largely evangelize the mainline churches."

While academic women may have rich visions for church life, they sometimes find themselves with no place to share this vision and with little power in forming it. This then becomes a double sadness—to know what it could be like and to be defined out of making a significant contribution. One woman involved in a dynamic evangelical church during graduate school remembered with sadness that "the fact that I was a graduate student in theology was completely overlooked in my church." A married man also working on his doctorate received a great deal of attention and many opportunities to teach, but she noted that "it never occurred to anyone to ask her" to teach.

A number of the women who remain involved in conservative congregations noted the complexity that this connection posed for several aspects of their lives. Many of these women had been raised or converted in that denomination and had very close personal ties—familial, friendship or mentoring relationships—that remained important to them. For these women, family and church or denomination are integrally related. For some, it simply would be impossible to leave because of the fracturing of relationships their departure would cause. A few of these women worshiped in other churches but would not sever their ties with their denomination. For example, one woman wrote,

> *There are lay people in [my denomination] that have faithfully prayed for me for twenty-eight years. I receive regular telephone calls, cards, small Christmas gifts. They now regularly e-mail me. It is mainly because of them that I do not feel free to leave the [denomination] because it would be like divorcing them. They pray for me regularly.* ✍

In conservative denominations that are ambivalent about women's roles, some academic women found themselves treated and honored as exceptions, with all the complexity that identity brings. One woman noted that some of her greatest encouragers had been high-profile churchmen with conservative positions on women who nevertheless encouraged her to study and advocated that the denomination provide financial support for her academic studies.

For a number of women, multiple ties and fissures within their denomination were a source of deepest pain. Having been nurtured into a theological and missional identity in a certain denomination, encouraged by denominational leaders to pursue further studies or even having received denominational funding for studies, they found that the ground had subsequently shifted under them. Their own denominations had moved toward more restrictive roles for women and no longer had any place in which their academic and leadership gifts were usable or welcome. Their communities could not employ them as professors or as pastors. These decisions have left women feeling deeply betrayed by the churches that shaped them and by the communities to which they had given their lives and energies. Because personal bonds often remained significant, these issues continue to be very painful. Most of the women have found employment outside their denomination, but church connections remained extremely difficult.

Among women who were converted in college, denominational ties are often much looser. Interestingly, few of these women had much experience with fundamentalism and, at times, were mystified when fundamentalist assumptions showed up in church life. Few adult converts to evangelicalism have much knowledge of the history of the institutions within which they eventually dwell and serve and are rarely in touch with the fundamentalist strand in certain traditions.

Approximately one-third of the women we surveyed were ordained or licensed within a particular denomination, and a number had experience in pastoral ministry, clear evidence of the importance of the church in the formation of academic evangelical women. Because their denominations were closed to having women in positions of authority, however, some women had sought out alternatives to pastoral ministry and had found a place in the academy. One woman wrote, "I believe I may have pastoral gifts, but these have not been affirmed, and I have not cultivated them in a traditional pastoral role because of the sexism in the evangelical subculture from which I have come." Another commented, "I have a call from God to build the church. Because I was not able to get a pastorate after graduation from seminary (because of my gender) and because I was offered a job in a seminary, I fulfilled my call through forming and pastoring pastors." Another woman, who had served for a decade in pastoral ministry in a conservative denomination, found academic work in an evangelical seminary to be a much better fit. She wrote,

> I . . . find, as a woman, that the credentials required for [a professorial role] seem to help with the "woman in authority" thing that is so difficult in our culture. Whereas I was often considered a "pastor-ette," I've never been classed as a "professor-ette."

Despite the importance of megachurches to contemporary evangelicalism, almost none of the women we surveyed were involved in such congregations. Because these churches are influential and often have extensive teaching ministries, this is a significant issue. While some are open to women in leadership, many limit women's roles in the church to particular areas and populations. Women faculty in evangelical colleges and seminaries now find themselves dealing with a generation of young students, nurtured in high-profile megachurches, who are more conservative about women's roles than students were a decade or two ago.

The vibrancy, energy and commitment within evangelical congregations can be winsome.[9] Clearly, women appreciated the vigor and willingness to take risks for the sake of the gospel that are evident in the evangelical world. Even women who had moved away from evangelicalism into mainline churches spoke of appreciating parts of evangelicalism: its "emphasis on petitionary prayer, the priesthood of all believers, fellowship, practical care of one another in the congregation." Most of the women found a place somewhere between mainline and evangelical life but fitted perfectly in neither.

Some have found mainline denominations to be as troubled by gender issues as

---

[9]In his study, Christian Smith notes that "evangelicals are the most active of all the comparison groups." He describes contemporary evangelical efforts to "try to change American society to better reflect God's will" through participation in various forms of religious, social and political activism; voluntarism in the local community; giving money to assist the poor and to spread the gospel; and working to defend a biblical worldview. Christian Smith, *American Evangelicalism: Embattled and Thriving* (Chicago: University of Chicago Press, 1998), p. 39.

is the evangelical world. Said one woman who works in mainly liberal church and academic settings and is herself ordained,

> *The stained-glass ceiling is firmly in place, and articulate women still are likely to be labeled "strident" and "unfeminine" in both places [church and academy]. However, the conflict is often framed as a "personality" issue (that just happens to repeat itself along gender lines) rather than a conflict over authority. For instance, my colleague at church is quick to label me "controlling" if I want to be involved in something he'd rather define as his "turf."*

When encountering patriarchal and paternalistic dynamics in mainline congregations, the sense of betrayal is also acute because of the public stands that suggest more equality than is actually present. The patronizing though well-intentioned character of many church interactions can be extremely trying. Several women commented about such experiences and added, "I'm not going to be in an organization that does not consider me to be an adult."

For the sake of preserving community, women often hesitate to directly challenge patriarchal statements in the church. In some situations, women know that the underlying intentions are better than the actual expression. Patriarchal language and practice, however, can become a deep barrier to worship; and if a number of incidents come in quick succession, a woman can feel a deep ache of betrayal with people she considers friends. Noninclusive language, demeaning jokes or stories, cavalier treatments of difficult biblical texts and slams against the feminist movement become sources of significant pain. When these practices occur within a sermon, there is almost no way to challenge them publicly. While it is possible to identify the issues in academic circles, it is more complex in church situations where identifying such concerns can easily be viewed as undermining a pastor's authority.

When they have found it, women deeply value the support and love of a church community. Those who experience such community will endure quite a lot for the sake of preserving valued relationships and a place of refuge. Sexism, patriarchalism and other irritants are overlooked for more intangible support, encouragement and a shared experience of rich worship. However, the problems become exacerbated when one's own students are also present in the congregation. How are we to respond when students hear or experience problematic gender assumptions? How are we to be mentors in such situations? Silence or long-suffering "niceness" hardly seems sufficient when our commitment is to the shaping of students for discipleship or ministry.

Commitments to creating and sustaining community can make dissent and criticism within any institution quite difficult. Evangelical churches and schools value "niceness," and women who speak their minds or identify problems risk quick marginalization if they do not find ways to temper their criticisms. Simply to name or describe troubling circumstances can be interpreted as adversarial or aggressive. Pressures to maintain an image of peaceful, well-functioning community can powerfully discourage dissent, and in these situations, people do not readily learn how to disagree with civility or grace.

As we noted previously, some women deal with the problems of living on the boundary by bracketing certain questions or by bracketing questions in a particular context; for example, the ambiguities of scholarship or feminism may be bracketed in church. Bracketing is easier if the worlds in which one lives have little overlap. As a strategy, bracketing can heighten a sense of isolation while it simultaneously allows a person to function within multiple communities. A person can make moral or theological sense of what she is doing as long as she does not have to explain it to anyone else. If there were a safe community that bridged different worlds, the bracketing would no longer be necessary. Almost everyone who has graduated with a Ph.D. in a theological field lives in numerous different intellectual worlds, and bracketing is a strategy for people that value very different communities or organizations and want more than a marginal identity in each one.

Elaine Storkey described her struggles with similar tensions. She writes that she had invited women from her school setting to come with her to church because

> I believed they would hear the Christian gospel more fully there, and be drawn to God. But when one woman took up the invitation, the effect was not what I had, naively, expected. Her comment afterwards was simply, "Gosh!" and I suddenly saw the service through her eyes. Men had taken charge of everything—the sermon, the service, the prayers—and the hymns, language and liturgy had all embodied exclusively male language. It had been alienating for a woman. She looked at me with bewilderment, and I could see she was thinking—"How can a feminist like you . . . ?"
>
> I suppose it was about then that I realized that I was not living an integrated life. I had accepted the church as it was, and not applied the same standards to it that I had applied everywhere else.[10]

Another woman commented poignantly, "I cannot take my brain, my gender or my vocation to church, and there is not a lot left of me after that. I turn more and more to contemplative spirituality as a source of grounding and inner strength." Increasingly, women are turning to contemplative spirituality—wherever it may be

---

[10]Elaine Storkey and Margaret Hebblethwaite, *Conversations on Christian Feminism: Speaking Heart to Heart* (London: Fount, 1999), p. 11.

found—in Catholic retreat houses, Celtic pilgrimages or Taizé services. A sense of commitment to church remains strong, but there is also a deep weariness with long struggles, as is evident in the following comment.

> *I am so tired of fighting the battles . . . that I have limited patience when people raise the issues of women in ministry, inclusive language and so on. But I know I don't fit in real liberal settings. So I often feel like I don't fit. But I believe there are those moderate places out there. I just have to find them.*

Another woman who had grown up Roman Catholic and later had become an evangelical explained that she had grown so weary of the evangelical fights that she had returned to Roman Catholicism, "where although they won't ordain you, they value your intellect." She continued, "But if you push on me, you'll find I'm an evangelical underneath." A woman, quoted in *Defecting in Place*, gave a response that represents the combination of alienation and commitment a number of women expressed: "I love the church. I have no anger. Just a growing emptiness."[11]

Finding solidarity with laywomen in church can sometimes be difficult for women who teach in theological studies. It is not always possible to talk seriously or theologically about gender concerns or feminist tensions with laywomen or even with women who deal with feminist issues at work. Laywomen often leave those issues behind at work and enter a different world in church. They do not necessarily want to press the gender boundaries, especially if those boundaries are only symbolic, because in doing so they may sacrifice what power they do have. Academic women live in a more unified world and are often troubled by the absence of conversation partners in their churches.[12]

The women we surveyed expressed much ambivalence about church life and experience, but this problem is not confined to evangelical women. Many theologians feel lonely in church. And many lay people feel marginalized and excluded by academic theological language. Church and community of some sort, however, were important to almost all of the women we surveyed. Small prayer groups suffice for some women whose church situations are very unsatisfactory, but small groups do not necessarily fulfill the role of church for those who are hungering for authentic Christian community.

---

[11] Winter, Lummis and Stokes, *Defecting in Place*, p. 45.

[12] Feminist critiques of church can be very compelling to academic women, especially in conservative ecclesial situations that are difficult. Feminist visions of community, discoveries of the insights and experiences of other women, and analyses of patriarchy in religious institutions can become important resources for hope and interpretation.

FRIENDSHIP NETWORKS

Nobody nurtures me in the church. . . . Without my developing professional network and a small network of profound friendships, I could not survive. ✒

I think [the role of professional and friendship networks] has varied throughout my life. Because I have been on the "outside" most of my life (i.e., considered a liberal in a very conservative school or being considered very conservative in a more liberal context), I have sort of had to depend on a small group of like-minded souls or go it on my own. ✒

Exceptionally important to women were the more informal associations that make the difference between a lonely and a shared journey; these relationships enabled women to survive and even to thrive. Many women identified a small group of friends, especially other women, to whom they turned for support and guidance. They described their dependence on structured times for meeting, prayer, conversation and sometimes study.

Commenting on their professional and friendship networks, one woman explained that they "play a crucial and primary role in sustaining my identity and in validating my concerns and commitments." Another woman commented, "I depend on a constant core of friends, a woman's prayer group that meets biweekly [and] a group of women friends at church." Though married with a child, another described herself as "on the edge of every social institution" and grateful that her "friends and husband help me to see my own better self. They reassure me that I am not losing my mind." These people, she explained, were the ones by whom she is "nurtured, edified, reproved, encouraged and corrected."

Often women described how they had assembled small groups for spiritual nourishment. One commented,

I have become very interested in spiritual formation over the years and find myself gravitating to classical writings for my own spiritual nourishment and participating in silent retreats. I meet with a group of four friends twice a month, where we participate in Lectio readings. These individuals have helped to keep me sane over the years. ✒

Levels of isolation varied significantly among the women we surveyed. Isolation often seemed to reflect a combination of personal and institutional dynamics, though it was somewhat unpredictable. A few women turned to some form of therapy for help. One said that she had been taught as a fundamentalist child to survive alone and that "therapy has helped but not cured me." For a surprising number of women, there was just one person in each of their lives who had made the difference in their ability to persevere and to flourish.

PARACHURCH ORGANIZATIONS

It would be hard to overestimate the role of parachurch organizations for the women we surveyed. Many had been shaped by InterVarsity Christian Fellowship, but a number also mentioned L'Abri, Young Life, Campus Crusade and various campus fellowship groups. Parachurch organizations were important in some of the conversion stories and in much of the discipleship. In a significant number of cases, they helped to form Christians who cared about academic life. Parachurch groups rarely move persons toward specific denominations, however, and this proved to be an interesting dilemma. An interdenominational orientation fits the evangelical world, which tends to transcend denominations. Schools hiring in theological areas, however, often look for faculty formed in a particular tradition.

A number of women expressed deep appreciation for the role of InterVarsity in their experience. In many cases, it provided opportunities for growth, leadership and responsible intellectual engagement with the world of Christian faith. As one woman noted, "I cannot speak highly enough of my IVCF experience. The opportunities were endless. The IFES [International Fellowship of Evangelical Students] also encouraged me greatly."

In her book *Fundamentalism and Gender* Margaret Lamberts Bendroth provides historical insight into why InterVarsity has been able to shape women for further theological study without necessarily dealing directly with evangelical resistance to women's authority.

> The growing popularity of "inductive Bible study" among conservative Protestants also owed much to female Bible teachers. . . . In this method students and teacher analyzed a text without notes or commentaries. Together they examined a biblical passage, asked questions of it, and applied it to a practical problem. Rebecca Price, a Biblical Seminary graduate, brought the method to Wheaton College in the 1930s. Jane Hollingsworth, a graduate of both Wheaton and Biblical Seminary, established inductive Bible studies in the work of InterVarsity Christian Fellowship, a national evangelistic organization for college students, during the 1940s. Many observers agreed that this pupil-oriented method allowed women to lead Bible studies without undue exercise of intellectual authority.
>
> Bible teaching formed the basis for feminine networks and leadership as well as careers for women in fundamentalist circles. The clustering of fundamentalist women in religious education is not surprising, given women's longstanding leadership in that field.[13]

---

[13]Margaret Lamberts Bendroth, *Fundamentalism and Gender, 1875 to the Present* (New Haven, Conn.: Yale University Press, 1993), p. 86.

THE GIFT OF HUMOR

Surviving and flourishing in any community requires a sense of humor. An ability to laugh at oneself and to see the humor in ridiculous situations keeps things in perspective. Such humor is helpful only as it is also tenderhearted; as it moves toward the cynical, it can become deeply destructive to all. But being able to take kidding and to do it in return is extremely helpful. Women who are not "continually offended" and who let love cover a multitude of sins find it easier to survive in fallen communities.

Such a posture does not solve everything, however, and being told to "get over it" or that "it was only a joke" rings quite hollow when the joke and the reality are not very far apart or on days when the journey has been particularly difficult. It is also difficult to remain good-humored when, after one has been generous and gracious and only eventually raises an issue, someone else is quickly offended and asks, "What's the big deal?"

Fearful of being labeled a humorless feminist and yet frustrated at not being able to be truthful, a woman can find it very difficult to take up the right mode of speech. But developing a sturdiness is important, and sturdiness that can laugh is even better. One evangelical woman who has worked for years first in very conservative and then in very liberal academic settings wrote, "A sense of humor gets you through a lot."

CONCLUSION

These, then, are the threads that hold us together. Within community, family and church, we encounter voices of confirmation and sometimes those of disconfirmation. Often, friends and family see wider horizons than we can imagine for ourselves. Women have found a variety of ways to sustain their call and commitment, but as deeply relational beings in the image of the triune God, we are profoundly disturbed to encounter the absence of community and conversation in the very heart of Christian congregations and theological thinking. Women, committed to the church, long for safe places for life-giving conversation and for more vibrant communities of faith and discourse that recognize the multiple worlds we inhabit.

We have, in the past five chapters, attempted to describe and analyze the personal, social, cultural and institutional contexts within which evangelical women have been formed and within which we now teach and serve. We have used various historical, sociological and interpersonal lenses to map the terrain over which the "good" woman travels and to examine the communities in which she dwells.

In the next two chapters, we will look closely at the theological landscape in an effort to prime the pump of conversation across evangelical and feminist boundaries. We are hopeful that this will be helpful to evangelical institutions, faculties and students and, in particular, to evangelical women who dwell on multiple boundaries. We hope it will also help our more feminist colleagues for whom the resources of evangelical theology have often been obscured from view.

| 6 |

EVANGELICAL AND FEMINIST MAPS

Redefining the Theological Interior

———

Ever so many tales might be told of woman positioned as difference at the edges
of the world, of woman positioned as difference at the edges of the text.
I read the overlapping cartographies of modernism and postmodernism,
a feminist familiar with the languages of both. I do not live on these maps,
but I visit them from time to time, hoping that,
as one map overlays another, as the maps shift back and forth,
something unexpected and new might be found.
JEFFNER ALLEN, in *Women, Knowledge and Reality*

The sects called evangelical were the first agitators of the woman question . . .
[by convincing women of] their prodigious influence, and consequent
responsibility, in the great work of regenerating a world lying in wickedness.
ABOLITIONIST LYDIA MARIA CHILD, quoted in *Women of Spirit*

Finally we come to theology, within which the discourse that so shapes evangelical
institutions takes place. How does living on both evangelical and feminist maps
change a woman's theological perspective? Is it possible to do theology from both
maps, or must one methodology be chosen and the other bracketed? Are the hidden assumptions of evangelicalism incompatible with doing feminist theology, or
is there something fresh and important that can emerge from this sharing of perspectives? We believe the latter—that a rich theological perspective can be gleaned
from the interaction between the two. Feminism asks questions regarding our horizontal space: how do we function as men and women under God and within the
natural world? Feminism also attempts to nurture that sacred space which is hos-

pitable to women and other alienated people. Evangelicalism continues to make urgent the vertical dimensions of faith—that God is really there, both hidden and revealed, and that we live in the world but not of it—and the existential importance of conversion and appropriation of faith. The shared space, however, within which these important insights can claim attention is not yet large or very hospitable.

Much contemporary theology emerges out of questions of identity and, for us, important reflection arises out of the praxis of living on the boundary. In this and in the following chapter, we dialogue in particular with those writers who have thought through some of the complexities of being evangelical and feminist, or who would claim to be both, and with women who have had a formative evangelical training that still influences their theological expression. We also interact with particular evangelical and feminist writers who have helped to define the theological discussion.

As a group, the evangelical women we surveyed had less exposure to feminist theology than we had anticipated. A considerable number deal with feminism only around the edges of their work or by looking at the issues exclusively from historical or hermeneutical angles, although there are indications that this situation has been changing over the period during which this book was being written. In several evangelical schools, previous conflicts over feminism had primed the institution to react negatively to the slightest hint of feminism, and this has certainly complicated the experience of women who are now engaging gender issues. Some of the lack of engagement with feminism is due to institutional location. Where churches and colleges are still struggling with basic issues of equality and where gender questions spark deep passions, it is easy to be labeled a feminist when suggesting very mild changes to the status quo or when raising concerns about inclusive language or about the use of exclusively male imagery for God.

Nevertheless, almost two decades ago, when Esther Bruland described the solidarities existing between feminism and evangelicalism, she was hopeful that there would be an increasing number of women and men who would claim to be both.[1] Also in the mid-1980s, David Scholer and Randy Maddox argued that feminist and evangelical theology and hermeneutics had profound affinities.[2] Certainly most women in theology are considered feminists of some kind, though perhaps this is less the case

---

[1] Esther Byle Bruland, "Evangelical and Feminist Ethics: Complex Solidarities," *The Journal of Religious Ethics* 17, no. 2 (1989): 139.
[2] See Randy L. Maddox, "The Word of God and Patriarchalism," *Perspectives in Religious Studies* 14, no. 3 (1987): 208; and David M. Scholer, "Feminist Hermeneutics and Evangelical Biblical Interpretation," *Journal of the Evangelical Theological Society* 30, no. 4 (1987).

in the related disciplines of biblical studies, ethics and church history.

For some evangelicals, a woman who teaches a class on Bible or theology to both men and women is automatically a feminist, whether or not she owns the label. A woman can find herself suddenly labeled a feminist even when she has had a long tenure in a particular institution, if the institution in which she teaches takes a turn toward a more conservative position. The women and men who have been through the Southern Baptist controversies over the last two decades can readily testify to this. One does not have to be very radical—all one needs to do is to support women in leadership—to find oneself under suspicion in these and similar institutions.[3]

Some evangelical academic women deal with selected feminist concerns indirectly, as noted earlier. While issues of equality, justice, voice, pedagogy, power and recognition are feminist issues, they are also part of broader discussions and can be engaged without identifying them as feminist. This allows women to tackle hard issues without increasing the resistance to those concerns by locating them within a suspect framework. Similarly, while maintaining a theologically orthodox framework, women are able to pick and choose among various insights that come from feminist theology without having to work with a totally coherent whole.

The narrow specialization of many academic disciplines also makes it possible to avoid key doctrinal debates unless a woman deliberately decides to enter the fray. Perhaps it is not surprising then, that for some women, a great deal of controversy can be bracketed for the sake of survival and effective ministry. Sometimes simply getting up to teach in a contested situation is an act of courage; to reflect on feminist questions in a sustained and systematic way would be too costly and too painful.

When women were more actively engaging an evangelical feminism, they were usually located in Wesleyan, evangelical left or evangelically oriented mainline seminaries. Less common was evangelical feminist reflection in the more Reformed evangelical institutions. The few women in these schools are in the difficult position of breaking new ground in communities that are as much "family" as work environments. One woman for whom this was the case described her slow and painful move to more feminist understandings: "I wasn't putting it together. I was at an impasse. I knew the right thing to say in order to be a part of the system. I had been schooled in it." Yet using the familiar arguments became more difficult as she more fully acknowledged her identity as a woman and a daughter of God. She

---

[3]Interestingly, it was a handful of men in the 1980s who articulated the evangelical case for feminism; works by David Scholer and Randy Maddox were particularly noteworthy. See also the defining work of the 1970s, Letha Scanzoni and Nancy Hardesty, *All We're Meant to Be: A Biblical Approach to Women's Liberation* (Waco, Tex.: Word, 1974).

wanted to express herself not just in solidarity with "women out there"; she wanted to define her own conflicted situation in feminist terms as well. In these contexts women are reflecting constantly on their identities and on their relationship with the traditions that have formed them. As this woman suggested, the process can be a painful one of discovering and finding authenticity within the limits of a particular community. What sometimes emerges is not so much a new theology but a new spirituality and a renewed sense of solidarity with women throughout Christian history and across denominational boundaries.

Before an evangelical feminist theology can be engaged, it is important to address issues of legitimacy and authority. Although feminist theology and evangelicalism are both renewal movements within the church—each is concerned with justice and the eradication of evil, and each is intent on explicating meaning out of the details of the text—the polarity between the two is great. Perhaps this is the case because the stakes are very high in both directions. If women are ontologically and eschatologically equal with men (and equal heirs in Christ, as the third chapter of Galatians asserts), then patriarchy weighs very heavily on human history and on women's and men's lives.

If evangelical egalitarians are wrong, as is commonly believed by conservative evangelicals and by many conservative Roman Catholics, then egalitarians and feminists are in danger of disrupting deep-rooted gender roles and idolatrously reimagining God in human image. When we spoke with a prominent, gifted and conservative Baptist theologian, it was this danger she emphasized: that women, by grasping beyond their callings, were in danger of falling again into Eve's deception. And if deceived, women may be trying to change something contrary to both nature and the will of God.[4] J. I. Packer, regarded by many as a major evangelical moderate of recent times, has argued similarly against making women presbyters by citing I Timothy 2:12-14, among other reasons. Packer asserts that Paul viewed the stories of creation and Fall "as disclosing universal truth about the two sexes." He writes, "I am as emphatically for women's ministry as I am against turning women into men by making presbyters of them."[5] Views of headship, authority and deception remain highly polarized.

Although there is little middle ground, advocates of diverse positions are often present in a single evangelical institution. Further exacerbated by the presence of

---

[4]For most evangelicals, male headship is understood as a *creation* issue, however headship is exercised. See Sally K. Gallagher, *Evangelical Identity and Gendered Family Life* (New Brunswick, N.J.: Rutgers University Press, 2003).

[5]J. I. Packer, "Let's Stop Making Women Presbyters," *Christianity Today*, February 11, 1991, pp. 18-20.

the teaching woman herself, the differences between the positions create a gulf that a profession of faith does not readily bridge. Elouise Renich Fraser expresses this bind when she says,

> Most of all, I didn't want to be forced to choose between evangelicalism and feminism. Despite my vigilance, I feared being co-opted by nonevangelical agendas, thus making myself unacceptable within evangelical circles.[6]

Women do become "unacceptable" very quickly in certain evangelical contexts and cannot easily prove that they are not deceived. Protestations to the contrary can be taken as evidence of guilt, and the common evangelical recourse to call or vocation is ineffectual.

Reflecting on such contexts, Scholer warns that "the deepest motivating factors in the whole discussion of women and ministry in the NT and in the church today are not grammatical, lexical, exegetical, historical, or even hermeneutical in the traditional sense."[7] He argues that they arise, instead, from fears of women's power in ministry, from male insecurity and desire for dominance and from an inadequate understanding of God as neither male nor female. Even if Scholer's assertion is only partly correct, his assessment offers some reasons why careful exegesis and responsible hermeneutics have failed to challenge many people's gender assumptions.

It is not surprising, then, that when women have faced these issues, some have discerned a basic incoherence in the traditional evangelical position that gives experience a large place in conversion and piety but not in theology. Thus they insist that theology should incorporate experiential and subjective elements and be true to this central aspect of faith. "Evangelicals," said one woman, "need to reflect theologically on experience. So much of their theological reflection has been channeled into developing a rational apologetic for biblical authority." Another woman wrote, "I can't imagine doing theology except out of my experience. I'm more and more thinking that writing needs to be autobiographical to a certain extent."

While the evangelical subculture reveals deep tensions and paradoxes around women's issues, it is also in evangelical institutions that some of the fresh insights of the Pentecostal and charismatic movements have been incorporated. Many evangelical seminaries have very high student representation from these less mainstream churches and traditions. It is in these traditions that the depictions of Joel 2:28-29 and Acts 2:16-21 (that women as well as men will prophesy in the last days) carry

---

[6]Elouise Renich Fraser, *Confessions of a Beginning Theologian* (Downers Grove, Ill.: InterVarsity Press, 1998), p. 25.
[7]Scholer, "Feminist Hermeneutics," pp. 418-19.

theological weight. Here, too, is the promise that the Spirit will guide in ways that are not simply reinterpretations of previous eras.[8] Said one younger biblical scholar from this tradition,

> *This is not the place for a thorough discussion of the normative authority of covenantal texts such as the [Joel 2 passage] versus the situational authority of texts such as 1 Timothy 2:9-15, but let me at least say that I believe one of the radical truths of the New Covenant is that women will lead the New Israel.* ❧

Evangelical women also face questions about legitimacy and authority in more feminist settings. This is quite apparent in many descriptions we received of women's experiences in graduate school—of feeling silenced and of not having their concerns taken seriously. In addition, there is the disturbing experience of having one's position regularly misunderstood and misrepresented. Feminism often appears to be caricaturing classical orthodoxy. The tradition is sometimes portrayed by feminists in ways that do not ring true to evangelical experience. Feminists have argued, for example, that the tradition describes God as a transcendent judge or king. Nevertheless, within evangelicalism, there has always been a more richly biblical understanding of God, and this is certainly the case in lived experience. Transcendence and immanence are both a part of the tradition, even if the transcendent images have been the more powerful. One woman explained,

> *What I find interesting now, dealing with feminist critiques of theology, is that due to evangelicalism's strong biblical basis, which meant a critical and scholarly handling of the text, I imbibed and learnt a biblical rather than systematic theology and avoided some of the pitfalls of classical theology. For example, feminism and feminist theology critique the strong dualistic worldview that is so harmful to women and the world. While none of us can escape this Hellenistic intellectual heritage because it informs so much of the Western world, [at my evangelical seminary] the Hebraic holistic understanding of life came through and dualistic thought itself was critiqued.* ❧

This woman continued,

> *It strikes me [as] somewhat ironic that evangelicalism is not seen as a friend to feminists—to put it mildly! But it actually . . . has the potential to offer to women something of the richness of the biblical tradition, which is such a valuable resource.* ❧

---

[8] It is interesting to note that Miroslav Volf, who offers rich insights into the Trinity and gender, had a Croatian Pentecostal/evangelical upbringing. See chap. 4 of Miroslav Volf, *Exclusion and Embrace: A Theological Exploration of Identity, Otherness and Reconciliation* (Nashville: Abingdon, 1996).

Much academic feminism is rooted in liberal feminist theology. In her early work, which was definitive for almost two decades, Rosemary Radford Ruether described feminism's sources as located in and reacting to the liberal tradition, the Marxist critique and Romanticism.[9] She did not include the evangelical revivalist tradition—much harder to categorize intellectually—and this omission, in her writings and in that of other feminists, is evident to evangelicals.[10]

Some women are critical of contemporary expressions of evangelical feminism because it only attempts to carve out a very narrow space that is safe for evangelical egalitarians. One woman expressed her frustration by commenting, "I dislike the tone of much evangelical feminism. It boxes and stereotypes too easily, and I think I'd like to keep my borders between groups a little more fluid and flexible." We also think it will be helpful to seek out further dialogue across both maps and between life-worlds, testing claims to justice, compassion and integrity within the stories, narratives and liturgies of our collective biblical and theological experience. In this chapter then, we look at patriarchy, self, evil, eschatology and church—aspects of theology addressing our identities, communities and practices—in the context of ambiguity and finitude. In the following chapter, we will examine the doctrines of Christ, God, Scripture and truth—the transcendent categories that speak of divinity and authority.

CRITIQUE OF PATRIARCHY

By patriarchy we mean not only the subordination of females to males,
but the whole structure of Father-ruled society: aristocracy over serfs,
masters over slaves, king over subjects, racial overlords over colonized people.
Religions that reinforce hierarchical stratification use the Divine
as the apex of this system of privilege and control.
ROSEMARY RADFORD RUETHER, *Sexism and God-Talk*

---

[9]Rosemary Radford Ruether, *Sexism and God-Talk: Toward a Feminist Theology* (Boston: Beacon, 1983), pp. 41-45.

[10]Some of the earliest evangelical contributions to feminist theology, for example, came from Hardesty, who studied and wrote on the lives of nineteenth-century evangelical women. Others have recently discovered the richness of the tradition and the women within it, bringing to life the stories of the Wesley women, Esther Edwards Burr, Phoebe Palmer, Florence Nightingale and others. More recently, Ruether has given a paragraph to the work of Scanzoni and Hardesty and some attention to the role of nineteenth-century evangelicalism in an essay in the *Cambridge Companion to Feminist Theology*. In this work, however, while various forms of feminism are discussed, evangelical feminism is not addressed. See Susan Frank Parsons, ed., *The Cambridge Companion to Feminist Theology* (Cambridge: Cambridge University Press, 2002), p. 10.

The following snippet of conversation, overheard recently by one of the women in the study, suggests the ongoing power of patriarchal interpretations. A precocious young boy, who has not had any exposure to fundamentalist teaching, and his friend were discussing the problem of evil. "I know the answer," he said. "It is original sin. Eve ate the apple and that's where all the evil comes from. It was *Eve's fault.*" Later he pondered his mother's failings and, half-laughingly, half-seriously, wondered aloud if this was the "Eve factor."

Christian theology has always been concerned with sin. Feminist theology, however, has shifted the discussion and discovered a new, more basic and primitive collective form of sin: patriarchy. Patriarchy, as Ruether describes it above, is ubiquitous. For some women the realization of this depth of oppression has come as a sudden change of consciousness, like conversion, while for others it has been a gradual process, more like peeling back the layers of an onion. Evangelical women, too, critique the patriarchal tradition, albeit in a sometimes more guarded manner. One respondent explained, "I am not ready automatically to assume that men's sin is a result of patriarchy as opposed to basic sinfulness, although if I look closely enough, I'm sure I could find patriarchy underneath many difficult situations."

Evangelical women are especially troubled by certain conclusions common in particular strands of feminism, namely, that patriarchy is defined as the primary evil, that women's separation from men is understood to be the only redemption and that patriarchal texts should be excised from Scripture on the basis of women's experience.[11] A respondent who no longer considers herself an evangelical but who had worked as a missionary in the Two-Thirds World said, "There is a propensity for evil within us which is even greater than us. So I can't stay too long on the evils of patriarchy."

For many evangelicals, an analysis of Genesis 1—3 remains more complex than it is for nonevangelicals. Feminists often portray the Genesis story as the root cause of patriarchy. Ruether, for example, concludes that

> the Hebrew myth of Eve has had much greater cultural impact that that of Pandora, since Christian theology has understood it to be divine revelation and hence has taken this rather odd folktale with consummate theological seriousness.[12]

---

[11]Ruether, for example, advocates this approach to Scripture in *Sexism and God-Talk*, p. 23. Elisabeth Schüssler Fiorenza, in her work, takes a different approach and insists that women need to go outside the canon to the reconstituted experience of the first-century church to gain a deeper understanding of gender and Christian origins. See Elisabeth Schüssler Fiorenza, *In Memory of Her: A Feminist Theological Reconstruction of Christian Origins* (New York: Crossroad, 1983), pp. xvi-xix.

[12]Ruether, *Sexism and God-Talk*, p. 166.

Feminist writers have identified and critiqued the long theological tradition that blames Eve for the downfall of the human race and has given rise to an understanding of woman as essentially deceived, weak, properly subordinate to men and not fully made in the image of God. It is true that there are numerous theological texts affirming this view. Evangelicals might agree that Scripture has been misused, but they are unlikely to relativize or to dismiss the Genesis narrative—or call it odd. Ancient narrative it may be, but inspired nevertheless.

Instead, evangelical women work with the received text whether or not it is difficult and troubling. Readings of Genesis have given us the tradition of inferior image and the dominion of men over women, especially when Genesis 3 is taken prescriptively. When this same passage is read descriptively, however, it sheds light on women's puzzling acquiescence to patriarchy throughout recorded history. Thus Genesis itself can be a liberating document for women in its realism and in its affirmations of equality, the goodness of creation and the equal role of men and women in procreation and stewardship. It may be the evangelical propensity to "stay with" the text that helps in discerning new or deeper interpretations. The domination of women by men can be interpreted as a profound expression of the brokenness of relationships and harmonies at every level of the social order, the creation and the cosmos. This realization can also be understood in light of God's alliance with the weak in incarnation and crucifixion. Patriarchy, then, becomes a part of the larger networks of suffering that find their final meaning and resolution in Christ. Nevertheless, women in the study also recognized the long history of a different interpretation—what one woman called "hemangelical"—and the powerful effect these patriarchal interpretations have had in human history. The need to read the stories of women *in memoriam* and against the history of interpretation that produced them can also be affirmed.[13]

For women not committed to an understanding of Scripture as authoritative, this evangelical exercise can be interpreted as bad faith. For them Genesis is better exorcised by deconstruction than by reconstruction. Some feminists and some evangelicals will thus feel themselves to be on opposite sides of a great divide—methodologically and theologically.

Nevertheless, both movements share a view of the world as deeply flawed, in need of redemption and completion, in need of justice and liberation. The important work of feminists like Phyllis Trible, who work closely with the biblical text,

---

[13]For a defense of reading a text *in memoriam,* see Phyllis Trible, *Texts of Terror: Literary-Feminist Readings of Biblical Narratives* (Philadelphia: Fortress, 1984).

shows the validity of the evangelical "hunch" that the Bible is worthy of fullest engagement. And ironically, it has been feminist exegesis that has so often opened the inspired text to new and refreshing readings.

SELFISHNESS, SACRIFICE, SIN AND SELF

What women may find unacceptable about the Lutheran system
is the sense that one must be continually breaking oneself and
basing oneself on one who is not oneself. . . . Rather should one speak of
continuity and growth from within oneself.

DAPHNE HAMPSON, in *Feminist Theology: A Reader*

The earliest days of contemporary feminist theology can be traced to Valerie Saiving Goldstein's critique of Reinhold Niebuhr's description of "the human situation."[14] Niebuhr had defined sin as pride, but Saiving argued that women were more inclined to "give up the self" than they were inclined toward sinful self-centeredness. From this point on, a great deal of attention has been given to a woman's propensity to deny the self, even when she has not yet developed a self, and to the social and family expectations that have been imposed on women in already fragile states of development. Feminism has deconstructed and reconstructed the feminine self. Feminist writings have nurtured women's power of creativity and fertility, reclaiming women's power and women's voice. But the "grammar" of feminist theology, and of feminist theology classes in particular, can appear individualistic and selfish to a woman coming from an evangelical background, even when the material is experienced as empowering at another level.

Feminist theology has, with some legitimacy, placed a great deal of emphasis upon the re-finding of the self. Hampson deplores the rhetoric, evident in some evangelical and reformed expressions of piety, that encourages the destruction of the self. Must the self be destroyed to come to God? she asks.[15] Recognizing and resisting oppression, abuse and imposed roles and expectations are part of feminist understandings of liberation that many evangelicals can affirm.[16] Yet the weight

---

[14]Valerie Saiving Goldstein, "The Human Situation: A Feminine View," *Journal of Religion* 40, no. 2 (1960).

[15]Daphne Hampson, "Luther on the Self: A Feminist Critique," in *Feminist Theology: A Reader*, ed. Ann Loades (Louisville, Ky.: Westminster John Knox, 1990), pp. 221-24.

[16]Catherine Clark Kroeger and Nancy Nason-Clark report that abuse rates for churchgoers are no different from those outside the church. See Catherine Clark Kroeger and Nancy Nason-Clark, *No Place for Abuse: Biblical and Practical Resources to Counteract Domestic Violence* (Downers Grove, Ill.: InterVarsity Press, 2001), p. 20.

placed on the self (with emphases on discovering transcendence within and on the self's constructed character rather than its essence) conflicts with the biblical grammar of losing one's life to gain it and the tradition of dying to oneself to find oneself. On the other hand, the move to deconstruct individual essence could be a helpful effort if it is associated with an affirmation of existence rooted in God's being and communion.[17]

Feminist emphases on self also conflict with the needs of more community-based cultures. The feminist critique *has* been a proper corrective to versions of self-worth founded on social status, class, race or station. Recent feminist theology has also been more attentive to community, nurture and the empowerment of all people, and these themes provide some balance to the self-in-liberation emphasis.

One feminist response to Niebuhr's identification of sin with pride has been to suggest that a woman's propensity to give up the self is also sin; failing to take responsibility for themselves and their worth, women commit what can only be termed the mirror image of the sin of pride. An evangelical propensity to suspect that self-deception is universal, however, will find this response inadequate. Failing to assert oneself may be a sign of bondage more than an expression of a virtue that was at times assumed for women, but is it really sin on a par with pride?

Cynthia Crysdale, in a new look at the cross and its meaning, openly addresses questions that hold in tension the need to acknowledge women's oppressor and oppressed status.[18] Roberta Bondi does similar work in her essay titled, "Out of the Green Tiled Bathroom: Crucifixion," in which she gives personal testimony to the ongoing pain, woundedness and guilt that resulted from internalizing a false obligation to sacrifice.[19]

An overemphasis on self-sacrifice *has* caused anguish for women in particular. Living on the boundary requires an ongoing internal dialogue that recognizes the narcissistic tendencies in all people as well as the resulting necessity of making sacrificial choices and examining one's conscience for spiritual blindness. Nevertheless, there is an obvious need for some self-centeredness to maintain coherent bodily existence and moral agency. A robust sense of self is a necessary, though not sufficient, condition for supporting others and for creating good community.

---

[17]See, e.g., John D. Zizioulas, *Being as Communion: Studies in Personhood and the Church* (Crestwood, N.Y.: St. Vladimir's Seminary Press, 1997).

[18]Cynthia S. W. Crysdale, *Embracing Travail: Retrieving the Cross Today* (New York: Continuum, 1999).

[19]Roberta C. Bondi, *Memories of God: Theological Reflections on a Life* (Nashville: Abingdon, 1995), pp. 111-44.

Evangelical women, however, often mention mothers, women of previous generations and missionary stories as sources of inspiration. Some women have
themselves worked sacrificially as missionaries. The question then arises, How
are contemporary notions of self reconciled with these historical voices? How
can contemporary women compare their lives with those of Susannah Wesley,
Sarah Edwards, Esther Edwards Burr or Dorothy Day? The *Diary of Esther Edwards
Burr,* for example, is an extraordinary window into the eighteenth-century life of
a woman at the heart of evangelical revival, danger and newly formed academic
institutions. Her life was very full and rich, albeit lived within traditional confines, and cut tragically short.[20] Evangelical women are sometimes forced to in-
terrogate feminism: Were these women less selves, or less authentic, for not having consciously grappled with the evils of patriarchy? Or is there something
about all our lives that is diminished by our lack of the community and the solidarity they experienced? How can we compare the possibility of a "voice" now
to the voice many women had in the past, even under patriarchy, because their
communities were more cohesive? Does finding a voice have to be at the expense
of previous generations, or do women hope to bring these historical realities to
voice as well, even when they are largely lost to contemporary hearers in their
day-to-day inflections? Sensitivity to the complexity of these questions is also
important when evangelical feminists engage women today who have given up
much for their husbands, families and churches and have accepted subservient
roles because they saw such choices as biblical.

And yet the critique of patriarchy is deeply compelling, as is the insight offered
by Saiving and others about women's difficulty in acquiring a self to sacrifice. Fraser
has eloquently described, for example, the long struggle to balance oppressive
voices from the past with a need for wholeness and authenticity in the present.[21]
The truth is perhaps more complicated. Is it not possible to have both pride and
a lack of self? And does not the absence of a formed self lead to other sins—jeal-
ousy, fear and revenge? The grammars of self and sacrifice are not easily resolved.
The need for a strong sense of self can be affirmed on psychological, physical and
spiritual grounds. Nevertheless, evangelicals and indeed many others admire most
those who have sacrificed themselves for the kingdom. The theology of self takes
us near to the heart of the mystery of *imago Dei,* the close resemblance we bear to
divinity and thus to the harm that can be perpetrated either when we deny the na-

---

[20]Carol F. Karlsen and Laurie Krumpacker, eds., *The Journal of Esther Edwards Burr, 1754-1757* (New
Haven, Conn.: Yale University Press, 1986).
[21]Fraser, *Confessions,* pp. 42-46.

ture of our being or when we use the power inherent in *imago Dei* to control and oppress others.

Sarah Coakley speaks to this tension, arguing that some measure of "vulnerability" or "dependence" on God is proper to piety and is not necessarily an acquiescence to male ways of seeing. Responding to Daphne Hampson, she writes,

> An undiscriminating adulation of "vulnerability" might appear to condone, or even invite such evils. . . . But what I am suggesting is that there is another, and longer-term, danger to Christian feminism in the *repression* of all forms of "vulnerability," and in a concomitant failure to confront issues of fragility, suffering or "self-emptying" except in terms of victimology. . . . Only . . . by facing—and giving new expression to—the paradoxes of "losing one's life in order to save it," can feminists hope to construct a vision of the Christic "self" that transcends the gender stereotypes we are seeking to up-end.[22]

Coakley notes that this proper sense of vulnerability is developed not by acquiescence to male authority, but in the difficult practices of prayer and contemplation.

The complex issues of sin and sacrifice suggest that additional questions should be asked. Is it possible to separate individual transgression entirely from corporate sin or systemic evil? In recent theological conversations—especially among evangelicals—a more corporate understanding of sin is allowing a move away from a male-female dualism toward understanding the ways in which we all are caught up in patterns and structures of oppression.

Where feminism and evangelicalism might concur, then, would be on the corporate nature of sin and of our redemption. It can be argued that we all are bound by forms of structural evil in which we participate both willingly and unknowingly. Vincent Bacote speaks to this when he writes, "Evangelicals can ill afford either to ignore corporate sin or to recognize it only when it comes to roost in their comfort zone."[23] But equally important is a recognition that salvation from sin is not an individual acquisition on our part; rather it is incorporation into the communal life of the Trinity and the incarnate life of Christ in the church. Cherith Fee Nordling articulates a corporate understanding of salvation when she writes,

> The idea of a dyadic, privatized relationship with God—particularly as an expres-

---

[22]Sarah Coakley, *Powers and Submissions: Spirituality, Philosophy and Gender* (Malden, Mass.: Blackwell, 2002), p. 33.

[23]Vincent Bacote, "What Is This Life For? Expanding Our View of Salvation," in *What Does It Mean to Be Saved? Broadening Evangelical Horizons of Salvation*, ed. John G. Stackhouse Jr. (Grand Rapids: Baker Academic, 2002), p. 110.

sion of salvation—is theologically impossible for Christians. Because God in his own being is one God in three Persons, there is no possibility of relating to God as the divine, solitary Other. Relationship with God is always and forever participation in the preexisting *koinōnia* of the divine Persons.[24]

Moving away from naive understandings that "Eve did it" (and therefore women must be subordinate and must sacrifice themselves) toward a more corporate understanding of sin and participation in the structures of grace helps to emphasize the seriousness of human failing, the salvation that comes from beyond and the corporate nature of belonging to Christ. This belonging entails a measure of sacrifice from everyone, but sin and grace, bondage and salvation will be linked. For some men and women this will mean a dramatic conversion and change of the inner self; for others it will involve a more subtle change of heart. For all, it will be a move toward community and mutual relationship.

EVIL

Feminism does not, on the whole, interact explicitly with evangelicalism, but feminists do interact with a theological tradition that is still clearly expressed within evangelicalism. In particular, feminism offers a rigorous critique of male individualistic dualisms that divide humanity into those whom God looks after, now and especially after death, and an unregenerate group who are vulnerable at all times to the wrath of God. Evangelical boundary keeping can encourage a theology that comfortably countenances a terrible fate for the unelect and a protected path for those who are "in." Thus evangelicalism is most criticized by liberals, including feminists, for the heartlessness and superficiality of its theodicy. Pious statements about God's plan for our lives, about how we will never be given more than we can bear and about all things working together for good are sometimes misunderstood as entirely callous claims. Evangelicals appear to implicate God in any number of evils. One woman wrote,

> *Evangelicalism is a fix-it theology, and there are some things in life that cannot be fixed. People only have to look around to know that! To say that God can bring good out of evil is not the same as saying God allows the evil and in some way sanctions it for our benefit—to make us better people. You can keep a God like that who is vindictive and who doesn't hurt when we do and can so easily inflict pain upon us.* ✍

---

[24]Cherith Fee Nordling, "Being Saved as a New Creation: Co-Humanity in the True Imago Dei," in *What Does It Mean to Be Saved? Broadening Evangelical Horizons of Salvation,* ed. John G. Stackhouse Jr. (Grand Rapids: Baker Academic, 2002), p. 118.

With other liberation theologies, feminist theology has brought to consciousness the church's part in the evils of the past and present. Feminism has compared
nurturing practices and gentler values of women with the images of a "warrior Yahweh." Process feminism has embraced visions of God that do not require God to
be implicated in evil; in these interpretations, God, in fact, has little power.

Feminists find that forms of evangelical triumphalism grate against sensitivity to
suffering and ignore the importance of compassion. Conservative Christianity is associated, in many feminist minds, with an oppressive meta-story that has manipu-
lated and coerced classes and genders of people into accepting and tolerating domination. Hence feminist postmodern thinkers work to deconstruct the tradition, and
some feminist theology sees itself as cleansing orthodox conceptions of faith.

Evangelicals, however, may still want to identify with those who use the language of being saved from a tragedy or a misfortune. One may wish to thank God
for her or his liberation without suggesting that God has not looked favorably on
a neighbor who was not liberated or healed. All sectors of the Christian tradition
have, at some time, affirmed the paradoxical nature of Christian faith—the mystery
of encountering God on the mountaintop and in tragedy. In believing that our theologies are unfinished, we affirm that, in some inextricable way, we can grieve and
be grateful at the same time. Scripture is filled with people who have thanked God
for rescuing them from whales, slavery, barrenness or enemy swords. Evangelical piety is replete with sober moments of gratitude for salvation from danger in missionary encounters, while simultaneously living with a daily dose of tragedy. Faith
may require that we dare to ask for resurrection and healing, as did Mary and Mar-
tha, while knowing that we all suffer and die.

It is helpful, however, to see these expressions of trust as they are interpreted by
those outside the tradition, by those for whom the stories of tragedy and grace are
not easily combined. Moreover, the postmodern feminist critique is very appropriate in cases where trust is used as an excuse for keeping others in states of bondage
or in unacceptable danger. Perhaps it is in worship that the mystery of gratitude,
petition and grief can be most successfully combined. In worship, we can enter into
God's care and into mutual bearing of affliction, whatever our situation. It is interesting, therefore, that so many women in the survey were moving toward more liturgical churches after sojourns in quite different ecclesial traditions.

Feminism, in its far-reaching critique of patriarchy, provides new depth to understandings of evil. It helps us to see that women are not lone or individual players
but intimately connected in the web of relationships and dominations. Evangelicalism affirms the language of grace, the ultimate care of God, the powers and prin-

cipalities, and the supernatural and natural in-breaking of God. All of these insights are needed in any proper theological discussion of evil. On the boundary between the movements or "ways of seeing," patriarchy can be viewed as a kind of spiritual power of evil. Evangelical lenses will see resistance to patriarchy in the context of a cosmic struggle even larger than our own constructions, devices and desires; and, in so doing, they will also help to explain the ubiquity of the patriarchy that feminism has so aptly described.

The strong missionary connections within evangelicalism provide another window through which to look at the problem of evil. On the other side of evangelicalism's "happy clappy" praise songs is its long involvement with other cultures. Missionary activity has often been caricatured and misunderstood by outsiders, and evangelicals have at times been guilty of cultural insensitivity. Engagement with other cultures and Christian communities, however, offers a fuller picture of how these issues are interpreted within the everyday practices of faithful Christians in very difficult circumstances. One woman explained that the Christians she knew in Africa would always insist that God is good and would start every class and every meeting with this affirmation. Yet, she noted, their lives were *all* marred by the tragedy of war, AIDS, polygamy or abuse. If the poor do have a hermeneutical advantage, then their combining the grammars of praise and gratitude with daily tragedy should act as a window to the nature of God and to a godly reaction to evil.

In the period since 9/11, and as the world faces constant danger and the presence of unidentified evil, there is more need than ever to seek the grace that can be found around the edges of suffering. False and superficial meta-stories of the good and the evil must also be rejected, while habits of seeing the world in terms of God's goodness and compassion can be identified and cultivated.

ESCHATOLOGY

But what of the sad insufficiencies of human finitude and the
consequences of social evils that take the lives of little children and cut off adults
in the prime of life [?] . . . What of the whole tragic drama of human history,
where so few have been able to snatch moments of happiness and fulfillment in
the midst of toil and misery? . . . Do their achievements live on only in our
fading memories, or is there some larger realm where the meaning of their
lives is preserved? The appropriate response to these questions is agnosticism.
ROSEMARY RADFORD RUETHER, *Sexism and God-Talk*

I am very uneasy with the very easy alliance between evangelicalism and political conservativism/ patriotism/ warmongering.

Differences in eschatological understandings are played out in American reactions to events in the Middle East, and the worldwide evangelical movement is to some extent drawn into these interpretations.[25] The problems Karl Marx may have observed in traditional piety—that it offered hope in the next life, so the injustices of the present could be ignored—fade into insignificance when compared with the enthusiasms of those who read and live by interpretations of a dispensational pretribulation rapture of the Left Behind series. Living within a story that culminates in the book of Revelation can be quite challenging. One respondent noted, "I am distressed about the self-congratulatory tones of evangelicals and appalled by their fear-based decision making in everything from voting to choosing between educational options for their children."

Feminist theologians' responses to conservative forms of eschatology have been radical, as the above quotation from Ruether illustrates. Feminist eschatology has pointed out the great injustices done in the name of religion when only a future hope is given any place in the Christian life. These injustices affect the poor, women and the earth especially. Feminism has thus often emphasized the loss of justice here and now and has complained that the church has looked only to the future and that it has used this future hope to legitimize patriarchy and other evils. Like other liberation theologies, feminist theology has emphasized finitude, embodiment and temporal justice more than eternal life. For some feminist theologians, the whole eschatological imagery of Scripture has been seen as seductive and as undermining of true justice. Ruether, for example, says,

> Instead of endless flight into an unrealized future, I suggest a different model of
> hope and change based on conversion or *metanoia*. Conversion suggests that, while
> there is no one utopian state of humanity lying back in an original paradise of the
> "beginning," there are basic ingredients of a just and livable society.[26]

Is there any point of compromise or discourse between these two eschatological models? An eschatology that emphasizes justice now at the expense of the future robs the faithful of their hope, their sense of eternity and their ongoing relationship with God whatever the future might bring. Such a view minimizes the transcendent aspects of our present existence. On the other hand an eschatological emphasis on life after death at the expense of justice and salvation here and now is accompanied by an indifference to issues of justice and social responsibility. The

---

[25] See Robert Jewett and John Shelton Lawrence, *Captain America and the Crusade Against Evil: The Dilemma of Zealous Nationalism* (Grand Rapids: Eerdmans, 2003).
[26] Ruether, *Sexism and God-Talk*, p. 254.

future-based premillennialism so popular in evangelical churches is also difficult to reconcile with ecological responsibility. For many premillennialists, the earth as we know it will be destroyed; hence efforts toward its care are largely viewed as wasted.

Because the resurrection is central to Christian faith, any approaches that relativize this hope are problematic. Nevertheless, feminist theology has properly emphasized the importance in the biblical tradition of embodied life here and now. God cares about release from bondage and slavery; much of the Old Testament narrative concerns issues of justice and liberation. The prophets railed against inequality, and there has been a long tradition woven in and out of the biblical narrative that demands justice and an end to oppression in this life.

More thoughtful reflections on the end times are largely unheeded in the public arena, but an "emerging" eschatological vision is shared in its general outline by a wide cross-section of theologians and faithful Christians. Rather than embracing a vision of an earth destroyed in fire and war, to be replaced by God's new creation, this scriptural vision insists that the new heavens and the new earth will be here on earth, albeit a transformed earth. In this eschatological vision, continuities as well as discontinuities with the present are important. There has been a renewed interest in the eschatology of Revelation 21 and in the unfinished nature of the cosmos and the "groans for its renewal" as described in Romans 8. Humanity's future will be worked out in a New Jerusalem come to earth, though in a world that is changed irrevocably. This is a vision both feminists and evangelicals can affirm. All who believe that such an eschatological vision is informed by biblical wisdom find a hope that is as yet mysteriously unfinished in the visions of the apocalypse.

This eschatological vision is not a truncated feminist nature ecology, and interestingly, feminist voices are now more diverse on this topic. The feminism of a few decades ago held very loosely to a diffuse idea of transcendence, emphasizing, as Ruether does, a solidarity with the earth and with finitude.[27] Today, in some circles, a new synthesis is appearing, a new trinitarian transcendence over the old patriarchal models. Catherine LaCugna was one such voice. So also is Valerie Karras, a feminist patristic scholar who critiques the eschatology of Ruether and Sallie McFague while adopting a somewhat transformed "hermeneutics of suspicion."

I propose an eschatology, and in fact an entire theological model, which is *truly* top-

---

[27]Ruether, for all the deficiencies of her eschatology in evangelical terms, has nevertheless been an important feminist voice in contemporary Christian ecological thought. See Dieter T. Hessel and Rosemary Radford Ruether, eds., *Christianity and Ecology: Seeking the Well-Being of Earth and Humans* (Cambridge, Mass.: Harvard University Press, 2000).

down, as opposed to the apparent top-down theology of patriarchal Christianity. . . .
The forgotten voices I am recovering are those of the early Christian East, articulating a theology of a tri-personal God who truly is simultaneously immanent and transcendent.[28]

This trinitarian theology of end times emphasizes the Spirit's call to the new community of the end and the promise of embrace here and now.

CHURCH

Churches that fall within the evangelical spectrum are widely diverse in institutional structure and appearance: they include megachurches, Pentecostal congregations, small emergent groups, Brethren assemblies holding Communion every Sunday, Salvation Army corps that do not baptize, nondenominational community
churches and evangelical congregations within mainline denominations. As a movement evangelicalism has flourished in parachurch organizations—especially on
high school and college campuses. Because much of the energy of the evangelical
movement is youth-oriented and parachurch, ecclesiology has often been a low priority in evangelical doctrine; church attendance and commitment, however, have
been strongly emphasized. The universalizing aspect of evangelicalism has tended
to emerge from the large parachurch and missions organizations and outreach
rather than from church or denominational structure, or from conscious attention
to signs of the universal church.

The lack of an explicit ecclesiology is not necessarily associated with open and
inclusive organizations; evangelicals have always taken boundaries seriously and,
hence, also the vetting of who is a genuine believer and who is not. Thus evangelicals, to the extent that they are the children of the Reformation, take seriously the
priesthood of all believers. Leaders come and go, but the small and informal group
at prayer perhaps best characterizes evangelicalism, its strength and its ecclesial
weakness; here there is confidence that Christ is with us, where two or three are
gathered in Christ's name. As a result, individualism survives within tight-knit
groups, and attention to the larger church is often absent. Faith can be nurtured
ahistorically, looking neither backward nor forward. And ironically, in spite of the
heavy emphasis on institutions in evangelical identity, there is also an abiding suspicion of the structures required to maintain theological coherence across cultures
and historical perspectives.

---

[28]Valerie Karras, "Eschatology," in *The Cambridge Companion to Feminist Theology*, ed. Susan Frank Parsons
(Cambridge: Cambridge University Press, 2002), p. 249.

While the vertical dimension of God's being with us as individuals, or as two or three gather, may be strong, a more communal sense of God's presence in the sacramental community and in the historical witness is weak. Perhaps for this reason, evangelicals morph easily into nonbelonging believers or emergent alternative groupings. This also means, though, that issues surrounding women cannot be dealt with conclusively. Without "institutional memory" questions are not settled in either direction for very long. And the questions do not go away, perhaps because, as we have discovered, gender plays a silent though important part in evangelical identity.

A feminist theology of church was first oriented around issues of ordination rather than around a comprehensive critique of the institution or around the development of a distinctive ecclesiology. While the movement for the ordination of women had some of its roots in the nineteenth-century evangelical revivals, it was successful in the mainline denominations only in the second part of the twentieth century. Ironically, at the end of the nineteenth century, some women in more sectarian, holiness or Wesleyan churches were being ordained.[29] Later backlashes against women in ministry have all but obliterated this memory in many evangelical institutions.[30] In mainline churches, ordained ministry has changed as women have entered the ranks. There are fewer opportunities for full-time or fully funded ministry, and ministers of the future will more often combine their pastoral duties with secular vocations.[31] Nevertheless, mainline and some evangelical communities celebrate the increasing numbers of women in ordained ministry and the consecration of a few women to the rank of bishop. Making the situation even more complex is that for different reasons and motivations, in both feminist and evangelical circles, a radical egalitarianism is never far from the surface, calling into question the validity and necessity of hierarchies and separate ordained ministry.

Since the 1970s, the so-called third wave of feminist theology has been more attentive to aspects of systematic theology and has continued to address historical issues important to ordination, especially in looking at the presence of women leaders in the early church. The ecclesial issues of language and discourse have been widely addressed as significant in defining the worshiping space in

---

[29]See, e.g., Nancy A. Hardesty, *Women Called to Witness: Evangelical Feminism in the Nineteenth Century* (Nashville: Abingdon, 1984).

[30]Margaret Lamberts Bendroth, *Fundamentalism and Gender, 1875 to the Present* (New Haven, Conn.: Yale University Press, 1993).

[31]See Frederick W. Schmidt, *A Still Small Voice: Women, Ordination and the Church* (Syracuse, N.Y.: Syracuse University Press, 1996).

ways that might be more hospitable to women.[32] Inclusive-language liturgies, prayers and Bible translations are a part of this endeavor. While mainline denominations now use inclusive language regardless of any underlying patriarchy in the institution, evangelical churches and institutions have been much less inclined to do so, especially when applied to the name of God and used within Bible translations.

Within the mainline and evangelical world, experiences of alienation from the church are common among academic women. Letty Russell describes herself as often alienated—but still deeply committed.[33] Dealing with alienation is an ongoing enterprise, more difficult than rewriting liturgies and working for ordination. It involves confronting a culture that subtly excludes or disempowers in any number of structural, liturgical and linguistic practices and forms. Or it may arise out of the absence of connection and deep spirituality afforded by a particular congregation. Either way, identifying and curing alienation is no ordinary task, especially when the goal of church is universal togetherness rather than separation.

While alienation is the common human condition, we expect—perhaps especially as women committed to church—that our *church* experience will be otherwise. The high expectations clash with the often low level of real community and equality and with the homogeneity of many church and institutional fellowships.[34] And if, as we suspect, evangelicalism includes a large cultural component, one can define oneself out by moving beyond the cultural limits in very subtle ways. Even when this does not occur, however, the theologically educated evangelical woman will find herself straddling cultures—literally living on the boundary, or on the edge of maps, bringing together in *her person* only the diverse practices and cultures that constitute church across the spectrum. And this in itself is alienating, when the common ground is sometimes only oneself.

Dealing with alienation has taken other directions as well. In evangelical circles there is an intense interest in postmodernism and the "postmodern church," in the

---

[32]Susan A. Ross says, "There is much less work done by feminists in sacramental theology—and I would add in ecclesiology—than in some other areas of theology." See Susan A. Ross, "Church and Sacrament: Community and Worship," in *The Cambridge Companion to Feminist Theology*, ed. Susan Frank Parsons (Cambridge: Cambridge University Press, 2002), p. 226.

[33]Letty M. Russell, *Church in the Round: Feminist Interpretation of the Church* (Louisville, Ky.: Westminster John Knox, 1993), p. 11.

[34]Natalie Watson said something similar when she noted that the idea of "flourishing and right relation are not what comes to mind when the majority of women reflect on their experience of church." She describes this as the vision of what the church ought to be and what it has begun to be in some places. See Natalie K. Watson, *Introducing Feminist Ecclesiology* (New York: Sheffield, 2002), p. 117.

experience of Generation X and in the "emergent church" movement.[35] This may well be the direction of the future—the energizing cusp of future-church. Emergent church spills out into small communities centered around alternative worship or large Christian rock festivals attracting thousands of teenagers and twentysomethings. In the older age group the phenomenon of "believing without belonging" is increasing among men and women, sometimes weary after many years of church battles and politics. Whatever the reasons, there is a fragmentation of church at a time when believers most long for a cohesive story and a place of refuge and healing. Real community, in or out of church, is often elusive, especially for theologically trained women. And interestingly, even the emergent church movement is mostly dominated by very charismatic men.[36] Perhaps for this reason established mainline churches look attractive, as we discovered among the women in the study. Whatever their deficiencies, these churches are open, reliable, often sacramental and less resistant to women with vision. Sometimes, too, the burden of holding a church together on the strength of individuals' beliefs can become tiring. The communal space of the universal church, however elusive, beckons.

With alienation, though, often comes a sense of solidarity with others who are similarly not included in the hierarchical "establishment" of church. Thus a number of women have developed scenarios of church as shelter for the outcast, a place of hospitality and grace, a round table open to all.[37] For such women, issues of justice and inclusion are central, and they offer a prophetic word calling the church to the radical equality the Scriptures espouse. Russell, for example, encourages the addition of justice as a fifth mark of the church along with unity, catholicity, holiness and apostolicity.[38] Feminist writers have reacted to the challenges of church life in a variety of ways: sometimes advocating separation, as in the women-church movement, and sometimes forming groups that provide solidarity around the edges of a congregation. In this, too, there are interesting connections with the small groups

---

[35]See Dave Tomlinson, *The Post-Evangelical* (Grand Rapids: Zondervan, 2003); John William Drane, *The McDonaldization of the Church: Consumer Culture and the Church's Future* (Macon, Ga.: Smyth & Helwys, 2002); Michael Riddell, *Threshold of the Future: Reforming the Church in the Post-Christian West* (London: SPCK, 1998); Brian D. McLaren, *The Story We Find Ourselves In: Further Adventures of a New Kind of Christian* (San Francisco: Jossey-Bass, 2003).

[36]A preliminary attempt to remedy this is evident in The Emerging Women's Leadership Initiative. See <www.emergentvillage.com>.

[37]See, e.g., Russell, *Church in the Round;* Christine D. Pohl, *Making Room: Recovering Hospitality as a Christian Tradition* (Grand Rapids: Eerdmans, 1999); Serene Jones, *Feminist Theory and Christian Theology: Cartographies of Grace* (Minneapolis: Fortress, 2000); and Letty M. Russell, "Hot-House Ecclesiology: A Feminist Interpretation of the Church," *The Ecumenical Review* 53, no. 1 (2001).

[38]Russell, *Church in the Round*, p. 136.

that help evangelical churches to flourish. But for every small group there remains the problem of the unity and catholicity of the church. In what way do participants *belong* in the larger sense? The evangelical feminist woman may indeed find herself a part of several diverse groups asking this question.

Meanwhile, discussions of ecclesiology in the wider theological community have moved toward models and images of community. The church is the body of Christ, and in the Trinity is a concept of ontological "being in communion."[39] In the church, community is not a construction from below; rather, it comes as a gift with the real presence of Christ and the Spirit within the gathered community, known in works of love and in the shared sacrament and prayer. Jürgen Moltmann, for example, identifies the church by the three-fold *presence* of Christ in prayer and sacrament, in the poor and in the eschatological community of the Lamb.[40] By faith, Christians experience this as reality and not just as the sociological phenomenon described by outside observers of trends in church life. The real presence of Christ in community can also remove from us the burden of trying to maintain boundaries and togetherness based exclusively on identical beliefs.

Nevertheless, at a time when there is a great deal of theological enthusiasm for the mystical and the relational aspects of faith centered on the presence of Christ among us, there is also increasing difficulty in realizing that community. Both feminism and evangelicalism have tended toward separatism and toward small-group identity against a larger whole. This problem is a microcosm of the problem of the church at large, recognizing that universality, openness and inclusivity are the eschatological promise at the marriage supper of the Lamb, but having, in the meantime, to opt for small groups of fellow believers around the edges. Feminists choose between alienation in the larger structure and the false closure of a small support group.[41] Evangelicals, too, may wonder what the small group that feels like church has to do with the greater political or public dimensions of the church. For both feminists and evangelicals, the larger church may at times espouse a vision of Christ that is at odds with their own, making more troubled the relationship between them.

---

[39]See, e.g., Zizioulas, *Being as Communion*, and Miroslav Volf, *After Our Likeness: The Church as the Image of the Trinity* (Grand Rapids: Eerdmans, 1998).

[40]Jürgen Moltmann, *The Church in the Power of the Spirit: A Contribution to Messianic Ecclesiology*, trans. Margaret Kohl (San Francisco: Harper & Row, 1977), pp. 121-22.

[41]Interestingly, although women-church is the most well-known movement of women apart from church structures, evangelicals have always organized in parallel women's groups, from the very successful nineteenth-century missions organizations to the Women's Aglow of today. Although these groups might not see themselves as feminist, they have tended to fulfill similar functions of support and solidarity and resistance. See R. Marie Griffith, *God's Daughters: Evangelical Women and the Power of Submission* (Berkeley: University of California Press, 1997).

The separatism that is born of a profound alienation from disappointing institutions may begin as prophetic; however, it can become sectarian and closed in the longer run, hence the boundary, the unclear maps and the sense of unease when crossing these boundaries in both directions.[42] Must women choose between small-group solidarity and alienation in the larger communion? Reinterpreting the signs of the ancient church or the marks of the Reformation church can be helpful, but it does not necessarily offer adequate guidance in the process of resistance and re-creation required to be a woman in the church at large.

If indeed we are constituted in community, then the small groups, even on the edges, are valid, but we must always be seeking the universality of the more mixed gathering. The feelings of alienation, ephemerality and incompleteness are those of the church both experiencing and not yet experiencing fulfillment. Small groups are strengthened by a sense of the connections between the group and the whole and between the group and the tradition and by the sense of eschatological promise. These connections are best fostered by the larger church and by teaching institutions, which themselves have not always been welcoming but, at their best, do provide the links that keep the inner spirit of community and mission alive.

Perhaps the image of the holograph can help us to understand the relation between small local groups and the larger church. The local is not a part of the whole, nor is it connected to the whole, but it contains the whole as a reflection. The connection to the whole, however, needs to be explicit and lived out. Churches are communities of memory in increasing levels of organization. The smallest prayer group needs to foster an awareness of these larger structures, of historical mandates and of our context in the social and natural world—the catholic and apostolic nature of the church.

The emphasis on the larger context, however faith is played out, gives us an awareness of the need for open structures of welcome to the larger world, both Christian and otherwise. The church does not exist only for itself or its members. It should be a place of refuge and shelter and hospitality, where works of love are done and transformation and holiness are sought. Both the sacrament and prayer define its existence.

Evangelical understandings of the importance of the sacraments, especially the Eucharist, to the life of the church have been diverse. A number of evangelical theologians are now arguing that the Eucharist characterizes the people of God, not in

---

[42]Natalie Watson (using the work of Iris Marion Young) cautions that in any human context, community—especially small communities—can be subtly oppressive. See Watson, *Introducing Feminist Ecclesiology*, p. 49.

an artificial and ritualistic sense, but as the natural center-point for a renewed understanding of the world, as resistance to the powers of the world, as recognition of Christ's presence in the Spirit and as anticipation of the future. The Eucharist has also been the subject of much feminist re-interpretation and deconstruction, especially in churches that still insist on male presidency at the communion table.[43] In addition, the sacramental nature of community and of works of love, mercy and justice have been re-emphasized.

While many evangelicals point to prayer as their primary means of sensing Christ's presence, less common is testimony to the significance of the Lord's Supper. One woman in the survey, however, described how the small evangelical sect to which she had belonged as a child excluded women from positions of influence and authority, but fully included them in the heavenly vision associated with Communion services. Eschatological hope, prayer and visions of the church can intersect powerfully for evangelical women. For many evangelicals, Communion is self-consciously and exclusively symbolic, and there is a resistance to the participatory elements that the Roman Catholic and the Orthodox traditions have always insisted on. Eucharistic renewal is a point where feminist evangelicals might help educate the contemporary church in the direction of a fuller appropriation of the sacrament. Eucharist is physical, it is attractive to postmodern people, and it can act as a powerful expression of resistance to overwhelming materialism and false hope.

In light of all of this, what might we expect in terms of a theology of the church in the early twenty-first century? We can expect that the church will continue to surprise us, as Vatican II astonished the world and the church, as feminists have brought new life and interpretation to particular dogmas and Scriptures and as the Pentecostal and charismatic renewals have inspired recent generations. Evangelicals bring to the subject of church both an expectation that God is doing something new and an openness to some experimentation. Feminism has challenged us to listen to the small still voice of the Spirit, or of wisdom, in lonely places. Wherever the church is gathered, it will be oriented around the story of Christ. Here too, emergent postmodern evangelicalism and feminism agree that in acting out the drama of Christ, the church is made manifest. We come to inhabit the story of Christ, and this is the witness to God in our midst.

CONCLUSION

Evangelical academic women attempt to do theology in contexts that are not often

---

[43]Ross, "Church and Sacrament," p. 226.

open to feminist voices, contexts where the very presence of women as theological leaders can raise alarm that "natural" gender balances have been upset. Sometimes the effort required to stay in the conversation is all-absorbing. What theologically trained women are able to do must be accomplished between the cracks, so to speak, and will be in some way a dialogue between a feminist consciousness and a biblically informed life-world. Looking back and forth across this divide, our theological intuitions are sharpened and the dialogue becomes richer as vertical and horizontal dimensions of faith are informed by evangelical understandings and feminist insights.

We steer a course in which the feminist critiques of patriarchy, of sin defined as pride, of a superficial theodicy and of future eschatology are modified by an evangelical awareness of God's presence with us on the journey. God's mercy meets us as we experience sin and evil within social structures, God meets us in solidarity with our suffering, and God meets us eschatologically in the renewed earth of the kingdom of God.

Although evangelical settings are not always welcoming of this dialogue and may view divergence from old patterns with some wariness, the tensions become more pronounced when we move into the area of God-talk, theories of the atonement, Christology and Scripture. Nevertheless, it is here that far-ranging discussions—even significant arguments—are occurring among evangelical men. These discussions help to open up a space where old modernist theological assumptions can be challenged. In the next chapter we outline the beginnings of an evangelical-feminist dialogue in these areas.

| 7 |

CONTINUING THE
THEOLOGICAL DIALOGUE

Finding a Home for Eve

—⊶⊷—

What would feminist exposition look like if it saw
God as the ultimate Author of the Bible? . . .
Evangelicals affirm the orthodox belief that God is not sexual
and is neither male nor female—or, perhaps better, that God is
imaged in *both* male and female human beings together.
We affirm that doctrine readily, and then go ahead and depict God as male.
Not "mostly" as male, the way the Bible indeed does, but *always* as male.
As a rule, it seems, evangelicals never depict God as female,
even metaphorically and rarely even as transcending the
categories of male and female. But the Bible does.
Where are the women? More basically, where is the female, the feminine, the "not-
male" in the Bible, in our churches and families, and in God?
JOHN G. STACKHOUSE JR., in "Finding a Home for Eve"
(emphasis added)

Evangelical schools are often places of intense theological discussion and, in some
of these institutions, the debates over Calvinism, charismatic gifts and evolution
have been replaced by new conversations about the atonement, the nature of evangelicalism, subordination in the Trinity and the openness of God. These questions,
though framed in distinctly evangelical ways, resonate with concerns evident in
other parts of the Christian community. Interestingly, they make feminist theological analyses more palatable to evangelicals because there is significant overlap in the
issues raised. For example, critiques of the penal theory of the atonement coincide

with feminist concerns about the connection between violence and God. Arguments about the subordination (or nonsubordination) of the persons of the Trinity have wide-ranging repercussions for hierarchical relationships in society at large, especially in gender relations. The openness of God debate addresses issues of human freedom, ecology, the human-divine interface and the problem of evil—areas in which process feminism has previously spoken. In fact, many theological issues under discussion in the academy today were first raised by feminist theologians.

We are, however, also entering a new phase in feminist scholarship. While the feminism of the last few decades was somewhat ambivalent about the transcendent God, preferring to reconstruct images of God from within the self rather than from Scripture, there are signs that this is reversing. The "hermeneutics of suspicion" has been turned against feminism itself, asking the question, What if God is really there, really revealing Godself to us? What if, as John Stackhouse asks above, God is the ultimate Author of the Bible? Some of this return to the transcendent, for want of a better word, is influenced by encounters with Eastern Orthodoxy and by renewed interest in patristics.[1] A new orthodoxy is emerging, but it is one that is well acquainted with and sympathetic to postmodernism and feminism; an example is the so-called radical orthodoxy movement. This theology is fresh, compelling and experiential; it has the marks of the Spirit and can be vigorously engaged by evangelicals attempting to integrate transcendence and feminism. We turn now to look at some of these areas most associated with the feminist critique—Christology, God, Scripture and the nature of truth itself.

CHRISTOLOGY

A lot of men are drawn to Jesus because of the concept of sacrifice. . . .
That is not a big thing for me: I am profoundly grateful that Christ died,
I am full of admiration and so on, but that is not my point of engagement.
It is more on this level of sheer intimacy and love.

ELAINE STORKEY, *Conversations on Christian Feminism*

Evangelical women in the survey were aware of the feminist christological debates, though few of them were very disturbed by the maleness of Christ. This may be related to the fact that a high Christology is taken for granted in evangelical institutions. If evangelicals err theologically, it is on the side of a docetic Christ, thus de-emphasizing Christ's humanity and hence his gender. There is, however, an in-

---

[1]Sarah Coakley, Roberta Bondi and Valerie Karras are some of the authors doing very interesting work with the ancient Christian tradition.

creasing evangelical awareness of the need to encounter the human Christ. Evangelicals are acknowledging that weaknesses in ecclesiology and in theodicy result in part from an insufficient emphasis on Jesus' humanity.

A fuller theology of the cross requires a more complete reappropriation of the humanity of Christ. Jesus did not simply treat women well, which might be construed as patronizing; he entered into women's experience, suffering with them and being alongside them in ways that are often overlooked. The story of the woman at the well and her testimony that Jesus knew her life (Jn 4) is an example. Others include the woman who anointed his feet, whose motives were understood only by Jesus, and the women who remained with Jesus at Calvary. The mystery of power and powerlessness shows God entering into powerlessness to overcome evil. Here women may have the hermeneutical advantage in understanding and embracing Jesus, regardless of his gender difference. Like women, Christ suffered shame; given his social marginality, Jesus rarely experienced any advantage in his maleness.

Questions about Christology cut close to the evangelical bone; admitting a degree of psychological unease with a male savior would be quite difficult on most evangelical campuses. The psychology can work both ways, however. In their conversations on Christian feminism, evangelical Elaine Storkey and Roman Catholic Margaret Hebblethwaite discuss the added emotional advantage that the maleness of Christ has for them as women. They suggest that there is a degree of attraction to the person of Jesus that would not be present if the savior were female.[2] They note also the strong connection between Jesus and the women who were his disciples. Interestingly, the emphasis on being drawn to Jesus' humanity requires an engagement with the Gospels that is sometimes missing in the more Epistle-driven evangelical culture. Evangelical feminism can certainly affirm the current trend toward retelling the story of the Gospels, emphasizing the narrative and meditating on Jesus' life and encounters.

Even so, in their conversation, Storkey and Hebblethwaite recognize the importance for persons of various racial and ethnic backgrounds to reconceive of Jesus as nonwhite. These women resolve the theological tension regarding Jesus' *male* identity, however, by asserting that the point of the incarnation was the assumption of humanity and not maleness. Nevertheless, minimizing the significance of Jesus' maleness is not necessarily sufficient for women who have experienced abuse from

---

[2]Elaine Storkey and Margaret Hebblethwaite, *Conversations on Christian Feminism: Speaking Heart to Heart* (London: Fount, 1999), chap. 4.

a man. Neither is it convincing in church circles where the bar to women's ordination is the maleness of Christ.[3]

While several women in the survey expressed reservations about forensic substitutionary theories of the atonement, they did not necessarily suggest a coherent theory to put in its place. Until very recently, evangelicalism has assumed the substitutionary and even penal nature of the atonement, affirming the need for a payment made to God on our behalf. This has been at the heart of evangelical theology, but it is not a popular part of the Christ-story in feminist theology. Feminists have argued that the worship and the ethos that emerge from substitutionary atonement can be harmful to women who already feel worthless or have suffered sexual abuse.[4] At its worst, the penal theory evokes images of a God who is intent on wrath and destruction of the individual, prevented only at the last moment by the intervention of the Lamb, Jesus. Battered women are only too ready to believe that God is always angry, and these penal stories can exacerbate the difficulty in appropriating God's grace. One woman described her shift in understanding.

> *Jesus' death was inevitable given sin, but [it was] not required by God's grace. Death is required for humanity to see God. I have moved completely from a substitutionary atonement because of the emphasis on grace. Substitutionary atonement is tied for me to family violence and my own deep sense of unworthiness. I needed to leave it.*

Several others stressed the solidarity of Christ with us in the atonement or frankly admitted they "do not understand it." Some acknowledged a substitutionary dimension to Christ's death but denied the forensic or penal aspect. Another woman said of the cross, "I don't define it all. I don't have a problem with substitutionary atonement. It is just inadequate in itself. I struggle with this one—so I just can't give a specific answer. I understand it in all its dimensions, not just one."

With the widespread evangelical reflection on the cross in recent years, more room has been opened for constructive theological discussion. Joel Green and Mark Baker, for example, address these questions in *Recovering the Scandal of the Cross*. In this work, they point to the wide variety of cultural and biblical metaphors for the cross, and they find no scriptural mandate for elevating a penal theory above all

---

[3]Of course, in evangelical churches with a limited sacramental emphasis, the bar to women's ordination is more often Pauline passages or a hierarchical creation theology, than it is the image of Christ.
[4]This is one of those psychological equations, however, that may appear to be obvious on the surface but works differently in practice. Some women who work with abuse cases will testify that abused women are quite able to make a distinction between the Jesus who saves and the men who abuse.

others. Moreover, they argue, familiar evangelical interpretations of the atonement owe much to truncated understandings of sin as individual acts of disobedience. "This identification of sin with acts of disobedience has too easily been coupled in the United States with widespread cultural norms of autonomous individualism," they suggest.[5] As a result, it becomes "possible to conceive of salvation apart from any notion of human transformation."[6] They deny neither the representative nature of Christ's atonement nor the part that disobedience has to play in human sin. Rather, they point to crosscultural understandings of atonement (for example, in shame-based cultures), to the wide variety of meanings associated with sacrifice in Scripture and to the resonances of Christ's cross in less individualistic societies. Removing the penal theory from its central place in evangelical discourse does not, they argue, remove the scandal of the cross. But the good news of the cross must be retold in each generation and each new context—always depending on the Spirit's working "through the community of God's people."[7]

In a similar way, Chris Marshall, in *Beyond Retribution*, has argued that Paul does not see Jesus' death as a vicarious punishment that appeases God's wrath; rather, God's justice is vindicated by overcoming oppressive powers, forgiving those who are guilty of collaboration with the enemy and restoring all humans to covenant relationship with God. Jesus bears our sin in costly solidarity with us and in that sense represents us. But the cost is the natural consequence of sin, not an imposed extra penalty. Like Green and Baker, Marshall argues that penal theories of the atonement give too little emphasis to the healing that Jesus achieves and too much emphasis to the efficacy of punishment.

> Paul himself does not understand the atonement as a matter of penal substitution as *conventionally understood*. He does not view Christ's sacrificial death as an act of vicarious punishment that appeases God's punitive wrath.
>
> It is true, to begin with, that Paul sees a *substitutionary dimension* to Christ's death. But it is substitutionary not in the sense of one person *replacing* another, like substitutes on a football team, but in the sense of one person *representing* all others, who are thereby made present in the person and experience of their representative. . . . Paul's understanding seems to be that when Christ died, in some mysterious way fallen humanity died with him and through him.[8]

---

[5]Joel B. Green and Mark D. Baker, *Recovering the Scandal of the Cross: Atonement in New Testament and Contemporary Contexts* (Downers Grove, Ill.: InterVarsity Press, 2000), p. 201.

[6]Ibid., p. 202.

[7]Ibid., p. 219.

[8]Christopher D. Marshall, *Beyond Retribution: A New Testament Vision for Justice, Crime and Punishment* (Grand Rapids: Eerdmans, 2001), p. 61.

Again, the suspicion that the "answer" is to be found in the text, and not in constructions outside the text, has paid off. J. Denny Weaver and others who are advocating a nonviolent atonement have resuscitated the Christus Victor strand of
atonement thought. The theory Weaver calls "narrative Christus Victor" suggests
that Jesus came to overcome evil and the powers and principalities of evil. This he
did in his life, and it is exemplified in every dimension of his work. According to
this understanding, Jesus did not come to die, was not slain by the Father and was
not a substitution for the vengeful God; rather, his death was inevitable as one who
opposed evil with more purity and consistency than is possible for any human. In
his life and death he saved us, mysteriously, and may be our representative, but he
is not the substitute victim.[9] As these ideas are discussed on evangelical campuses,
room will open up for more investigation of gender concerns in atonement theology. Certainly the pastoral considerations of atonement theory include those of
justice and the politics of retribution and war, as much as gender, as Weaver and
Marshall discuss. Loosening the connection between penal atonement theory
and evangelical faith can deepen and strengthen our Christology. Other metaphors
and models privilege our deep communion with and participation in Christ, and
through Christ in God. They emphasize the connections and interconnections of
Christ with the whole creation, both as Creator and Redeemer.

In spite of a generally high Christology, another dimension of the evangelical
ethos is the strong presumption of a relaxed and friend-like relationship with Jesus:
"What a friend we have in Jesus, all our sins and griefs to bear," proclaims the familiar hymn. While this relationship gives great comfort, it can also, at times, be
strangely superficial. Elouise Renich Fraser describes how this song "stuck" in her
throat one day long after she had completed theological training and was teaching
theology at a seminary. Her strong reaction revealed to her the ambivalence she had
come to feel about Jesus. In the subsequent difficult work she did in coming to
terms with Jesus, she learned to see him in the despised and unattractive crowd with
whom he mixed. She realized that "Jesus is a stranger to men *and* to women."[10] Fa-
miliarity was balanced by the otherness of Jesus. A few women in the survey also
described their existential struggles as they recognized simultaneously how much
was at stake and how little they really knew Jesus in the way that is presupposed in
the language of the hymn.

The work of teaching theology often means defamiliarizing students and our-

---

[9] J. Denny Weaver, *The Nonviolent Atonement* (Grand Rapids: Eerdmans, 2001).
[10] Elouise Renich Fraser, *Confessions of a Beginning Theologian* (Downers Grove, Ill.: InterVarsity Press,
1998), pp. 101-3.

selves with the language we have grown too accustomed to using. In this process of defamiliarization, feminist insights and questions can be very helpful.[11] The defamiliarization often needs to come from multiple directions—seeing Jesus' humanity when we have become accustomed to the divine identity of God and Christ; affirming his divinity when the connection between the human man and Jesus is too familiar. In this task, we are assisted by the questions of alternative maps or frames of reference.

GENDER AND DIVINITY

I see God as love, not power. The hard lines are softer now. Truth is important, but I once saw the world as black and white, and now [I see] more gray.

I do not believe that the solution to the exclusion of women in the church will be achieved by re-naming God "mother." But I do believe that correctly understanding the metaphor of "father" in a patriarchal setting will correct all sorts of doctrinal error.

At the heart of feminist theology has been a deconstruction of the male God and an accompanying search for other God-images. Feminist imagery of God has been free moving, as found in Mary Daly's *Beyond God the Father* and Sallie McFague's *Models of God*. In breaking away from older images of God, feminists have felt free to bring to life metaphors of God that they believe are more emancipatory. Feminist theology has intentionally been theology from the human side of the divine-human interface, theology that places experience before revelation.

Accompanying this revolution has been a renewed emphasis on religious language and grammar and, in particular, on the place and function of metaphor. In mainline, liberal and feminist liturgies, God-images have been used quite eclectically. Forgotten, overlooked or mistranslated images of God—in particular, images of God as mother—have been redeemed or remembered. In evangelical circles, as Stackhouse's comment at the opening of the chapter observes, the metaphors and images have remained almost exclusively male, even where inclusive language in reference to human beings has been adopted.

Feminism has highlighted links between abuse and religious patriarchy. All of this has encouraged imaginative rediscovery of self and of God—part theology and part therapy. Models of a less authoritarian, less autocratic God, who is more inti-

---

[11]The work of defamliarization in theology is mentioned by a number of theologians. In particular, see Alister E. McGrath, *Theory*, vol. 3 of *A Scientific Theology* (New York: T & T Clark, 2003), pp. 36-43.

mately bound to the creation and less controlling of the future, have been embraced. Feminist evangelicals, however, have been more cautious, committed to drawing images of God from Scripture. One woman, for example, in critiquing the eclectic appropriation of images found in feminist spirituality, explained,

> *There seems to be a [weakness in terms of] things making sense—some spiritualities seem to me to have conflicting rationales. Rather, anything goes. But while all experiences may be described, and it would be arrogant to suggest there is only one explanation of events, I believe only in one God, not many, and that God is not of our creation.*

A debate also continues around the merits of calling God "Father" and imaging God as father. Is *father* just a human word, used in the text to image something of God who is really "totally other," or does the father image have greater priority because it is biblical? Feminist evangelicals have often felt as if they were negotiating a boundary where there was very little common space, defended by feminists who were mistrustful of any male imagery on the one side and evangelicals who denounced any female imagery on the other. Kathryn Greene-McCreight takes up the argument against dropping "father" language when she critiques feminism for not being true to the narrative revelation of God in the Old and New Testaments.[12] Another woman expressed a similar sentiment when she wrote,

> *My question is, to what extent can we say that God as Father is just one possible image of God but not essential for understanding God or Christ's relationship with God? And if we conclude this, then what are we saying about what Jesus was doing when he utilized this picture? To what extent was he contextualizing and to what extent may we? And what are the implications for this?*

Marianne Meye Thompson suggests that the biblical language of fatherhood should be maintained, as a part of the revelation of God in the wider scope of God's covenantal relationship with Israel and extending eschatologically to the future when we will know and understand this fatherhood more clearly. In other words, we do not understand the meaning of the fatherhood of God by observing human fathers, nor do we learn lessons on fatherhood by modeling God; rather, the biblical sense of fatherhood is gleaned only from the as-yet-unfinished story itself. God is still other and still not male. Thompson insists, however, that this in no way exhausts the imagery that can be used of God.

---

[12]Kathryn Greene-McCreight, *Feminist Reconstructions of Christian Doctrine: Narrative Analysis and Appraisal* (New York: Oxford University Press, 2000).

If there were greater emphasis today on the biblical narrative in which the Fatherhood of God takes on texture and shape, and fewer spurious arguments for why God could never be imaged as a mother or with feminine imagery, our theological discourse would be enriched.[13]

Valerie Karras, an Eastern Orthodox theologian, argues that the old language for the Trinity is more feminist than that of current liturgies that refer to the Trinity as Creator, Redeemer and Sanctifier. This language, she maintains, is "anthropocentric" and Western in its love of oppositions rather than complementarity. Furthermore, the new language divides up the interconnectedness of the Trinity.

> It would be equivalent to telling a woman that, although she thinks of herself most existentially and fundamentally as the mother of her children, we have decided to categorize her and refer to her only by her occupation as a physician. Ironically, then, the traditional names are more feminist, in the sense of interpersonal relationality, than the feminist names.[14]

She argues, however, that the male language is moderated in Orthodox theology in a number of ways: for example, by its emphasis on human deification and by its willingness to use metaphors for mother and father interchangeably.

The academic discussion continues. On the boundaries, however, evangelical men and women will respond more positively to a feminism that acknowledges transcendence and to a liturgical space that finds good theological sense in the traditional titles for God, among others. Neither men nor women, however, are always operating out of good theological sense. The feminist journey often involves anguish and anger and requires deep healing. Sometimes the healing is facilitated by an enthusiastic embracing of the feminine dimensions of God, not because God is a woman, but because this image is important at a particular point in time. In the survey, several women spoke of having been inspired by the fourteenth-century work of Julian of Norwich. One young respondent, then still a graduate student said, "Doing a comprehensive exam on Julian of Norwich had a major effect on me. I saw Christ as mother. I saw the feminine side of God."

The twentieth century was deeply influenced by the experience of, and subsequently by a new theology of, the Holy Spirit. This rediscovery of the third person of the Trinity, together with Karl Barth's return from liberal experientialism to rev-

---

[13]Marianne Meye Thompson, *The Promise of the Father: Jesus and God in the New Testament* (Louisville, Ky.: Westminster John Knox, 2000), p. 184.

[14]Valerie Karras, "Eschatology," in *The Cambridge Companion to Feminist Theology*, ed. Susan Frank Parsons (Cambridge: Cambridge University Press, 2002), pp. 247-48.

elation, eventually resulted in a rediscovery of the Trinity itself. Evangelicals have been enthusiastic in their reappropriation of trinitarian theology; Colin Gunton, Robert Jenson, Catherine LaCugna, Jürgen Moltmann, Miroslav Volf and Thomas Weinandy are widely read and discussed in evangelical seminaries and by evangelical theologians.[15] In some evangelical circles, however, the new emphasis on the Trinity has almost exclusively concerned questions about the subordination of its members.[16] The subordinationist view has asserted that if the Son is subordinate to the Father, so also can women be properly subordinate to men—without implying, in any sense, a diminution of status or worth. These arguments are another example of the ongoing importance of gender in evangelical theological concerns and of claiming divine mandate for hierarchical gender relations.

The contemporary emphasis on the Trinity has also been enthusiastically embraced by women—not necessarily in its more rationalistic and technical aspects, but because the rediscovery of the Trinity has again emphasized the unity and diversity of the Godhead and above all the personhood and community of God's being. The love of God is communal, embracing, nonhierarchical and inclusive of the creation and the cosmos; it is certainly not only a formal relationship between the Father and a single individual. Salvation and transformation involve participation in intra-trinitarian love and in the body of Christ in the church, deeply communal and transformational experiences. Volf uses the perichoretic nature of the persons in the Trinity to argue that gender roles, though rooted in the differences of the "sexed body," are as fluid and interchangeable as the different members of the Trinity.

> Instead of setting up ideals of femininity and masculinity, *we should root each in the sexed body and let the social construction of gender play itself out guided by the vision of the identity of and relations between divine persons.* . . . It is precisely the one triune God in whose image all human beings are created who holds the promise of peace between men and women with irreducible but changing gender identities.[17]

---

[15]See Colin E. Gunton, *The Triune Creator: A Historical and Systematic Study* (Grand Rapids: Eerdmans, 1998); Robert W. Jenson, *Systematic Theology: The Triune God* (New York: Oxford University Press, 2001); Catherine M. LaCugna, *God for Us: The Trinity and Christian Life* (San Francisco: Harper, 1993); Jürgen Moltmann, *The Trinity and the Kingdom: The Doctrine of God*, trans. Margaret Kohl (Minneapolis: Fortress, 1993); Miroslav Volf, *After Our Likeness: The Church as the Image of the Trinity* (Grand Rapids: Eerdmans, 1998); and Thomas G. Weinandy, *The Father's Spirit of Sonship: Reconceiving the Trinity* (Edinburgh: T & T Clark, 1995).

[16]For a refutation of some evangelical arguments for subordinationism, see Kevin Giles, *The Trinity and Subordinationism: The Doctrine of God and the Contemporary Gender Debate* (Downers Grove, Ill.: InterVarsity Press, 2002).

[17]Miroslav Volf, *Exclusion and Embrace: A Theological Exploration of Identity, Otherness and Reconciliation* (Nashville: Abingdon, 1996), p. 182 (emphasis in original). Volf defines *perichoresis* as "the idea of divine 'mutual indwelling' that results from 'self-giving' " (p. 181).

The turn in some parts of feminism to an engagement with a revealed God, and the accompanying suspicion that divinity is behind the creation and the Scriptures, opens up more room for feminist evangelical reflection. Throughout its history, Christianity has adopted culturally appropriate images for God, and the Scriptures use multiple metaphors for God. There are strong arguments for looking closely at father images and at the same time adopting additional ones in liturgy and prayer. Abandoning the exclusive use of male language can be deeply liberating. At the same time, however, it is important to recognize that eclectic language for God is sometimes used in ways that bear no connection to the revealed God and make sense only in terms of projection. Evangelical feminism will continue to affirm that God is God and will be there ahead of us.

Within evangelicalism, the sometimes bitter debate now raging between open and traditional theists has also provided a space for evangelical feminism that is not defined primarily by feminist literature. The work done, and the dialogue opened, by theologians like Greg Boyd, John Sanders, and Clark Pinnock probably could not have been initiated by an evangelical woman.[18] The openness of God critique of classical orthodoxy, however, is interesting because it owes much to feminist efforts at the dismantling of Calvinism and yet attempts also to stay true to the biblical narrative—more true, openness theologians claim, than Calvinism is. Here we find another instance of space opening up for biblical feminism to be part of a wider debate, though it comes considerably after the initial critique of the tradition was articulated. While this space exists, individual evangelical women teaching in evangelical institutions may find it difficult to join the conversation unless leaders in their schools are also involved in this debate. One woman, however, noted, "I like process theology for its emphasis on relationality. God's omniscience is in holding all possibilities, not in foreknowledge. But I still believe God is 'in charge.'" This woman makes the connection between a high view of God's "control," so common in evangelicalism, and an inadequate theology of suffering.

> *Evangelicalism is inadequate in its dealing with the realities of life's suffering, and I think that is directly related to its theology of "God is in control"—one of those lies that is perpetuated as truth. God as sovereign is not the same thing as in control. Try 1 John 5:19.* ✍

Regarding the openness of God, evangelicals are asking important questions.

---

[18]See Clark H. Pinnock, *Most Moved Mover: A Theology of God's Openness* (Grand Rapids: Baker, 2001); John Sanders, *The God Who Risks: A Theology of Providence* (Downers Grove, Ill.: InterVarsity Press, 1998); Gregory A. Boyd, *God of the Possible: A Biblical Introduction to the Open View of God* (Grand Rapids: Baker, 2000).

Are we just exchanging one set of metaphysical errors for another? Is the under-standing in process and feminist theology of God as always "luring" us toward material and spiritual perfection really a good image of God's work in the world? These complex questions and conversations suggest once again that concerns ini-tially raised by feminist theologians have wide-ranging resonance in the larger church.

Nevertheless, evangelicals often work in contexts where doctrinal boundaries are carefully guarded, and the boundary-marking work of organizations like the Evan-gelical Theological Society continues. "Evangelicalism stops you [from] going all the way with feminism," said one woman. In evangelical settings, women continue to ask questions like, Where does imaging of God end and projection of self onto God begin? What is given and transcendent, and what can legitimately be con-structed and imagined? One respondent, commenting on the limits of God-language, explained, "We can embrace the full range of biblical metaphors for God, but no further."

A particularly poignant place where these theological conversations become far more than academic discussions is in the practice of community prayer. Evan-gelical feminist women can find themselves pressed to choose between prayer communities that recognize the spiritual power of prayer but do so in very pa-triarchal language, and more liberal and inclusive communities that have little confidence in the efficacy of petitionary prayer. Women on the boundary might agree with Sarah Coakley, who argues for an orthodox feminist understanding of God and Trinity that mixes trinitarian interconnectedness and vulnerable inter-communion with God through the Spirit—a feminist transcendent image of God in practice.

> What I have elsewhere called the "paradox of power and vulnerability" is I believe uniquely focused in this act of silent waiting on the divine in prayer. This is because we can only be properly "empowered" here if we cease to set the agenda, if we "make space" for God to be God. Prayer which makes this "space" may take a va-riety of forms.[19]

In practice, attitudes to prayer—like our understandings of God—can disclose quite distinct religious life-worlds. Prayer is perhaps most plausible for those who believe in a God who moves in response to our actions and petitions but who has ultimate redemptive power.

---

[19]Sarah Coakley, *Powers and Submissions: Spirituality, Philosophy and Gender* (Malden, Mass.: Blackwell, 2002), p. 34.

SCRIPTURE AND AUTHORITY

In America, I believe that the most important variables between an evangelical and an almost-evangelical are the authority and inspiration of the Bible, and the unique role of Jesus Christ in the salvation of humanity. In my experience, these are the two elements of orthodoxy that are most quickly sacrificed by the evangelical-on-their-way to becoming a universalist. ᴥ

Scripture is very special. It is not like reading Plato. It is revelation from God, but the book is written by people and translated by people, men mostly. It is complicated trying to understand it, involving the human and divine. I don't have any specific theory. [Understanding] scripture was and is a communal task, and [it] needs the Holy Spirit as well. ᴥ

Probably most troubling to evangelical women who are considering feminism are the differences in approach toward Scripture. All of the women surveyed mentioned the high place of Scripture as an evangelical distinctive, though they also emphasized the importance of appropriate exegesis and interpretation. Fraser, an evangelical theologian, captures the ambivalence women nevertheless often feel about Scripture: "For years I feared difficult passages. They were time bombs waiting to explode, activating voices from my past. The best way to protect myself was to avoid them altogether."[20] Fraser explains that in her experience, Scripture has never been completely affirming or consoling. For every page or paragraph that is good news, there are other words and voices that trouble and disturb us; important passages are sometimes set in the midst of patriarchal relationships.[21] Similarly, one woman in the survey expressed her struggle with identity and commitment to the Word when she commented, "My evangelical roots are deep! But I need to work on the difficulties that are real . . . in what it means for Scripture to be God's revelation."

For many feminists, the core Scripture can be culled, the wheat can be taken from the tares, and readers need not restrict themselves to the canon but can also add liberating voices from the tradition on an equal footing. This stance toward Scripture is clearly problematic for many evangelical women. One of the women in the survey noted that although she found Elisabeth Schüssler Fiorenza's work helpful, in the end the women came out looking better than Jesus. Several commented that Rosemary Radford Ruether's "canon within a canon" was unsatisfactory.

Evangelicals might well embrace certain feminist voices, but they will not quickly discard parts of the text, even where they are difficult. Boundary living encourages a

---

[20]Fraser, *Confessions*, p. 56.
[21]Ibid., pp. 59-61.

dwelling within the text, placing and drawing the received narrative back together. One woman explained that she was an evangelical because of her high view of the authority of Scripture and her commitment to "living under the Word." Another woman, however, noted the implicit preference among evangelicals for some parts of Scripture over others, recognizing that she herself did not often use I Timothy 2:11-15 as "a devotion piece." Such preferences are frequently revealed by the choices made regarding which texts receive attention and which are quietly overlooked.

But if there is some ambiguity in the surveyed women's embrace of Scripture, it is also apparent in the constant reflection that takes place around hermeneutical matters within evangelicalism more generally. One woman identified the tension between the intellectual and the experiential as well as the need to bring them together and to recognize God's presence in the questions as well as the texts:

> *In many evangelical circles the split between the spiritual and intellectual is very great. In other words, faith is what you have instead of reason. . . . The Enlightenment [and] the relativism that comes with it [are] such a threat that they [evangelicals] leap the other way and talk about God's command; there's a whole kind of approach that is very assertive. To me there's been this real meshing with the spiritual. And I'd even say my intellectual questions are part of God's Spirit at work in me.* ✍

In her interesting work on fundamentalism and evangelicals, Harriet Harris devotes an entire chapter to examining hermeneutical ambiguities. She notes the persistent tendency of evangelicals to objectify the text and its meaning, while nevertheless living in a space that finds great pleasure in the *experience* of the text and of the community.

> Evangelicals today are under a similar strain: the highly experiential nature of their faith is not apparent in their apologetics; their personal interaction with scripture cannot be detected in their defense of inerrancy and their "objective" readings of the biblical text; from the fear of subjectivism they have subordinated religious experience to empirical and rational demonstration.[22]

"Yet," observes Harris, "the way in which scripture functions in their lives is one of their primary joys."[23]

In the boundary between feminism and evangelicalism, the interaction between Scripture and experience can be affirmed. Scripture is not accepted out of the blue. It is accepted because our relationship with God is bound to our coming into the

---

[22]Harriet A. Harris, *Fundamentalism and Evangelicals* (Oxford: Clarendon, 1998), p. 321.
[23]Ibid., p. 322.

scriptural story and because we recognize in the biblical narratives a truth and a story that preceded us, rather than something of our own construction. Experience and narrative then become a common and unlikely bond between feminism and evangelicalism. Said one woman for whom the struggle has been long and acute,

> I continue to wrestle with Scripture, attempting to describe the balance between essence and form. The form, as Calvin said, sounds like God's lisp. The essence is God's unblemished voice. But is it even possible to hear the voice without the lisp, both then and now? I am still working on this one. ✑

Another woman described her struggles with how to see the Scripture as authoritative, given her understanding of its genesis:

> But I would see the Bible as a vehicle and not the source. I think the source of our belief is Jesus Christ himself and the experience of people who walked with him and walked through the resurrection. . . . Then the question is, how do we enter into the story? I no longer see the Bible as some evangelicals want to have it—as . . . the source of truth. . . . I distinctly remember the light going on—that in fact it was the church that had created the Bible and not vice versa. The Bible was really a product of a community who had granted it authority. ✑

However much evangelical women might struggle with issues of scriptural authority, there is an overwhelming assent to the text. Scripture remains for most of the women in our survey an "abiding love," God's revelation and a source of empowerment for ministry, even while there is an associated "sense of grieving" when one can no "longer read scripture in a pre-critical way."[24]

As noted previously, an aspect of feminist biblical interaction, often overlooked by evangelicals, has been the recovery of the text. Much feminist biblical criticism works with the received text, highlighting neglected stories in which women act decisively or redemptively, bringing to light "texts of terror," using auxiliary literature to illuminate the text's meaning and documenting the complex situation of women under Old Testament law. Feminist criticism has brought new life to texts; connections and drama rarely seen before are made visible. The lives of Tamar, Hagar, the unnamed woman in Judges and others have a new place in our lives since reading Phyllis Trible's *Texts of Terror*.[25] Feminists like Trible remind us to listen not just to the forgotten stories, but to the details as well. In this close attention to the text

---

[24]Ibid., p. 321.
[25]Phyllis Trible, *Texts of Terror: Literary-Feminist Readings of Biblical Narratives* (Philadelphia: Fortress, 1984).

and in the expectation that it will speak to us anew, feminists and evangelicals form an unlikely alliance.

Some feminist evangelical women work specifically on this boundary, describing the ways in which Scripture critiques itself as a hermeneutical standard. When asked how she dealt with the patriarchal material in Scripture, one woman's response was to emphasize the culture-bound character of the patriarchy. Another commented, "This [the patriarchy] is a misreading of Scripture," and she was very aware of "the texts in the canon that critiqued it." She and others have observed that Jesus critiqued the Old Testament text and spoke of a Comforter who will further inspire us, that Paul cautioned against believing him unless he was speaking the gospel, that Peter claimed Paul was hard to understand and that the Old Testament prophets reinterpreted the tradition. The discerning of the spirits has always been necessary, as much in evangelical fellowships as in feminist circles.

Other women have found alliances between a narrative approach to Scripture and evangelical understandings of the unity of the canon. Fraser describes how important it was to her to treat the Bible finally as a unity: "Discovering the unity of the Bible just as it is goes hand in hand with discovering the unity of my life."[26] Hers is a good expression of the narrative insight that in telling the story of Scripture, we inhabit it and indwell it in ways that both make sense of our lives and are life-forming at the same time. Narrative, however, is not a panacea for all theological difficulties,[27] and indeed sometimes obscures questions of truth, historicity and inspiration.

To be true to the accounts we received, however, we must acknowledge that there were several women for whom a high view of Scripture was no longer persuasive. One woman saw her former evangelical identity in terms of control and scriptural authority.

I suppose coming to a different view of the Bible was what made me no longer identify as an evangelical. For example, Scripture—I am really not hung up on the authority of Scripture, so important to evangelicalism as a control device rather than an enabling one. Feminists use authority in terms of our own authority, but it is in an empowering sense rather than controlling of others. So when people say they believe in the authority of Scripture, I hear them saying they believe that there is a set of rules, guidelines, set in stone, that we have to follow and by which we judge everything and everyone. The realities of our lives are made to fit into the grid of Scripture whether they fit in or not.

---

[26]Fraser, *Confessions*, pp. 59-60.

[27]See Amy Plantinga Pauw, "Review of *Feminist Reconstructions of Christian Doctrine* (by Kathryn Greene-McCreight): Narrative Analysis and Appraisal," *Theology Today* 58, no. 2 (2001): 248.

In her book *Strength for the Journey,* Diana Butler Bass describes a striking epiphany whereby, for the first time, she felt she really understood what the Bible was about. For her, though, this required leaving evangelicalism and the interpretative stranglehold she believes it has on the text. She recounts her experience at a Bible study on Matthew 22:34-46 in a mainline Episcopal church.

> I remember looking around the room in stunned silence as it occurred to me that, for nearly fifteen years, I had been reading the Bible through a particular interpretation of the text—and had largely been ignoring the words of scripture itself.
>
> I wanted to shout, "No, this cannot be! Jesus told us the point of the whole thing? Love? How do you love God and your neighbor? How can I love myself? Have I gotten it wrong for all these years?"[28]

Suddenly, she realized, "the point was not about what you believe about Jesus but what you do in his name. The point was love." Many evangelicals can identify, at least in part, with her experience. After years of struggle to "get it all right" and to discover truth by rational methods (employing very intense but also very rational approaches to Bible study), one can find Jesus' commandment to love a new and liberating insight, accessible to all whatever one's level of theological sophistication. While the command to love challenges us to live differently, it can also lead us back to the text in a more prayerful and contemplative manner.

A number of women admitted that they had not yet worked out their theology of Scripture, choosing to live from day to day depending on Scripture and making it authoritative. One woman explained,

> *I have not finally concluded [anything] about my view of Scripture. I believe Scripture to be a revelation from God, and by that I do not mean to take Scripture out of critical scrutiny. But rather I am trying to work out how God reveals in Scripture, given the issues raised by critical biblical scholarship and in particular by feminist scholarship and re-reading. I cannot bring myself to throw books or bits of it out because they are not liberating to women.*

Even women who have endured harsh gender-related backlash within conservative traditions often enthusiastically endorse Scripture. One claimed to have become a feminist by reading the Bible. Another spoke of her deep love of Scripture, "that she will not allow to be taken from her," though she also remembers the time when her institution was in the hands of "inerrantist cudgels." A professor in bib-

---

[28]Diana Butler Bass, *Strength for the Journey: A Pilgrimage of Faith in Community* (San Francisco: Jossey-Bass, 2002), pp. 136-37.

lical studies, who has observed the struggles of others but has never experienced her own over Scripture, wrote,

> *I love the Bible. I have loved it all my life. I have never been afraid of it, experienced it as threatening or had anybody succeed in persuading me that they were better interpreters of it than I was, even when I was a child and uneducated. I always knew that I could figure out what it meant if I tried hard enough and prayed about it, and I have always been certain that when I figured out what it meant it would be good news for me. This must be a result of very early parental relationships and Sunday school teachers plus some huge dose of grace; I can't imagine what else it could be. This makes it hard for me to have an existential appreciation for the struggles of other women. I know because I have heard and believed their stories that many (most?) women have been abused by the Bible and its interpreters. I know that the concept of authority is a problem and that women need to trust their experience. I know all this, but I have no existential connection with this knowledge. I am constantly (and successfully) fighting the impulse to say to women who raise these issues that they should get a life.* ✑

It is the case that within the evangelical academic world, questions of hermeneutics are under continual discussion. While there is widespread consensus that Scripture is uniquely authoritative and that it underpins all our theological activities, it is also from Scripture that the difficult metaphors and Pauline directives originate. It is in Scripture that God is encountered and that we come face to face with troubling cultural perspectives. Frequently, the life-giving Word of God is also used to draw hierarchical analogies for Christian life and society. If we look at the long view of God's work in the world, listen to the Spirit, enter into the story of God incarnate in Jesus and listen to conversation partners inside and outside the tradition, Scripture speaks with hope and with redeeming and transforming power. When a deep respect for the Word is combined with certain feminist insights, the result can be both powerful and liberating.

QUESTIONS OF TRUTH, POSTMODERNITY AND PLURALISM

> *I suppose for me in my research, I am interested in truth that is both theological and feminist at the same time. But truth is, of course, more than this.* ✑

> *I have grown in my appreciation of the power and influence of human subjectivity on understandings of truth. I see insights gleaned from the social sciences and other disciplines as windows into knowledge, which is the starting place for truth.* ✑

What I appreciate about the social sciences, feminism and postmodern thought are the new questions they pose to the search for truth, which can help—through utilizing new frameworks of understanding, new epistemologies and new questions—to expand a fuller understanding of knowledge as the quest for truth continues. ❧

To the extent that evangelicalism is rooted in twentieth-century fundamentalism, it is a modernist movement attempting, in places, to transform itself for a postmodern world. The defenders of evangelical orthodoxy in the twentieth century placed a very heavy emphasis on rational, propositional, well-ordered thought and biblical interpretation. The many forms of feminism, however, have tended to be innovative and theologically creative, rather than dogmatically rational. Almost all the women we surveyed suggested that truth is broader than evangelicalism has tended to admit, and they were impatient with dogmatic, modernist understandings of truth. They emphasized the limited power of human beings to know the truth, the need for subjectivity in accessing partial truth, the importance of epistemological humility, and the rootedness of truth in God who is known relationally.

Even in the wider evangelical movement, evangelicals are critically and readily engaging postmodern ideas, perhaps because truth is so important to evangelicals and because postmodernism so often appears to represent a deliberate relativist undermining of any realist metaphysics. Said one woman,

I rather enjoy postmodern thinking. I do not agree that there is no absoluteness or characterizable definition to God and the spiritual. The tension for us is holding gently what we have learned from Scripture, history and our own experience with the reality that we are finite and in a universe defined more by relational dynamics than by objectivity. This should humble us, but this does not mean that God is not the definer. As interpreters, errors will be made, but God is not created out of our interpretations. God is and God is revealed through Christ and our own experience. We can humbly seek to know God, and God responds to this seeking with being known. ❧

As mentioned previously, Nancey Murphy has written at length about the positive effects of postmodernity as a mediating epistemology, "beyond fundamentalism and liberalism."[29] Fundamentalism/evangelicalism and liberalism, she claims, are variant forms of modernist foundationalism. Liberals build their theologies on feelings, and evangelicals on scriptural propositions. Both need to heed the postmodern antifoundationalist epistemology that allows a more dynamic, more inter-

---

[29]Nancey Murphy, *Beyond Liberalism and Fundamentalism: How Modern and Postmodern Philosophy Set the Theological Agenda* (Valley Forge, Penn.: Trinity Press International, 1996).

connected view of the world and enables us to move beyond the polarizations that have characterized American religious life. Other evangelicals enthusiastically engaging postmodernism include Stanley Grenz, who has written a widely read "primer."[30] John Drane, Leonard Sweet, Dave Tomlinson, John Franke, Brian McLaren and Michael Riddell are authors who come out of, or appeal to, the emerging evangelical postmodernist experimental church culture.[31] In the twenty-first century world of "posts-" (postliberalism, postmodernism, postfoundationalism), room is being opened for an ecumenical and interconnected evangelicalism, potentially able to embrace feminist and other methodologies and theologies as partners in the search for truth.

One woman noted that postmodernity's "web epistemology," moving back and forth from the particular to the general, corresponded well with the way she used to do inductive Bible study in her evangelical campus group. She commented further,

> *As to the postmodern, I struggle to find a way to speak intelligently about my understandings of truth in a discussion where no universals are allowed. The liberating position of being able to look at all sides of an issue without feeling trapped by one mode of thought has been a great advantage of the postmodern world. Yet I maintain for myself an understanding of what I call "capital T" Truth. Just because I do believe in absolutes does not mean I have to limit my interaction with the postmodern world. But it also does not mean that I embrace everything that comes along.*

A considerable number of other women who responded to the survey endorsed this sentiment. It is not that "anything goes," but discussion and wide-ranging interaction bring the greatest opportunity for truthful living and knowing. On issues of truth, however, evangelicals are often caught outside the margin of tolerance in liberal communities. Believing in the possibility of truth becomes the only unacceptable position, however irenically one holds to it. One woman remembers with some exasperation the arguments she had in graduate school. "I was bemused and told him that I thought it was funny that I was talking about what I believed and noth-

[30]Stanley J. Grenz, *A Primer on Postmodernism* (Grand Rapids: Eerdmans, 1996).

[31]See John William Drane, *The McDonaldization of the Church: Consumer Culture and the Church's Future* (Macon, Ga.: Smyth & Helwys, 2002); Leonard Sweet, ed., *Church in Emerging Culture: Five Perspectives* (Grand Rapids: Zondervan 2003); Michael Riddell, *Threshold of the Future: Reforming the Church in the Post-Christian West* (London: SPCK, 1998); Dave Tomlinson, *The Post-Evangelical* (Grand Rapids: Zondervan, 2003); and Stanley Grenz and John R. Franke, *Beyond Foundationalism: Shaping Theology in a Postmodern Context* (Louisville, Ky.: Westminster John Knox, 2001); Brian D. McLaren, *The Story We Find Ourselves In: Further Adventures of a New Kind of Christian* (San Francisco: Jossey-Bass, 2003).

ing more, and he was telling how I should believe, yet I was the one accused of being imperialistic."

Also noted with appreciation by a number of women was the evangelical emphasis on the way in which sin, and not just human finiteness, puts limits on our knowing. One wrote, "I see sin and self-interest, not to mention finitude, putting severe limits on anyone's claim to be in possession of the truth."

As noted earlier, quite a few women expressed difficulty with older, modernist versions of truth.

> *Historical evangelical notions of truth seem very propositional in nature with little connection with the subjectivity of human knowledge. . . . Historical evangelical notions of truth locate truth in a set of concepts and ideas which are binding regardless of the human subjectivity and experience they reflect.* ✍

> *I write against an evangelicalism that views itself as the defender of God and truth. . . . We do "see through a glass darkly" at present. I think the problem with the practice of evangelical notions of truth has been that such notions have been misapplied or dogmatically repeated rather than being applied to our life situations. I also believe that truth can be complicated and that in our social reality we find truths seem to be competing with each other. Not all life-decisions are simple and obvious.* ✍

Murphy suggests that we can test religious truth in the same way we test scientific paradigms, by the pervasiveness of the story and by their success as research programs. The life of faith, she argues, is a bit like an experiment in whether the claims of Christianity work. Overall, we continue to believe because we see the fruits of belief. This requires more patience, however, than many churches and academic institutions are prepared to allow. It can take generations to "test" some theological ideas. For example, is the idea of God as mother a helpful one—a liberating construct, a window into a reality previously locked to our view, a useful device for breaking the hold of patriarchy on our lives and for redeeming the concept of God, a penultimate linguistic metaphor—or is it a harmful and idolatrous misreading of Scripture and the tradition? When do words become idols, and when are they merely limited metaphorical expressions? While feminist evangelical women might want more freedom to use images eclectically in some circumstances and liturgies, as evangelicals they will also always be testing and wondering where the truth lies.

"God is truth" was the answer several women gave on the subject of truth. Others reconciled divergent claims to truth by recognizing the unity that exists beyond us in God. One wrote,

Of course the question remains as to external sources of truth. . . . Here I think is where faith is paramount but not opposed to reason or experience. Essentially I believe in God— I do so partly because such a notion has always been in me, and I do not know from where or how, but partly because I believe I have encountered God in person. Once one allows the possibility of God, then belief in miracles, a virgin birth, a resurrection and life after death are not problematic intellectually. 🖉

Another response was very similar:

I do see a tension between different truths and I have not figured out exactly how it all fits. Truth in Scripture for me begins with a full understanding of a loving God who has chosen to work in and be a part of the world. The model of relationships and treatment which Christ exemplifies and Scripture specifies can only enhance human experience. 🖉

Evangelical women with strong Wesleyan connections and commitments affirmed the diverse tradition within which they worked, and they comfortably embraced a wide range of sources of truth. One woman said that she "gleaned for truth from whatever source is available—like Wesley."

The Wesleyan quadrilateral enables me to work with an awareness of the tradition, experience and reason, as did the biblical writers. Revelation is experienced by human beings. 🖉

Another observed, "I am less inclined to propositional truth because of my Wesleyan/Arminian background, and I see truth as more than doctrine or philosophical position."

For many women, the issues of truth, Scripture, church and community are linked, and there was a desire for a more integrated approach to knowledge. Incarnation in community as a prerequisite of knowing was emphasized by some and is evident in this woman's comment.

Truth is what the Christian community, engaged in a careful process of discernment through biblical study, prayer, reflection and discussion of personal/social experience, claims to believe in a particular time and place, and which informs and transforms the community's behavior. Thus, truth is social, contextual and transformative. Although raised in a conservative tradition, I am most comfortable with truth being less encased in dogma and more found in relationships—relationships with God and others. At this time, I have not the need to grasp the truth as tightly as I had earlier in my career, although now, ironically, I feel closer to understanding truth than I have ever felt before. 🖉

Many of the evangelical women in the survey affirmed the relational and experiential aspects of truth—those parts of being evangelical that have always been important but have often been overlooked in systematic theologies and in formal expositions of method. For this reason, several aspects of postmodernity are viewed as positive and enlightening developments which open up possibilities of creative research and cooperative dialogue that had been quite difficult within the systematic rationalizations of the modern era.

CONCLUSION

Is it possible to live on the boundary between evangelicalism and feminism or even to reclaim the boundary as the center? Is it possible to live within both worlds theologically? To raise these questions is to invoke a gospel space of surprising reversals and to live in the hope of the reality it proclaims. Choosing to live in this space means we will not be able to define ahead of time all that is good for us or exactly where the boundary of a hermeneutic would lie. Evangelical feminist women remain convinced of the received nature of the text and the power of the Word to form our lives. We are equally convinced that the prophetic voice reclaims that Word and reinterprets it in each generation under the power of the Spirit for women as well as for men. The voices we have heard from this boundary are passionate and discerning, concerned with grace and justice, oriented to the future, and always wondering and pondering, often in the midst of clutter and conflict. If there is a distinctive theology and a renewed spirituality emerging on the boundary, we hope and pray that it will be Christ-centered, egalitarian, life-giving and supernaturalist and that it will unite rather than divide the various facets of the church.

| 8 |

CONCLUSION

———

We have traveled over significant terrain in exploring the intersection of evangelical women, feminism and the theological academy. In identifying some of the personal, institutional and theological features of this terrain and in giving voice to the women who regularly negotiate the edges of these worlds, we have attempted to provide a fuller picture of life on the boundary.

Our conversations with the many women we have met along the way have left us both encouraged and troubled. We were deeply moved by the numerous accounts of hope and grace from women living not only on boundaries between maps, but often on larger culturally and religiously defined "fault lines." We also heard many agonizing stories; sometimes these issues break a woman apart. Nevertheless, women persevered and demonstrated faith and strength while working as pioneers in uncharted territory.

We are convinced that defining the territory, unmasking the gender tensions and identifying the difficulties and opportunities are important. These efforts help in answering the complex question Where are the good women? but they also help in finding companions for the journey and in reducing the sense of isolation. They provide a way to express the ambiguity of this space and to recognize that small efforts in acknowledging and addressing these complexities make a difference. To define the landscape and ourselves is also to resist, in some measure, the defining of women that has so often been a part of the theological territory.

In concluding, we also want to acknowledge that the space between maps continues to be a very interesting location. We inhabit not just a tense and conflicted space, but one that is theologically rich, full of grace and spiritually demanding. As an increasing number of sociological studies have shown, evangelicalism looks different when seen through the eyes of women, and evangelicalism will change, we believe, as women gain a stronger voice.

We have noticed, over the period of researching and writing this book, that the terrain is fluid and is shifting quite rapidly. In the evangelical academic world, there are now openings and opportunities for women's theological reflection, discussion and teaching that previously did not exist; simultaneously, however, there is a hardening of positions in a number of schools and denominations. While we are hopeful about some changes, it is also the case that the future for academic women in evangelicalism is less than clear. In the larger evangelical culture the situation is uncertain, and in several communities doors that were previously open to women have recently been closed. Some of the rapprochement that is possible in the small world of academia is not present in the larger culture, and the split between the church and the academy, if anything, has increased.

Significant numbers of well-trained and academically gifted women have left evangelicalism. Many were educated in evangelical colleges and seminaries. Only some of those who have completed or are pursuing Ph.D.s in theological disciplines persist in an evangelical identity. This represents an enormous loss to the evangelical community—of distinctive theological voices, spiritual insights and hard-earned wisdom.

Feminism has also shifted and broadened in recent years, embracing, in a new way, the particular and the local. The significant number of engaged and respectful descriptions of evangelical women written by nonevangelicals over the past few years is evidence of this trend. Feminism is now more willing to accept the ambiguity of gendered space and is less separatist in response to patriarchy and male domination. Many aspects of the more orthodox theological tradition are being reappropriated in careful and nuanced ways.

Moreover, in the Christian world at large, boundaries are now being shared and broken. Mainline publishing houses are deliberately seeking out moderate evangelical writers. Publishing houses long associated with evangelicalism have moved into Roman Catholic and mainline markets. A number of evangelical writers themselves are calling for a new catholicity. Within these shifting boundaries, there is some space for evangelical academic women to speak and even to help shape the movement for the twenty-first century.

As we were completing the book, we received several e-mails within a single week that reminded us of how very alive the issues are. Two were sent to Nicola in response to an article she had written that had been posted on a Victoria University Chaplaincy website since 2000. The first came from a young student who had just begun her studies at a Bible college in the United States. The student wrote,

> I recently read an article you wrote on the Internet about Christian feminism. I wanted to tell you that I really appreciate your viewpoints and [the] explanations behind them. I am so glad that I was able to read it.
>
> You see, I have been really wrestling with what my role is as a female. I considered myself a feminist in high school and studied a bit of secular feminism. I tried to keep my godly standpoints on the whole issue though. Then, in the fall of 2003, I came to [Bible college]. It has been difficult in some ways because I don't agree with some of their views. It is very conservative. I suppose I consider myself a conservative, nevertheless. . . . I am starting to become agitated at all the labels. The teachings here really emphasize the submission of women to men, that women may not teach in the church (at least they should never advise men) and [that] women should not work when they are married.
>
> All of this really aggravated me at first and then I was confused. I started thinking that maybe the ways I thought before were wrong. I thought God gave me a gift for creativity. . . . But suddenly I doubted all of that. I questioned myself. Were all my ambitions just pipe dreams? Was my independence just rebellion? I was confused and still am a little. ✑

This correspondence aptly describes the very mixed terrain encountered by young female students and raises significant questions about how they are being shaped and formed by evangelical institutions. Students have opportunities to draw from multiple traditions but clearly face tensions that touch the very center of their identity and future. They come with a fragile mix of questions and experiences, visions and dreams.

The second e-mail came from a woman, also in the United States, who had spent over thirty years in a Roman Catholic convent. No longer a nun, she had married and was interested in nurturing the spiritual life of other women. She wrote that she had come to understand her work in terms of seeking liberation for both men and women from patriarchy and that she was encouraged by the idea of "living on two maps." That women in such different circumstances resonated with some of the issues we have outlined was deeply important to us.

A third e-mail came from one of the women we had interviewed. As she was exploring additional options for teaching beyond the academy, she received a message from a female friend she had known most of her life. In the e-mail, her friend explained that she would not attend any Bible teaching or preaching offered by this professor if men were present at the meeting. Despite the fact that this teacher is one of the best in her field, the use of her gifts was being circumscribed, if not rejected, by a friend. The story is deeply painful but again illuminating of the struggles we face in trying to be faithful to God's call on our lives.

While acknowledging the ongoing difficulties, we also want to suggest that marginality is not an entirely negative condition. Being on the margins, or on the intersection of maps, does not necessarily mean that we must be marginalized or disempowered. It can and will mean disempowerment if creative resistance and constructive voice are not possible. We believe that on the margins or boundaries between maps we can bring different questions and experiences to light and that these might, in the end, have a more significant role than the scripts that belong entirely in one place or another. Living on the margins allows us to identify important ambiguities and difficulties because we have some distance from which to see our institutions and communities more clearly. We can often negotiate multiple worlds because we have had to learn several languages. As long as this window of opportunity exists within the evangelical world, we may be able to shape our institutions as much as they shape us, especially if we do it together.

While this is a hope and an opportunity in some evangelical schools, churches and parachurch organizations, we recognize that the possibility of influence and contribution is not always predictable. Even in communities that articulate commitments to gender equality, decisions and practices sometimes betray different assumptions and beliefs.

We end by summarizing our conclusions regarding the question Is evangelical feminism possible? In addition, we offer some suggestions about how our conversations and reflections might translate into practical responses. For men and women who have found this charting of the landscape helpful and who themselves want to be helpful to women seeking to live out a call within the theological academy, we offer some suggestions and challenges.

IS EVANGELICAL FEMINISM POSSIBLE?

A young woman, just beginning doctoral studies in theology, recently commented,

> *I get so frustrated when my conservative evangelical friends and my liberal friends speak badly about the other. They seem to be thinking, "Why bother with the conversation? What could we possibly have in common?" And I want to reply, "You have me in common and that should be enough for a beginning."* ❧

- Our conclusion, then, is yes, evangelical feminism is possible; we *embody* the overlap of the maps. We may not have worked out all the details and we may deal daily with conflicts and tensions, but it is possible to the extent that we are already bringing these assumptions and commitments together in being both feminist and evangelical. Both worlds are part of our identities, and for both worlds, it is helpful that some people are living in the intersection.

- As evangelicals reflect on these questions, their churches and educational institutions matter a great deal. They significantly shape the questions that will be considered and the types of theology that can be done. Theological reflection at the boundary of evangelicalism and feminism will flourish where pastors, school administrators and colleagues help to make a space for it to happen. This will require naming and addressing constraints and power dynamics that undermine women's voices and women's leadership; it will mean taking risks in allowing controversial topics to be addressed. In these efforts, we will be helped as we remember the Reformation heritage of charting new territory in response to the Spirit's call.

- Because many evangelical academic women have found church homes within evangelical congregations of mainline denominations, the disturbing specter of denominational schisms have additional, very personal implications. Women and men who have chosen to live in the overlap of maps may find that neither side of these church divisions has room for them.

- An evangelical feminism is possible both because parts of evangelicalism are interested in broader conversations and because the feminist theological movement is changing. While continuing to offer critiques of patriarchy and women's oppression, a number of feminist theologians are moving toward a stronger emphasis on the transcendence as well as the immanence of God. Increasingly, they are finding a place for "absolute dependence," transformation and *metanoia*, and the scandal of the cross. Conversations within evangelical feminism will look to Scripture as authority, not quickly jumping over hermeneutical challenges, but staying with the text long enough to glean fresh and redeeming insights.

- Theology that is both evangelical and feminist will look for the revelation of God that comes from outside ourselves. That God is incarnate, has spoken in the Word and is also heard as an inner voice of the Spirit raises complex hermeneutical challenges. It means we are always called to discernment, asking, Where does projection end and genuine Spirit-filled revelation begin? These questions do not have easy answers, and following the Spirit into truth might take us into surprising places.

- Recent academic conversations about "lived theology" and Christian practices are demonstrating that these are promising frameworks within which to continue important theological discussions across evangelical, feminist and liberal boundaries. Closer attention to the historical Christian tradition is providing unexpected links across divergent contemporary communities.

- Despite the fact that conversations within the evangelical world are widening, the gender assumptions within much of popular evangelicalism keep the door open to disappointing reversals, as has been seen in several conservative denominations in recent years. The covert nature of much gender conflict allows for quite sudden and unexpected appearances of its effects. We should not be surprised that our lived reality is very mixed.

- Because gender issues are so significant within evangelicalism, feminist critiques will rarely be uncontested, even where they are possible. Nevertheless, numerous feminist concerns and insights offer a source of ongoing challenge and thoughtful correction to many assumptions and practices within evangelicalism.

- Being feminist and evangelical also depends on some degree of interaction with and welcome from the feminist side. If feminist theologians allow their interest in the particularity of women's experiences to include evangelicals, then feminist theology also can be enriched by the evangelical emphasis on transcendence and transformation, by a critique of patriarchy that does not include a denial of the entire tradition and by the particular but not always predictable experiences of women in the evangelical world.

- The small number of evangelical women in academic disciplines related to theology means that most schools are still quite a distance from having a critical mass of women who can reflect on these issues together. Environments in which female professors and students flourish are those with a good mix of female and male colleagues, mentors and models.

PRACTICAL SUGGESTIONS FOR MOVING FORWARD

Sympathetic readers—whether concerned educators, colleagues, church leaders, spouses, parents or academically inclined women—may want to think further about the practical implications of having come to a better understanding of the experiences of evangelical women in the theological academy. We would like to help further the conversation about constructive responses to the concerns and issues that have been raised. The following comments are meant to be suggestive rather than comprehensive.

- The stories we heard regularly affirmed the importance of taking seriously women's calls to ministry and teaching. Every human being needs the help of others in imagining what they can become. Young women need encouragement in seeing beyond a limited horizon to the many options available and to where God may be leading. Pastors, youth workers, parents and teachers need to recognize the importance of taking seriously a young girl's theological interests and early intimations of God's call. Many promising, academically gifted female college students never pursue studies in theological areas. They are discouraged by both practical and internalized obstacles. Who are we losing when this happens? Could she have become the next generation's brilliant and faithful theologian, Christian ethicist or church historian?

- Parachurch organizations, especially campus ministries, were extremely important in helping many women move forward toward further theological education. Campus ministry staff members have very important roles as models and mentors. Seminaries committed to raising up a new generation of women in theological studies would do well to look closely at how they are training students who are preparing for campus ministry.

- We were struck by how important supportive husbands and other family members were to the women who stayed within evangelicalism and within the academy. Support was both verbal and practical and was especially important when childrearing was involved. Similarly the encouragement of parents and small groups of friends made it possible for women to press on in studies and teaching, even under very difficult circumstances.

- Small groups that met together for prayer and encouragement were indispensable to most of the women with whom we spoke. In these settings it is possible to share struggles, receive and provide encouragement, and reframe difficult experiences in ways that are both truthful and constructive.

- We were surprised by the number of stories suggesting that it did not take very many people to make a difficult situation bearable or even good; sometimes it was the presence of just one good friend, supportive colleague or coworker.

- A combination of high expectations and high support seemed to be most helpful to women in moving toward significant academic achievement. Mentors that demanded excellent work but also found ways to affirm women's tentative voices and initial efforts were especially valued.

- The world of academic study and work becomes compelling to some students not only through one-on-one relationships of mentoring, but also in classrooms and other gatherings in which a professor's love for a subject shines through his or her teaching. Women faculty members may especially need to be reminded that equally important to their mentoring relationships with individual students is their teaching, writing and research in forming the next generation of Christian leaders.

- Most of the women we surveyed identified male professors as their most significant mentors. The importance of this role for men cannot be overstated. Although there are complexities in cross-gender relationships between faculty and students, their importance to female students suggests that mentors particularly need to be creative and intentional in finding appropriate physical and social settings in which good mentoring can be done.

- Female models and mentors in evangelical theological schools are still scarce. The presence of a faculty woman allows female students to imagine themselves in such a role and helps male students discover the gifts and wisdom that women can bring to theological education.

- When female presence on a faculty is very limited, it can be exhausting for those women. Being tokens or pioneers is difficult; in such contexts women find themselves alternately invisible and a bit of a spectacle.

- It is not always easy to recognize how gender dynamics work in an educational institution, but it becomes easier to see them and to address them constructively as more women are present in a community and as more are present in decision making.

- Students look to faculty members as models as they develop their own sense of what it means to be faithful leaders within the academy and church. Among other things, students need to see gracious and respectful male-female professional relationships modeled.

- Faculty views on gender and their attitudes toward female colleagues, female students and women's concerns in general are very important, as is evident from the following conclusion outlined in *Being There*.

Faculty members . . . dominate the students' experience of the school. Students hear faculty statements about what is true and important far more often than any other messages; they regularly observe how faculty members conduct themselves; they have far more exchanges with faculty members—from which they learn what kind of arguments carry weight, which views gain respect, and what manners are acceptable—than they do with any other representatives of the school. . . . Faculty members, simply by being who they are as well as by doing the things they are paid to do, are the primary purveyors to students of institutional culture, with all its formative power.[1]

---

[1]Jackson W. Carroll et al., *Being There: Culture and Formation in Two Theological Schools* (New York: Oxford University Press, 1997), p. 272.

- Leaders in educational institutions that are seeking to increase the number of women faculty members can simultaneously affirm the value of having women present and silence their distinctive voices. This can occur among well-meaning leaders in well-intentioned institutions that have not fully considered what it means to welcome different kinds of people into the community. A striking example is when administrators or colleagues say that they are very pleased to have women on the faculty but then, in the same breath, also note their appreciation that none of the women are "feminists." This sends a strong message about what is expected of the "good woman," and marks certain discussions and concerns as out of bounds.

- Evangelical institutions are not necessarily used to hearing women speak with authority. A voice that is only assertive, distinctive or clear should not be interpreted as angry or aggressive. In close-knit academic communities it is also very important to distinguish dissent from betrayal.

- Given the gender conflicts within evangelicalism, it is not surprising that female faculty members encounter students who challenge their authority in any number of ways. Some students challenge women's authority to teach at all in a theological area; others challenge authority or competence more subtly by complaining about pedagogical style and assignments. All teachers encounter some challenges to authority, but a female professor often encounters far more than her share from students who have been shaped by teachings that limit women's roles. When the challenges become frequent or disrespectful in public, the school's administration should view it as more than an individual problem and address it at the institutional level.

- In evangelical academic communities that pride themselves on handling complex and difficult material, it is disappointing that feminist thought has received very little serious attention. The literature is extensive and diverse. An institutional culture can be created in which opposing or controversial positions are treated seriously and are presented in their strongest light. It is under these circumstances that critiques are most effective and that opportunities for real dialogue are opened up.

- An academic environment that encourages colleagues to collaborate and to engage one another's work is good for faculty and students and is especially good for women. One of our respondents quoted a student who asked her, "Do you people ever talk to each other?" A number of women mentioned how isolated they felt because colleagues never talked about their work with each other and never helped one another by constructively critiquing journal articles, essays or book manuscripts.

- A renewed interest in the historic Christian tradition is generating resources for exploring various models of women's leadership and authority. Historical accounts of educated, wise and prophetically gifted women need to be taken seriously.

- Evangelical academic women may be very well situated to write for the church in a voice that can be heard across denominations and traditions, whatever their theological discipline. Women's work on the boundaries of various traditions can open up opportunities for conversations with other Christian communities.

- For women and men to flourish within evangelical schools, it is very important that those institutions be flexible. In particular, school policies should reflect what evangelicals say to the larger culture about the significance of the family to human life. It is essential that schools recognize that faculty and students have responsibilities to dependents, and increasingly this will include aging parents as well as children. It is possible for women and men to combine an academic career and childrearing, but it is much easier if the schools within which they teach provide structures that allow for some flexibility in work load and publishing expectations during times when family responsibilities are particularly demanding.

- Among evangelical academics generally, there is a growing weariness with discussions of boundaries. Undoubtedly, some boundaries are important for identity; but perhaps instead of focusing on drawing boundaries, evangelicals in the theological academy could understand their task as one of identifying, preserving and helping to shape something distinctively evangelical for the sake of the larger church and kingdom.

- In their careful study of two seminaries, the authors of *Being There* concluded,

  The people who run schools and conduct their programs should listen intently to and look hard at themselves: What views of the world are explicitly or subtly announced and endorsed? What ideas and statements of norms and values go unchallenged? What patterns of behavior are required? Which are forbidden?[2]

---

[2]Ibid., p. 271.

In response to this, we offer the following additional questions for consideration and discussion:

- In what ways do our institutional policies and practices suggest to students how women and men should relate?

- How do chapel programs, classes and campus activities reinforce or challenge assumptions about gender?

- How are the family responsibilities of students and faculty taken seriously in academic expectations, scheduling and so on?

- Are there significant differences between gender assumptions within the classroom and in social occasions? What evidence do we have?

- Where in the curriculum are gender issues addressed? How are students helped to think theologically about gender relationships and roles?

- Are faculty members aware of the importance of their role as mentors? What resources will help them become better mentors?

- Are there sufficient numbers of female faculty members so that students have access to models of women who engage intellectual matters and theological fields vigorously, competently and faithfully?

- How is experimentation with pedagogical methods encouraged?

- What kinds of students are we producing, especially as we think about forming the next generation of pastors and Christian leaders? What gender assumptions are they bringing into ministry?

- What are we modeling to students as they catch glimpses of friendships among faculty members?

- How are we helping students to think about complex and contested issues?

In drawing this book to a close, we are reminded again of the gift of friendship among men and women. This has been an extended intrafamily discussion with multiple generations connected through complex but committed relationships. The story is not only about maps and boundaries. It is about family—beloved and troublesome. In the long years of writing this book, we have been sustained by many companions, by encouraging words and questions, by fresh insights into the biblical text and by love for Christ and church. We are deeply aware of the evidences of God's grace in the midst of the communities within which we live and serve. As we continue to live on the boundaries of multiple roles, affiliations, commitments and communities, we do so with a sense of call, responsibility and gratitude.

BIBLIOGRAPHY

Achtemeier, Elizabeth. "The Impossible Possibility: Evaluating the Feminist Approach to Bible and Theology." *Interpretation: A Journal of Bible and Theology* 42, no. 1 (1988): 45-57.

Aisenberg, Nadya, and Mona Harrington. *Women of Academe: Outsiders in the Sacred Grove.* Amherst: University of Massachusetts Press, 1988.

Alsdurf, Phyllis. "Evangelical Feminists: Ministry Is the Issue." *Christianity Today,* July 21, 1978, pp. 46-47.

Alvarez, Daniel Raul. "On the Possibility of an Evangelical Theology." *Theology Today* 55, no. 2 (1998): 175-94.

Ammerman, Nancy Tatom. *Baptist Battles: Social Change and Religious Conflict in the Southern Baptist Convention.* New Brunswick, N.J.: Rutgers University Press, 1990.

————. *Bible Believers: Fundamentalists in the Modern World.* New Brunswick, N.J.: Rutgers University Press, 1987.

Bacote, Vincent. "What Is This Life For? Expanding Our View of Salvation." In *What Does It Mean to Be Saved? Broadening Evangelical Horizons of Salvation,* edited by John G. Stackhouse Jr. Grand Rapids: Baker, 2002.

Balmer, Randall H. *Mine Eyes Have Seen the Glory.* New York: Oxford University Press, 1989.

Bartowski, John P. *Remaking the Godly Marriage: Gender Negotiation in Evangelical Families.* New Brunswick, N.J.: Rutgers University Press, 2001.

Bass, Dorothy C. " 'Their Prodigious Influence': Women, Religion and Reform in Antebellum America." In *Women of Spirit,* edited by Rosemary Radford Ruether and Eleanor McLaughlin. New York: Simon and Schuster, 1979.

Bateson, Mary Catherine. *Composing a Life.* New York: Plume, 1989.

Beaman, Lori G. *Shared Beliefs, Different Lives: Women's Identities in Evangelical Context.* St. Louis: Chalice Press, 1999.

Bednarowski, Mary Farrell. *The Religious Imagination of American Women.* Bloomington: Indiana University Press, 1999.

Belenky, Mary F., Blythe M. Clinchy, Nancy R. Goldberger and Jill M. Tarule. *Women's Ways of Knowing: The Development of Self, Voice and Mind.* New York: Basic Books, 1986.

Bellah, Robert N., Richard Madsen, William M. Sullivan, Ann Swidler and Steven M. Tipton. *Habits of the Heart: Individualism and Commitment in American Life.* New York: Harper & Row, 1985.

Bendroth, Margaret Lamberts. *Fundamentalism and Gender, 1875 to the Present.* New Haven, Conn.: Yale University Press, 1993.

Bineham, Jeffrey L. "Theological Hegemony and Oppositional Interpretive Codes: The Case of Evangelical Christian Feminism." *Western Journal of Communication* 57, no. 4 (1993): 515-29.

Bondi, Roberta C. *Memories of God: Theological Reflections on a Life.* Nashville: Abingdon, 1995.

Boyd, Gregory A. *God of the Possible: A Biblical Introduction to the Open View of God.* Grand Rapids: Baker, 2000.

Brasher, Brenda E. *Godly Women: Fundamentalism and Female Power.* New Brunswick, N.J.: Rutgers University Press, 1998.

Bridges, Linda McKinnish. "Women in Church Leadership." *Review and Expositor* 95, no. 3 (1998): 327-47.

Brow, Robert. "Evangelical Megashift." *Christianity Today,* February 19, 1990, pp. 12-14.

Brueggemann, Walter. *Testimony to Otherwise: The Witness of Elijah and Elisha.* St. Louis, Mo.: Chalice Press, 2001.

Brueggemann, Walter, William C. Placher and Brian K. Blount. *Struggling with Scripture.* Louisville, Ky.: Westminster John Knox, 2002.

Bruland, Esther Byle. "Evangelical and Feminist Ethics: Complex Solidarities." *The Journal of Religious Ethics* 17, no. 2 (1989): 139-60.

Burwell, Rebecca C. "Evangelicalism and Feminism: A Comparison of Nineteenth and Twentieth Century Feminist Thought." B.A. Honors Paper in Sociology, Houghton College, 1994.

Butler Bass, Diana. *Strength for the Journey: A Pilgrimage of Faith in Community.* San Francisco: Jossey-Bass, 2002.

Butler, Diana H. "Between Two Worlds." *Christian Century,* March 3, 1993, pp. 231-32.

―――. "An Evangelical Journey." Review of *Mine Eyes Have Seen the Glory,* by Randolph Balmer. *Christian Century,* April 28, 1993, pp. 459-60.

―――. *Standing Against the Whirlwind: Evangelical Episcopalians in Nineteenth-Century America.* Oxford: Oxford University Press, 1995.

Carr, Anne E. *Transforming Grace.* San Francisco: Harper & Row, 1990.

Carroll, Jackson W., Barbara G. Wheeler, Daniel O. Aleshire and Penny Long Marler. *Being There: Culture and Formation in Two Theological Schools.* New York: Oxford University Press, 1997.

Cazden, Elizabeth. *Antoinette Brown Blackwell*. Old Westbury, N.Y.: Feminist Press, 1983.

Charry, Ellen T. *By the Renewing of Your Minds: The Pastoral Function of Christian Doctrine*. New York: Oxford University Press, 1997.

Chopp, Rebecca S. *Saving Work: Feminist Practices of Theological Education*. Louisville, Ky.: John Knox, 1995.

———. "Situating the Structure: Prophetic Feminism and Theological Education." In *Shifting Boundaries: Contextual Approaches to the Structure of Theological Education*, edited by Barbara G. Wheeler and Edward Farley. Louisville, Ky.: Westminster John Knox, 1991.

Chopp, Rebecca S., and Sheila Greeve Davaney, eds. *Horizons in Feminist Theology: Identity, Tradition and Norms*. Minneapolis: Augsburg, 1997.

Christ, Carol P. *She Who Changes: Re-Imagining the Divine in the World*. New York: Palgrave Macmillan, 2003.

Christ, Carol P., and Judith Plaskow, eds. *Womanspirit Rising: A Feminist Reader in Religion*. San Francisco: Harper & Row, 1979.

Clifford, Anne M. *Introducing Feminist Theology*. Maryknoll, N.Y.: Orbis, 2001.

Clouse, Bonnidell, and Robert G. Clouse, eds. *Women in Ministry: Four Views*. Downers Grove, Ill.: InterVarsity Press, 1989.

Coakley, Sarah. *Powers and Submissions: Spirituality, Philosophy and Gender*. Malden, Mass.: Blackwell, 2002.

Cook, Sharon Anne. "Sowing Seed for the Master: The Ontario W.C.T.U and Evangelical Feminism 1874-1930." *Journal of Canadian Studies* 30, no. 3 (1995): 175-94.

Corley, Kathleen E., and Karen J. Torjesen. "Sexuality, Hierarchy and Evangelicalism." *TSF Bulletin* 10, no. 4 (1987): 23-27.

Crysdale, Cynthia S. W. *Embracing Travail: Retrieving the Cross Today*. New York: Continuum, 1999.

———. "Reason, Faith and Authentic Religion." In *The Struggle Over the Past: Religious Fundamentalism in the Modern World*, edited by W. M. Shea. Lanham, Md.: University Press of America, 1993.

Daly, Mary. *Beyond God the Father: Toward a Philosophy of Women's Liberation*. Boston: Beacon, 1983.

———. *Pure Lust: Elemental Feminist Philosophy*. Boston: Beacon, 1984.

Dayton, Donald. *Discovering an Evangelical Heritage*. Peabody, Mass.: Hendrickson, 1988.

Dayton, Donald, and Lucille Sider. "Evangelical Feminism: Some Aspects of Its Biblical Interpretation." *Explor* 2, no. 2 (1976): 17-22.

DeBerg, Betty A. *Ungodly Women: Gender and the First Wave of American Fundamentalism*. Minneapolis: Fortress, 1990.

Dorrien, Gary. *The Remaking of Evangelical Theology*. Louisville, Ky.: Westminster John Knox, 1998.

Drane, John William. *The McDonaldization of the Church: Consumer Culture and the Church's Future*. Macon, Ga.: Smyth & Helwys, 2002.

Elshtain, Jean Bethke. *Public Man, Private Woman: Women in Social and Political Thought*. Princeton,

N.J.: Princeton University Press, 1981.

Erikson, Millard J. *The Evangelical Left: Encountering Postconservative Evangelical Theology.* Grand Rapids: Baker, 1997.

Faludi, Susan. *Backlash: The Undeclared War Against American Women.* New York: Doubleday, 1991.

Fowler, Robert Booth. "The Feminist and Antifeminist Debate Within Evangelical Protestantism." *Women and Politics* 5, no. 2/3 (1985): 7-37.

Fox-Genovese, Elizabeth. *"Feminism Is Not the Story of My Life": How Today's Feminist Elite Has Lost Touch with Real Concerns of Women.* New York: Doubleday, 1996.

Fraser, Elouise Renich. *Confessions of a Beginning Theologian.* Downers Grove, Ill.: InterVarsity Press, 1998.

Fulkerson, Mary McClintock. *Changing the Subject: Women's Discourses and Feminist Theology.* Minneapolis: Fortress, 1994.

Futato, Mark D. "Yahweh the Patriarch: Ancient Images of God and Feminist Theology." *Journal of the Evangelical Theological Society* 42, no. 2 (1999): 314-15.

Gallagher, Sally K. *Evangelical Identity and Gendered Family Life.* New Brunswick, N.J.: Rutgers University Press, 2003.

Gallagher, Sally K., and Christian Smith. "Symbolic Traditionalism and Pragmatic Egalitarianism: Contemporary Evangelicals, Families and Gender." *Gender and Society* 13, no. 2 (1999): 211-33.

Garlett, Marti Watson. "Female Faculty on the Fringe: Theologizing Sexism in the Evangelical Academy." *Research on Christian Higher Education* 4 (1997): 69-97.

————. "Waiting in the Wings: Women of God in the Evangelical Academy" (Ph.D. diss., Claremont Graduate School, 1997).

Garry, Ann, and Marilyn Pearsall, eds. *Women, Knowledge and Reality: Explorations in Feminist Philosophy.* Boston: Unwin Hyman, 1989.

Giles, Kevin. *The Trinity and Subordinationism: The Doctrine of God and the Contemporary Gender Debate.* Downers Grove, Ill.: InterVarsity Press, 2002.

Gilligan, Carol. *In a Different Voice: Psychological Theory and Women's Development.* Cambridge, Mass.: Harvard University Press, 1982.

Glaser, B. G., and A. L. Strauss. *The Discovery of Grounded Theory: Strategies for Qualitative Research.* Chicago: Aldine, 1967.

Goldberger, Nancy R., Jill M. Tarule, Blythe Clinchy and Mary F. Belenky, eds. *Knowledge, Difference and Power: Essays Inspired by "Women's Ways of Knowing".* New York: Basic Books, 1996.

Green, Joel B., and Mark D. Baker. *Recovering the Scandal of the Cross: Atonement in New Testament and Contemporary Contexts.* Downers Grove, Ill.: InterVarsity Press, 2000.

Greene-McCreight, Kathryn. *Feminist Reconstructions of Christian Doctrine: Narrative Analysis and Appraisal.* New York: Oxford University Press, 2000.

Grenz, Stanley. *A Primer on Postmodernism.* Grand Rapids: Eerdmans, 1996.

————. *Renewing the Center: Evangelical Theology in a Post-Theological Era.* Grand Rapids: Baker, 2000.

Grenz, Stanley, and John R. Franke. *Beyond Foundationalism: Shaping Theology in a Postmodern Context.* Louisville, Ky.: Westminster John Knox, 2001.

Grenz, Stanley, and Denise Muir Kjesbo. *Women in the Church: A Biblical Theology of Women in Ministry.* Downers Grove, Ill.: InterVarsity Press, 1995.

Griffith, R. Marie. "The Affinities between Feminists and Evangelical Women." *The Chronicle of Higher Education,* October 17, 1997, pp. 6-7.

————. *God's Daughters: Evangelical Women and the Power of Submission.* Berkeley: University of California Press, 1997.

————. "Revising Our Assessment of Evangelical Women's Groups." *Tikkun* 13, no. 2 (1998): 18-20.

Groothuis, Rebecca Merrill. *Women Caught in the Conflict: The Culture War Between Traditionalism and Feminism.* Grand Rapids: Baker, 1994.

Grudem, Wayne. "A Response to Mark Strauss' Evaluation of the Colorado Springs Translation Guidelines." *Journal of the Evangelical Theological Society* 41, no. 2 (1998): 263-86.

Gunton, Colin E. *The Triune Creator: A Historical and Systematic Study.* Grand Rapids: Eerdmans, 1998.

Hagen, June Steffensen, ed. *Gender Matters: Women's Studies for the Christian Community.* Grand Rapids: Zondervan, 1990.

————, ed. *Rattling Those Dry Bones: Women Changing the Church.* San Diego: LuraMedia, 1995.

Hampson, Daphne. "Luther on the Self: A Feminist Critique." In *Feminist Theology: A Reader.* Edited by Ann Loades. Louisville, Ky.: Westminster John Knox, 1990.

————. *Theology and Feminism.* Cambridge, Mass.: Blackwell, 1990.

Hardesty, Nancy A. "The Communion of Saints and Sinners." In *Rattling Those Dry Bones: Women Changing the Church,* edited by June Steffensen Hagen. San Diego, Calif.: Lura Media, 1995.

————. *Women Called to Witness: Evangelical Feminism in the Nineteenth Century.* Nashville: Abingdon, 1984.

————. *Your Daughters Shall Prophesy: Revivalism and Feminism in the Age of Finney.* Brooklyn: Carlson, 1991.

Harding, Sandra, ed. *Feminism and Methodology.* Bloomington: Indiana University Press, 1987.

————. "Introduction: Is There a Feminist Method?" In *Feminism and Method,* edited by Sandra Harding, pp. 1-14. Indianapolis: Indiana University Press & Open University Press, 1987.

Harris, Harriet A. "After Liberalism: Fundamentalism in a Post-Liberal Context." *Theology* 100, no. 797 (1997): 340-48.

————. *Fundamentalism and Evangelicals.* Oxford: Clarendon, 1998.

————. "Fundamentalisms Comprehended." *Religious Studies* 32, no. 3 (1996): 421-24.

Harrison, Beverly Wildung. "The Early Feminists and the Clergy: A Case Study in the Dynamics of Secularization." *Review and Expositor* 72, no. 1 (1975): 41-52.

Hassey, Janette. *No Time for Silence: Evangelical Women in Public Ministry around the Turn of the Century.* Grand Rapids: Zondervan, 1986.

Hawley, John Stratton, ed. *Fundamentalism and Gender.* New York: Oxford University Press, 1994.

Hayes, Kathleen. "Opening up the Club." *The Other Side* 30, no. 2 (1994): 44-47.

Hayter, Mary. *The New Eve in Christ: The Use and Abuse of the Bible in the Debate About Women in the Church.* London: SPCK, 1987.

Hiebert, Paul G. *The Missiological Implications of Epistemological Shifts: Affirming Truth in a Modern/ Postmodern World.* Harrisburg, Penn.: Trinity Presbyterian International, 1999.

————. "Sets and Structures: A Study of Church Patterns." In *New Horizons in World Mission: Evangelicals and the Christian Mission in the 1980s: Papers Prepared for the Consultation on Theology and Mission,* edited by David J. Hesselgrave. Grand Rapids: Baker, 1979.

Hiebert, Paul G., and Eloise Hiebert Meneses. *Incarnational Ministry: Planting Churches in Band, Tribal, Peasant and Urban Societies.* Grand Rapids: Baker, 1995.

Hooks, Bell. *Teaching to Transgress: Education as the Practice of Freedom.* New York: Routledge, 1994.

Horner, S. Sue. "The Wind Shifts." In *Rattling Those Dry Bones,* edited by June Steffensen Hagen. San Diego: LuraMedia, 1995.

Hughes, Sheila Hassell. "Homosexuality and Group Boundaries in Contemporary Evangelical Feminism: A Historical Perspective." *Quarterly Review* 14, no. 2 (1994): 135-59.

Hunter, James Davison. *Culture Wars: The Struggle to Define America.* New York: BasicBooks, 1991.

————. *Evangelicalism: The Coming Generation.* Chicago: Chicago University Press, 1987.

Hunter, James Davison, and Kimon Howland Sargeant. "Religion, Women and the Transformation of Public Culture." *Social Research* 60, no. 3 (1993): 545-70.

Ingersoll, Julie J. "Engendered Conflict: Feminism and Traditionalism in Late Twentieth-Century Conservative Protestantism (Fundamentalism)" (Ph.D. diss., University of California, 1997).

————. *Evangelical Christian Women: War Stories in the Gender Battles.* New York: New York University Press, 2003.

Jamieson, Penny. *Living at the Edge: Sacrament and Solidarity in Leadership.* London: Mowbray, 1997.

Jenson, Robert W. *Systematic Theology: The Triune God.* New York: Oxford University Press, 2001.

Jewett, Robert, and John Shelton Lawrence. *Captain America and the Crusade Against Evil: The Dilemma of Zealous Nationalism.* Grand Rapids: Eerdmans, 2003.

Johnson, Elizabeth A. *Consider Jesus: Waves of Renewal in Christology.* New York: Crossroad, 1990.

————. *She Who Is: The Mystery of God in Feminist Theological Discourse.* New York: Crossroad, 1992.

Jones, L. Gregory, and Stephanie Paulsell, eds. *The Scope of Our Art: The Vocation of the Theological Teacher.* Grand Rapids: Eerdmans, 2002.

Jones, Serene. *Feminist Theory and Christian Theology: Cartographies of Grace.* Minneapolis: Fortress, 2000.

Karlsen, Carol F., and Laurie Krumpacker, eds. *The Journal of Esther Edwards Burr, 1754-1757.* New Haven, Conn.: Yale University Press, 1986.

Karras, Valerie. "Eschatology." In *The Cambridge Companion to Feminist Theology,* edited by Susan Frank Parsons. Cambridge: Cambridge University Press, 2002.

Keller, Catherine. *Apocalypse Now and Then: A Feminist Guide to the End of the World.* Boston: Beacon, 1996.

————. *Face of the Deep: A Theology of Becoming.* New York: Routledge, 2003.

————. *From a Broken Web: Separation, Sexism and Self.* Boston: Beacon, 1986.

Kellstedt, Lyman. "Simple Questions, Complex Answers: What Do We Mean by 'Evangelicalism'? What Difference Does It Make?" *Evangelical Studies Bulletin* 12, no. 2 (1995): 1-4.

Kelly-Gadol, Joan. "The Social Relation of the Sexes: Methodological Implications of Women's History." In *Feminism and Methodology: Social Science Issues,* edited by Sandra Harding. Indianapolis: Indiana University Press, 1987.

Keysar, Ariela, and Barry A. Kosmin. "The Impact of Religious Identification on Differences in Educational Attainment Among American Women in 1990." *Journal for the Scientific Study of Religion* 34, no. 1 (1995): 49-62.

Kimel, Alvin F., Jr., ed. *Speaking the Christian God: The Holy Trinity and the Challenge of Feminism.* Grand Rapids: Eerdmans, 1992.

Klein, Christa Ressmeyer. "Women's Concerns in Theological Education." *Dialog* 24, no. 1 (1985): 25-31.

Kroeger, Catherine Clark, and Nancy Nason-Clark. *No Place for Abuse: Biblical and Practical Resources to Counteract Domestic Violence.* Downers Grove, Ill.: InterVarsity Press, 2004.

LaCugna, Catherine M. *God for Us: The Trinity and Christian Life.* San Francisco: Harper, 1993.

Leonard, Juanita Evans, ed. *Called to Minister, Empowered to Serve: Women in Ministry and Missions in the Church of God Reformation Movement.* Anderson, Ind.: Warner Press, 1989.

Lerner, Gerda. *The Creation of Patriarchy.* New York: Oxford University Press, 1986.

————. *Why History Matters: Life and Thought.* New York: Oxford University Press, 1997.

Lilburne, Geoffrey R. "Christology in Dialogue with Feminism." *Horizons* 11, no. 1 (1984): 7-27.

Lindbeck, George A. *The Nature of Doctrine: Religion and Theology in a Postliberal Age.* Philadelphia: Westminster, 1984.

Lips, Hilary M. *Women, Men and Power.* Mountain View, Calif.: Mayfield, 1991.

Loades, Ann, ed. *Feminist Theology: A Reader.* Louisville, Ky.: Westminster John Knox, 1990.

Maddox, Randy L. "The Necessity of Recognizing Distinctions: Lessons from Evangelical Critiques of Christian Feminist Theology." *Christian Scholars Review* 17, no. 3 (1988): 307-23.

———. "Toward an Inclusive Theology: The Systematic Implications of the Feminist Critique." *Christian Scholar's Review* 16, no. 1 (1986): 7-23.

———. "Wesleyan Theology and the Christian Feminist Critique." *Wesleyan Theological Journal* 22, no. 1 (1987): 101-11.

———. "The Word of God and Patriarchalism." *Perspectives in Religious Studies* 14, no. 3 (1987): 197-216.

Maguire, Patricia. *Doing Participatory Research: A Feminist Approach.* Amherst: University of Massachusetts, The Center for International Education School of Education, 1987.

Maitland, Sara. "Ways of Relating." In *Feminist Theology: A Reader,* edited by Ann Loades. Louisville, Ky.: Westminster John Knox, 1990.

Malcolm, Kari Torjesen. *Women at the Crossroads: A Path Beyond Feminism and Traditionalism.* Downers Grove Ill.: InterVarsity Press, 1982.

Manning, Christel J. *God Gave Us the Right: Conservative Catholic, Evangelical Protestant and Orthodox Jewish Women Grapple with Feminism.* New Brunswick, N.J.: Rutgers University Press, 1999.

Marsden, George M. *Fundamentalism and American Culture: The Shaping of Twentieth-Century Evangelicalism 1870-1925.* New York: Oxford University Press, 1980.

———. *Understanding Fundamentalism and Evangelicalism.* Grand Rapids: Eerdmans, 1991.

Marshall, Christopher D. *Beyond Retribution: A New Testament Vision for Justice, Crime and Punishment.* Grand Rapids: Eerdmans, 2001.

McFague, Sallie. "The Ethic of God as Mother, Lover and Friend." In *Feminist Theology: A Reader,* edited by Ann Loades. Louisville, Ky.: Westminster John Knox, 1990.

———. *Metaphorical Theology: Models of God in Religious Language.* Philadelphia: Fortress, 1982.

———. *Models of God: Theology for an Ecological, Nuclear Age.* Philadelphia: Fortress, 1987.

McGrath, Alister E. *Theory.* Vol. 3 of *A Scientific Theology.* New York: T & T Clark, 2003.

Mickelsen, Alvera, ed. *Women, Authority and the Bible.* Downers Grove, Ill.: InterVarsity Press, 1986.

Milbank, John. *The Word Made Strange: Theology, Language, Culture.* Cambridge, Mass.: Blackwell, 1997.

Milbank, John, Catherine Pickstock and Graham Ward, eds. *Radical Orthodoxy.* New York: Routledge, 1999.

Miller-McLemore, Bonnie J. *Also a Mother: Work and Family as Theological Dilemma.* Nashville: Abingdon, 1994.

Millman, Marcia, and Rosabeth Moss Kanter. "Introduction to Another Voice: Feminist Perspectives on Social Life and Social Science." In *Feminism and Methodology: Social Science Issues,* edited by Sandra Harding. Bloomington: Indiana University Press, 1987.

Moltmann, Jürgen. *The Trinity and the Kingdom: The Doctrine of God.* Translated by Margaret Kohl. Minneapolis: Fortress, 1993.

Murphy, Nancey. *Beyond Liberalism and Fundamentalism: How Modern and Postmodern Philosophy Set the Theological Agenda.* Valley Forge, Penn.: Trinity Press International, 1996.

Neff, David. "A Call to Evangelical Unity." *Christianity Today* 43, no. 7 (1999): 49-50.

Noll, Mark A. *American Evangelical Christianity: An Introduction.* Oxford: Blackwell, 2001.

Noll, Mark, Cornelius Plantinga Jr. and David Wells. "Evangelical Theology Today." *Theology Today* 51, no. 4 (1998): 495-507.

Nordling, Cherith Fee. "Being Saved as a New Creation: Co-Humanity in the True Imago Dei." In *What Does It Mean to Be Saved? Broadening Evangelical Horizons of Salvation,* edited by John G. Stackhouse Jr. Grand Rapids: Baker Academic, 2002.

Oden, Thomas C. "Blinded by the 'Lite.'" *Christianity Today* 38, no. 10 (1994): 14-15.

Olson, Roger E. "A Forum: The Future of Evangelical Theology." *Christianity Today,* February 9, 1998, pp. 40-48.

————. "Postconservative Evangelicals Greet the Postmodern Age." *The Christian Century,* May 3, 1995, pp. 480-83.

Osborne, Grant R. "Do Inclusive-Language Bibles Distort Scripture? No." *Christianity Today,* October 27, 1997, pp. 33-39.

Packer, J. I. "Let's Stop Making Women Presbyters." *Christianity Today,* February 11, 1991, pp. 18-21.

Palmer, Parker J. *The Courage to Teach: Exploring the Inner Landscape of a Teacher's Life.* San Francisco: Jossey-Bass, 1998.

Parsons, Susan Frank, ed. *The Cambridge Companion to Feminist Theology.* Cambridge: Cambridge University Press, 2002.

Pauw, Amy Plantinga. "Review of *Feminist Reconstructions of Christian Doctrine* (by Kathryn Greene-McCreight): Narrative Analysis and Appraisal." *Theology Today* 58, no. 2 (2001): 246-48.

————. "The Word Is Near You: A Feminist Conversation with Lindbeck." *Theology Today* 50, no. 1 (1993): 45-55.

Perkins, Pheme. "Women in the Bible and Its World." *Interpretation: A Journal of Bible and Theology* 42, no. 1 (1988): 33-44.

Peterson, Margaret Kim. "What a Woman Ought to Think." *First Things* 82 (1998): 13-14.

Phillips, Timothy R., and Dennis L. Okholm, eds. *The Nature of Confession: Evangelicals and Postliberals in Conversation.* Downers Grove, Ill.: InterVarsity Press, 1996.

Pinnock, Clark H. *Most Moved Mover: A Theology of God's Openness.* Grand Rapids: Baker, 2001.

Pinnock, Clark H., and John B. Cobb Jr., eds. *Searching for an Adequate God: A Dialogue Between Process and Free Will Theists.* Grand Rapids: Eerdmans, 2000.

Pinnock, Clark H., Richard Rice, William Hasker, John Sanders and David Basinger. *The Openness of God: A Biblical Challenge to the Traditional Understanding of God.* Downers Grove, Ill.: InterVarsity Press, 1994.

Piper, John, and Wayne Grudem, eds. *Recovering Biblical Manhood and Womanhood: A Response to Evangelical Feminism.* Wheaton, Ill.: Crossway, 1991.

Placher, William C. *Unapologetic Theology: A Christian Voice in a Pluralistic Conversation.* Louisville, Ky.: John Knox, 1995.

Pohl, Christine D. *Making Room: Recovering Hospitality as a Christian Tradition.* Grand Rapids: Eerdmans, 1999.

Poythress, Vern S. "Two Hermeneutical Tensions in Evangelical Feminism." Portland, Ore.: Theological Research Exchange Network, 1991.

Poythress, Vern S., and Wayne A. Grudem. *The Gender Neutral Bible Controversy: Muting the Masculinity of God's Words.* Nashville: Broadman & Holman, 2000.

Rawlyk, G. A. *Aspects of the Canadian Evangelical Experience.* Toronto: University of Toronto Press, 1997.

Renegar, John D. "The Feminist Movement Within Theological Conservatism: A Survey and Analysis of Its Literature" (D.Min. thesis, Vanderbilt University, 1984).

Riddell, Michael. *Threshold of the Future: Reforming the Church in the Post-Christian West.* London: SPCK, 1998.

Ross, Susan A. "Church and Sacrament: Community and Worship." In *The Cambridge Companion to Feminist Theology,* edited by Susan Frank Parsons. Cambridge: Cambridge University Press, 2002.

Ruether, Rosemary Radford. *Sexism and God-Talk: Toward a Feminist Theology.* Boston: Beacon, 1983.

————. *Women and Redemption: A Theological History.* Minneapolis: Fortress, 1998.

Russell, Letty M. *Church in the Round: Feminist Interpretation of the Church.* Louisville, Ky.: Westminster John Knox, 1993.

————, ed. *Feminist Interpretation of the Bible.* Philadelphia: Westminster Press, 1988.

————. "Hot-House Ecclesiology: A Feminist Interpretation of the Church." *The Ecumenical Review* 53, no. 1 (2001): 48-56.

————. *Household of Freedom: Authority in Feminist Theology.* Philadelphia: Westminster Press, 1987.

Russell, Letty M., Pui-Ian Kwok, Ada Maria Isasi-Diaz and Katie Geneva Cannon, eds. *Inheriting Our Mothers' Gardens: Feminist Theology in Third World Perspective.* Philadelphia: Westminster Press, 1988.

Saiving Goldstein, Valerie. "The Human Situation: A Feminine View." *Journal of Religion* 40, no. 2 (1960): 100-12.

Sakenfeld, Katharine Doob. "Feminist Perspectives on Bible and Theology: An Introduction to Selected Issues and Literature." *Interpretation* 42, no. 1 (1988): 5-18.

Sanders, John. *The God Who Risks: A Theology of Providence.* Downers Grove, Ill.: InterVarsity Press, 1998.

Scanzoni, Letha, and Nancy Hardesty. *All We're Meant to Be: A Biblical Approach to Women's Liberation.* Waco, Tex.: Word Books, 1974.

Schmidt, Frederick W. *A Still Small Voice: Women, Ordination and the Church.* Syracuse, N.Y.: Syracuse University Press, 1996.

Scholer, David M. "Feminist Hermeneutics and Evangelical Biblical Interpretation." *Journal* of the Evangelical Theological Society 30, no. 4 (1987): 407-20.

Schüssler Fiorenza, Elisabeth. *But She Said: Feminist Practices of Biblical Interpretation.* Boston: Beacon, 1995.

———. *Feminist Theology in Different Contexts.* Maryknoll, N.Y.: Orbis, 1996.

———. *In Memory of Her: A Feminist Theological Reconstruction of Christian Origins.* New York: Crossroad, 1983.

———. *Jesus: Miriam's Child, Sophia's Prophet.* New York: Continuum, 1994.

———. *Motherhood: Experience, Institution, Theology.* Edinburgh: T & T Clark, 1989.

Schüssler Fiorenza, Elisabeth, and Shelly Mathews, eds. *A Feminist Introduction.* Volume 1 of *Searching the Scriptures.* New York: Crossroad, 1997.

Sequeira, Debra, Thomas Trzyna, Martin L. Abbott and Delbert S. McHenry. " 'The Kingdom Has Not Yet Come': Coping with Microinequities Within a Christian University." *Research on Christian Higher Education* 2 (1995): 1-35.

Shaw, Susan M., and Tisa Lewis. " 'Once There Was a Camelot': Women Doctoral Graduates of the Southern Baptist Theological Seminary, 1982-1992, Talk About the Seminary, the Fundamentalist Takeover and Their Lives since SBTS" *Review and Expositor* 95, no. 3 (1998): 397-423.

Smith, Christian. *American Evangelicalism: Embattled and Thriving.* Chicago: University of Chicago Press, 1998.

Spencer, Aida Besançon. *Beyond the Curse: Women Called to Ministry.* Nashville: Thomas Nelson, 1985.

Stackhouse, John G., Jr. "Finding a Home for Eve." *Christianity Today,* March 1, 1999, pp. 60-61.

———, ed. *What Does It Mean to Be Saved? Broadening Evangelical Horizons of Salvation.* Grand Rapids: Baker, 2002.

Stacy, Judith, and Susan Elizabeth Gerard. "We Are Not Doormats: The Influence of Feminism on Contemporary Evangelicalism in the United States." In *Negotiating Gender in American Culture,* edited by Faye Ginsburg and Anna Tsing. Boston: Beacon, 1990.

Staff, AAR Committee on the Status of Women in the Professions of the AAR. *Guide to the Perplexing: A Survival Guide for Women in Religious Studies.* Atlanta: Scholars Press, 1992.

Stafford, Tim. "The New Theologians: These Top Scholars Are Believers Who Want to Speak to the Church." *Christianity Today,* February 8, 1999, pp. 30-49.

Storkey, Elaine. *Origins of Difference: The Gender Debate Revisited.* Grand Rapids: Baker Academic, 2001.

———. *What's Right with Feminism.* Grand Rapids: Eerdmans, 1985.

Storkey, Elaine, and Margaret Hebblethwaite. *Conversations on Christian Feminism: Speaking Heart to Heart.* London: Fount, 1999.

Strauss, Mark. "Linguistic and Hermeneutical Fallacies in the Guidelines Established at the 'Conference on Gender-Related Language in Scripture.' " *Journal of the Evangelical Theological Society* 41, no. 2 (1998): 239-62.

Stroup, George W. "Between Echo and Narcissus: The Role of the Bible in Feminist Theology." *Interpretation: A Journal of Bible and Theology* 42, no. 1 (1988): 19-32.

Stuart, Elizabeth, and Adrian Thatcher, eds. *Christian Perspectives on Sexuality and Gender.* Grand Rapids, Eerdmans, 1996.

Sweet, Leonard, ed. *Church in Emerging Culture: Five Perspectives.* Grand Rapids: Zondervan, 2003.

Thompson, Marianne Meye. *The Promise of the Father: Jesus and God in the New Testament.* Louisville, Ky.: Westminster John Knox, 2000.

Tomlinson, Dave. *The Post-Evangelical.* Grand Rapids: Zondervan, 2003.

Trible, Phyllis. "Feminist Hermeneutics and Biblical Studies." In *Feminist Theology: A Reader,* edited by Ann Loades. Louisville, Ky.: Westminster John Knox, 1990.

———. *Texts of Terror: Literary-Feminist Readings of Biblical Narratives.* Philadelphia: Fortress, 1984.

Van Leeuwen, Mary Stewart, ed. *After Eden: Facing the Challenge of Gender Reconciliation.* Grand Rapids: Eerdmans, 1993.

———. "A Bit of Evangelical Evasion." *New York Times,* October 4, 1997, p. 15.

———. *Gender and Grace: Love, Work and Parenting in a Changing World.* Downers Grove, Ill.: InterVarsity Press, 1990.

Van Leeuwen, Mary Stewart, and Anne Carr, eds. *Religion, Feminism and the Family.* Louisville, Ky.: Westminster John Knox, 1996.

Volf, Miroslav. *After Our Likeness: The Church as the Image of the Trinity.* Grand Rapids: Eerdmans, 1998.

———. *Exclusion and Embrace: A Theological Exploration of Identity, Otherness and Reconciliation.* Nashville: Abingdon, 1996.

Weaver, J. Denny. *The Nonviolent Atonement.* Grand Rapids: Eerdmans, 2001.

Webber, Robert E. *The Younger Evangelicals: Facing the Challenges of the New World.* Grand Rapids: Baker, 2002.

Weinandy, Thomas G. *The Father's Spirit of Sonship: Reconceiving the Trinity.* Edinburgh: T & T Clark, 1995.

Wells, David. *No Place for Truth: Or Whatever Happened to Evangelical Theology?* Grand Rapids: Eerdmans, 1993.

Wells, David, and John Woodbridge. *The Evangelicals.* Grand Rapids: Baker, 1975.

Wessinger, Catherine, ed. *Religious Institutions and Women's Leadership: New Roles Inside the Mainstream.* Columbia: University of South Carolina Press, 1996.

Wheeler, Barbara G., and Edward Farley, eds. *Shifting Boundaries: Contextual Approaches to the Structure of Theological Education.* Louisville, Ky.: Westminster John Knox, 1991.

Winter, Miriam Therese, Adair Lummis and Allison Stokes. *Defecting in Place: Women Claiming Responsibility for Their Own Spiritual Lives.* New York: Crossroad, 1994.

Wuthnow, Robert. *Rediscovering the Sacred: Perspectives on Religion in Contemporary Society.* Grand Rapids: Eerdmans, 1992.

————. *The Struggle for America's Soul: Evangelicals, Liberals and Secularism*. Grand Rapids: Eerdmans, 1989.

Young, Iris Marion. *Justice and the Politics of Difference*. Princeton, N.J.: Princeton University
Press, 1990.

Young, Pamela Dickey. *Feminist Theology/Christian Theology: In Search of Method*. Minneapolis:
Fortress, 1990.

Zizioulas, John D. *Being as Communion: Studies in Personhood and the Church*. Crestwood, N.Y.: St.
Vladimir's Seminary Press, 1997.

Index